365
Main-Course
Salads

Carol Foster

A JOHN BOSWELL ASSOCIATES BOOK

HarperCollins*Publishers*

HarperCollins books may be purchased for educational, business, or sales promotional use. For information please write: Special Markets Department, HarperCollins Publishers, Inc., 10 East 53rd Street, New York, NY 10022.

FIRST EDITION

Series Editor: Susan Wyler
Design: Nigel Rollings
Index: Maro Riofrancos

Library of Congress Cataloging-in-Publication Data

Foster, Carol, 1950–
   365 main-course salads / Carol Foster. — 1st ed.
     p. cm.
   "A John Boswell Associates book."
   ISBN 0-06-017293-2
   1. Salads. 2. Entrées (Cookery) I. Title.
TX740.F84 1996
641.8'3—dc20
                                   96-44782

97 98 99 00 01 HC 10 9 8 7 6 5 4 3 2 1

Contents

1   **Classic Main-Course Salads**   **11**

Many of the world's greatest salads are included here, from American Cobb Salad, Crab Louis, and Taco Salad to Greek Salad, English Salmagundi, and Indonesian Gado-Gado, along with the classic dressings—Green Goddess, Thousand Island—that accompany them.

Not only chicken, but turkey, duck, and quail are featured in various inventive greened guises—Chipotle Chicken Salad with Mangoes, Chicken and Artichoke Salad, and Turkey, Cranberry, and Goat Cheese Salad to name a few.

Sizzling Southwest Steak Salad, Couscous and Lamb Salad with Mint–Red Currant Vinaigrette, and Italian Sausage and Cannellini Salad with Tomato-Fennel Vinaigrette represent several of the substantial but stylish dishes you'll find here.

These light and lovely salads include both fish—Oven-Roasted Salmon Salad, Two-Alarm Fresh Tuna Salad, and Halibut Salad with Avocados and Sun-Dried Tomatoes—and shellfish—Island Shrimp Salad with Macadamia Nuts and Coconut, Crab Cakes on Mixed Greens, and Skewered Scallop Salad.

Tortellini Salad with Blue Cheese Pesto, Pasta Salad Primavera, East-West Angel Hair Salad with Grilled Chicken, and Wagon Wheel Pasta with Tuna and Broccoli offer a sampling of the salads based on one of the world's favorite foods: pasta!

Healthful eating may be a benefit, but with combinations like Barley and Wild Mushroom Salad with Shaved Parmesan Cheese, Shrimp Tabbouleh, Confetti Lentil Salad, and Middle Eastern Chickpea and Roasted Vegetable Salad, all you'll notice is the great taste.

Introduction

Welcome to the glory days of salad. Basking in the height of their popularity, salads have emerged from a simple side dish to center stage at lunch, brunch, and dinner. More than any other food, salads have undergone a dramatic transformation in the last decade, and their versatility has made them the darling of daring chefs.

It wasn't long ago that salad-making lay on the bottom rung of the restaurant kitchen ladder. Thanks largely to the widespread influence of California cuisine, which emphasizes natural and local products, accepts adventurous combinations of ingredients, and stresses the importance of lightness and freshness, the creation of serious salads has been elevated to the ultimate culinary challenge. Trendy chefs strive to marry hot, warm, and cold ingredients; adapt salads to every season and to every ethnic heritage; and blend cooked and raw vegetables, greens, legumes, fruits, breads, pastas, fish, and meats into fresh, exciting combinations.

Salads offer vast opportunities for the novice and experienced cook alike, because while they invite creativity, no dish can be more simple, requiring only a good eye for what looks and tastes great together. In fact, many main-course salads require no cooking at all.

Main-course salads meet the needs of our fast-paced, nutritionally conscious lives. They include the components of traditional meals, but they don't require the hours it takes to prepare a meat, starch, vegetable, and side-dish salad. Most main-course salads are fresh, chic, and quick to prepare. Many can be made in one bowl, and even elaborate ones are assembled quickly compared to a traditional meal. Unlike preparing a roast or a stew that requires planning ahead for a number of people, salads can be an easy, spur-of-the-moment meal that can be made for one or eight with ease, a great convenience for helter-skelter households that are shrinking in size and mealtime organization.

Salad meals epitomize the way nutritionists tell us we should eat. With their bulk comprised of carbohydrates complemented by small amounts of protein and very small amounts of fat, main-course salads are nutritionally ideal.

As international travel has increased, so has our awareness of other cultures' tastes and once-foreign ingredients. Thanks to global marketing and technological advances, the array of fresh fruits, vegetables, and herbs at our doorstep these days is dazzling. Our choices used to be limited to a few types of lettuce and shrink-wrapped, tasteless tomatoes. Today we can choose from pomegranates and papayas, edible flowers and arugula, and blue potatoes and baby vegetables. Sun-dried tomatoes, radicchio, cilantro, jicama, and jalapeño peppers are among dozens of ingredients only occasionally heard of a decade ago. Today, they're commonplace in many large supermarkets.

Due to the freshness and inherent eye-appeal of most of these ingredients, salads are the easiest type of food to make tantalizing and beautiful. The secrets to creating fabulous salads are simple. Choose the freshest ingredients, store and clean them with care, and balance them to create an appealing combination. The information that follows, including a descriptive glossary of ingredients and information on how to choose, store, clean, and dress them, will arm you with all the information you need to create memorable meals from the salad bowl.

A GLOSSARY OF GREENS

Many of the recipes in this book call simply for "assorted lettuces." Here are some to choose from:

Arugula, also known as rugula and rocket, has small to medium slender, dark green, jagged-edged leaves with a sharp, peppery flavor. Choose small, young leaves, since old ones can be tough and bitter. Fresh from the garden, arugula keeps a week refrigerated; otherwise, it should be used within a day or two.

Belgian endive, also known as French endive and *witloof* (white leaf), refers to 3- to 5-inch-long, narrow spears of leaves that are creamy white with yellow tips and a slightly bitter flavor. Look for heads that are heavy, tightly packed, and pale. They are grown without light to prevent greening, and those with tinges of green will be more bitter. Available September through May, the peak season for Belgian endive is November through April.

Butterhead lettuce is a softly furled head of pale to medium green leaves that grow progressively larger from its tiny core to its large outer leaves. The lettuce is creamy soft in texture and mild in flavor. The two most common varieties are Boston and Bibb, both also known as butter lettuce.

Cabbage, a mainstay in coleslaw, comes in many varieties, but is most commonly sold as a round, tightly packed heavy head of crisp, pale green leaves that are mild in flavor. It's also available in purple with similar flavor, growth, and texture. Chinese or Napa cabbage is a tightly packed head of wide stalks with elongated, frilly leaves that are creamy white in color. It has a mild, sweet cabbage flavor. Savoy cabbage has evenly crinkled round leaves and makes a stunning, sturdy base for a salad.

Curly endive, also known as frisée and chicory, has jagged, frilly leaves on long, narrow stems. The leaves vary in color from off-white to medium green and are slightly bitter. Curly endive is available year-round.

Dandelion greens have bright green, jagged-edged leaves that are slightly bitter and tangy in flavor. They are available in the early springtime both wild and cultivated. Since older leaves taste excessively bitter, use only tiny young leaves that emerge well before flowering.

Escarole has broad, flat loose leaves that are a bit irregular with lightly curled edges held together by a sturdy stem. The leaves have a firm, slightly chewy texture and a mildly bitter flavor. Escarole is available year-round.

Flowers that are edible include nasturtiums, chive blossoms, day lilies, violets, roses, calendulas, marigolds, borage, dianthus, and geraniums. Although many are flavorful, they're used most frequently for a flourish of color in salads.

Fresh herbs are the aromatic leaves of various plants that, for the most part, do not have a woody stem. The most commonly used herbs in salads include basil, chives, cilantro, dill, mint, oregano, parsley, rosemary, sage, tarragon, and thyme. They should be used sparingly in salads, since their aroma will rarely be mellowed by cooking. Fresh herbs are increasingly available in groceries and supermarkets.

Iceberg lettuce is distinguished by extremely crisp, circular, tightly furled leaves that are about 90 percent water, resulting in a bland flavor but exceptional texture. It's available year-round, and it's the most durable of lettuces, lasting at least a week in the refrigerator.

Leaf lettuces, both green and red, are loose leaves held together by a sturdy stem. The leaves are curly, delicate in flavor and texture, and either solid green or tinged with ruby tips. Oakleaf lettuce, also delicate in flavor, is flatter than other loose-leaf varieties and resembles the softly jagged edges of the leaves of oak trees.

Mâche is also known as lamb's lettuce and corn salad, because it grows readily in cornfields. Its dark green leaves are soft in texture and so delicately nutty in flavor that they need to be accompanied by mild ingredients. Although mâche is prolific in the wild, it's highly perishable and therefore expensive.

Mesclun is not a green, but a mixture of piquant and delicate baby greens, herbs, and sometimes edible flowers. The ingredients vary in flavor from mild to peppery and from season to season, but since they are picked young, no flavors are overpowering. Young versions of greens that are too strong for a raw salad at maturity, such as kale, Swiss chard, and mustard greens, can be included in mesclun. Picked over, cleaned, and sometimes bagged, mesclun is widely available now in farmers' markets and many supermarkets. It provides a variety of textures, colors, and flavors in every handful, a delight for connoisseurs and a convenience for those in a hurry.

Mizuma has sharply jagged tender green leaves and a mildly bitter taste. It's often included in mesclun.

Radicchio is an Italian chicory that grows into small, round heads of curled burgundy leaves with strong white veins and a slightly bitter flavor. Seven- to nine-inch-long spearlike radicchio, known as Treviso, is also available. Although radicchio can be found in markets all year long, its peak season is mid-winter to early spring.

Romaine lettuce has creamy to deep green, long, oblong leaves that are loosely packed and have a mild, watery flavor. They are crisp and sturdy enough to cradle heavily textured or flavored ingredients. Available year-round, romaine is second only to iceberg lettuce in crispness and durability.

Spinach has coarse-textured leaves that vary from small and pale to large, deep green, and leathery. The large leaves should be stemmed before using. Due to their sturdiness, they hold up well in salads tossed with warm dressings. Spinach has a faintly musky aroma and is available year-round. Baby spinach has virtually stemless leaves, each the size of a silver dollar, and harbors no grit, which often accompanies regular spinach.

Watercress has small, round, deep green leaves with edible stems and peppery flavor. It can be found growing wild alongside streams with cool running water, and it's available commercially year-round in many parts of the country. Use the leaves and tender stems for salad. The tougher stems have a lot of flavor and make delicious soups, or minced fine and blended with cream cheese, a flavorful sandwich spread.

CHOOSING GREENS

Always choose greens that appear just-picked and small or average in size with no wilting, bruising, or yellowing. Fruits and vegetables, including lettuce, should feel firm and heavy for their size, indicating healthy water content.

In choosing salad ingredients, consider flavor, texture, and color. Too many assertive flavors will cancel each other out, and too much of any one will be overwhelming. Mild and assertive flavors should blend together to form a pleasing balance for the palate.

The same principle holds true for texture and color. If a salad is monochromatic and uniformly soft or crisp in texture, it will be boring and unappreciated. Balanced, lively contrast gives us the ability to enjoy texture and color.

In most areas of the country, customers have the option of choosing either hydroponically grown or organically grown produce. Hydroponically grown products are grown without soil, but in water with added nutrients. They are typically picture-perfect and clean, but many lack flavor. Organic produce is grown in soil, but without fertilizers, pesticides, artificial flavorings or colorings, or additives.

Since the size of lettuces and greens varies between seasons and growing areas, this book lists cups of torn greens instead of heads of lettuce. When more than 8 cups of greens are called for, a weight is also given. A general guideline for buying greens according to their yields follows:

1 average head or bunch	torn & lightly packed leaves
arugula (1 ounce)	1½ cups
butterhead lettuce (½ pound)	5 to 6 cups
curly endive (¾ pound)	10 cups
escarole (½ pound)	7 cups
iceberg lettuce (1½ pounds)	12 cups
leaf lettuce (½ pound)	10 to 12 cups
radicchio (½ pound)	6 cups
romaine lettuce (¾ pound)	8 to 10 cups
spinach (¾ pound)	12 cups
watercress (¼ pound)	2½ cups

STORING, WASHING, AND PREPARING GREENS

Before storing or cleaning salad greens, remove any outer leaves that may be damaged or that have brown spots. It's best to rinse greens just prior to using them to avoid decay from excess moisture, but some people prefer to clean them ahead of time for later convenience.

To clean iceberg lettuce, cut out the stem and run cold water into the stem end. Drain it stem side down. To clean curly endive, escarole, romaine, butterhead, and looseleaf lettuces, pull the leaves apart and rinse under cold water individually or swish them in a large bowl or sink filled with water. Dirt will sink to the bottom and the greens will float. Scoop up the greens before draining the water and spin them dry in a salad spinner or dry by hand with towels. Particularly gritty greens, such as spinach, may require repeated soaking, swishing, and draining. Delicate greens, including butterhead and baby lettuces, bruise too easily when spun dry, so they are better dried with towels.

If not using at once, wrap cleaned greens in a damp kitchen towel or paper towels and place in a plastic bag. The towels will protect the greens from too much moisture, which can cause bacterial growth and decay. Store in the coldest, most humid section of the refrigerator. Depending upon how delicate or sturdy the greens, they will keep 1 to 4 days. Iceberg lettuce will keep at least a week.

Most salad greens are best torn by hand, but some, such as romaine and radicchio, are fine if cut with a sharp knife. Shredded iceberg lettuce will develop brown edges, so shred it just before using. Some herbs, such as basil and mint, blacken quickly after cutting, so they should be cut just prior to using. Remove any tough stems from greens before serving.

DRESSING A SALAD

The one component that gives a salad cohesion is its dressing. In many salads, this is a simple vinaigrette, a temporary emulsion of oil, vinegar, salt, and pepper. Other salads may be coated in a heavier dressing of creamy mayonnaise, a stable emulsion of egg, oil, salt, and pepper. The dressing must complement the components of the salad in quantity, texture, and flavor, not overwhelm them or repeat them. A delicate salad of mâche and bay scallops needs a dressing light in texture and flavor; a salad of shredded cabbage and seasoned beef can handle an assertive mayonnaise. In general, choose a vinaigrette for a sharp effect and mayonnaise and other creamy dressings for a mellow effect.

Note: *Some dressings in this book, including the mayonnaises, are made with raw egg. While the acid from lemon juice or vinegar retards bacterial growth, it is important never to leave any dressing containing raw egg at room temperature. Use it immediately or refrigerate it and use within 2 days. Use only fresh eggs with no sign of a crack in the shell. Because of the possible threat of Salmonella — a bacteria that causes food poisoning — from raw eggs, U.S. Government officials recommend that the very young, the elderly, pregnant women, and people with serious illnesses or weakened immune systems not eat raw or lightly cooked eggs. Keep this in mind and consume raw eggs at your own risk.*

In all cases, use only enough dressing to lightly coat the ingredients. By its very name, dressing is coating, not substance. In most cases, dress the salad the moment before serving it. Vinegar, citrus juices, and salt pull water from tender greens, causing them to wilt and release nutrients.

Always choose a bowl large enough to maneuver ingredients without crowding them. If a bowl is too small, tender ingredients are likely to get bruised or spilled. Ceramic, glass, and hard plastic bowls make the best salad bowls because they are easy to clean. Despite its reputation as the ideal material for salad bowls, wood is porous and absorbs oil, which may become rancid over time.

A multitude of vinegars and oils are available today, and they reflect wide differences in quality and cost.

Choosing them well is critical to the quality of salads. Just as salad greens need to achieve a pleasing balance, so do dressing ingredients need to achieve a balance with each other and with the main components of the salad.

OILS

Olive oil is healthy, versatile, and prized throughout the world for use in salads and cooking. It's pressed from tree-ripened olives, resulting in an aromatic, monounsaturated oil. Olive oils are graded according to their levels of acid, which increases with each pressing. Cold-pressing olives with no heat, steam, or chemicals produces a naturally low-acid oil. The first pressing produces the finest, most expensive, extra-virgin oil that is only 1 percent or less oleic acid. It's fruity in aroma and ranges from pale to deep yellowish-green in color. In general, the deeper the color, the more intense the aroma.

The recipes in this book that benefit from extra-virgin olive oil's intense, fruity aroma call for extra-virgin. The remaining call for olive oil, in which case, use superfine, fine, pure, or light, depending upon your preference and pocketbook.

Olive oil should be stored in a cool, dark place for no more than 6 months. It will keep refrigerated up to a year, but it becomes cloudy and difficult to pour when chilled. Returning the oil to room temperature makes it clear and pourable again.

Nut oils, such as hazelnut and walnut, are full-flavored oils pressed from specific nuts. Because they are powerful with aroma that resembles roasted nuts, they're often cut with milder oils. In general, nut oils are best complemented by fruity vinegars or sherry vinegar. Because they're prone to turn rancid, store them in the refrigerator up to 3 months. They can be purchased in cans or bottles in specialty markets and some supermarkets.

Vegetable oils, such as corn and safflower, are almost tasteless and odorless. They are best used in salad dressings when blandness is desired or with ingredients that are highly spiced or dominating.

Asian sesame oil is dark and very strong with the aroma of roasted sesame seeds. Because it's overpowering, it's always cut with blander oils or soy sauce and other oriental ingredients. Don't confuse Asian sesame oil with the light, unassertive sesame oil made from raw white seeds that is sold in health food stores.

VINEGARS

Vinegars are the twice-fermented, sour liquids made from bacterial activity which converts alcohol or grains into a weak solution of acetic acid. The name is derived from the French *vin aigre,* meaning "sour wine," and you'll find vinegars made in every country that produces wine. In the seventeenth century, the French developed the process of fermenting wine in wooden barrels, called the Orléans process after the city where it was born. The best red and white wine vinegars are made by this natural process, although some lesser versions are made by artificially accelerating the fermentation.

Red wine vinegar is far more robust and assertive than white, which is lighter and sweeter. Champagne vinegar is even lighter than white wine vinegar. Sherry vinegar, made in Spain, is mellow and full-bodied, so it's best paired with strong ingredients. Highly aromatic balsamic vinegar, made in the Modena region of Italy, is actually made from white Trebbiano wine grapes, but it takes on the color of the barrels it's aged in, resulting in a deep red color. It's highly acidic, sweet, and mellow. Balsamic vinegar can be very expensive. Often a few drops of it are blended with red wine vinegar.

Cider vinegar is made from fermented apple cider, and delivers a very strong, fruity aroma. It should be used only with assertive ingredients. On the opposite end of the spectrum is rice vinegar, made from fermented rice. It's delicate and sweet, and should be reserved for delicate salad ingredients. Fruit and herb vinegars are made by steeping fresh berries or herbs in vinegar, and they tend to be aromatic, but delicate. They are available in specialty markets and supermarkets, but they are also easily made at home. Steep fruits or herbs in vinegar until the desired flavor is achieved. At that time, strain out the solids and store in the refrigerator in a clean, tightly covered container.

Although vinegars provide the acidic element in salad dressings most often, lemon and lime juice can do the same. Freshly squeezed lime juice is a must, since bottled lime juice contains sweeteners and other ingredients that alter the outcome of the dressing. Bottled lemon juice is not altered by extraneous ingredients, but fresh delivers truer flavor with more of its characteristic zestiness. All of the salads and dressings in this book assume the use of fresh lemon juice, except those in the chapter on instant salads, where bottled lemon juice is used to save time.

PRESENTING A SALAD

The look of a salad, perhaps more than any other food we eat, displays what flavors and textures are about to be enjoyed. Since most salad ingredients are unchanged by cooking, their appearance is straightforward and natural, making it easy for us to eat with our eyes first. Greens glistening with a splash of dressing, highlighted by vividly colored raw fruits and a small wedge of perfectly ripened cheese, present a picture that tempts us to the table.

There are two different ways of serving salad. One is informal, where all of the ingredients are tossed or blended together, and another is composed, in which combinations of diverse ingredients are arranged in a formal, attractive pattern. If the salad is to be tossed, varying the color and texture of the ingredients takes precedence over the shape of them. Shape becomes important when salads are purposefully arranged in rings, layers, or asymmetrical designs. Crescents of sliced papaya, large rounds of vine-ripened tomatoes, and ovals of steamed mussels require different treatment due to their shape as well as color. The juxtaposition of ingredients gives them visual distinction, and the overall effect of the assembly is most important.

Although all of the recipes in this book are written with instructions regarding presentation, they are meant only as guidelines. Often salads look especially striking on lettuce-lined plates, but if you prefer to serve them without liners or in bowls, do so. If you prefer to serve main-course salads in a family style, where food is put on a platter and diners help themselves, by all means do so.

In the chapters that follow, you'll find a full range of main-course salads to satisfy different palates, nutritional needs, and time constraints. I hope you'll have as much fun making and eating them as I have, and I hope you'll be inspired to create bold new full-meal combinations from the salad bowl.

Chapter 1

Classic Main-Course Salads

French Salad Niçoise, with its moist chunks of tuna, ripe tomatoes, green beans, and olives, and the all-American Chef's Salad, adorned with tender slivers of ham, cheese, and turkey, have long been familiar to us as salads that comprise an entire meal. Yet it took the impeccably chosen vegetables, baked rounds of cheese, and quickly grilled fish, chicken, and meats that defined the California style of cooking to bring main-course salads into the forefront of American culinary consciousness.

The availability in supermarkets of good olive oil, flavored vinegars, and assorted lettuces—including the mixed baby greens called "mesclun," pungent arugula, and bitter red radicchio—all helped this fresh, simple, and flavorful way of eating grow enormously in popularity. Another boost to the interest in main-course salads, which drove them onto the menus of all sorts of restaurants across the country, was our contemporary interest in eating lighter and healthier, with more vegetables and less fat and meat.

In this chapter, I include those salads that have gained a permanent standing in the repertoire. Some of these recipes, such as Cobb Salad, Palace Court Salad with Green Goddess Dressing, and "21"'s Lorenzo Dressing, originated in restaurants. Others that are immensely popular are American-ized versions of international dishes, such as Chinese Chicken Salad, Greek Salad, Taco Salad, and Italian Chop-Chop. And still others are mainstays in other countries, enjoyed in homes and restaurants, including Herring, Beet, and Apple Salad from Scandinavia; Caponata with Tuna Fish from Sicily; and Gado-Gado from Indonesia.

A few American salads in this chapter are so much a part of our culture that they hardly need recipes. All-American Potato Salad with Bacon, Old-Fashioned Chicken Salad, Tuna Fish Salad, and Egg Salad have been consistent home, deli, and picnic fare for decades. In this chapter, the standard recipes have been embellished a bit to make them a satisfying whole meal, and most benefit from an addition of bread.

With the popularity and diversity of salads on the rise, hopefully more main-course salads will join the ranks of the classics. In the meantime, enjoy these knowing they're the ones people have relied on for decades the world over.

1   CAESAR SALAD
Prep: 15 minutes   Cook: none   Serves: 6

Although Caesar salads have been around for decades, they are enjoying a resurgence in popularity. This restaurant classic has been updated to eliminate the coddled egg, which was a part of the traditional dressing. Instead of using questionably cooked eggs to thicken the dressing, adding mustard and using a food processor or blender to make the dressing thickens and emulsifies it. This salad calls for whole lettuce leaves for a dramatic presentation, but if you prefer your lettuce torn, use 3 cups torn lettuce per serving. To make the salad even more substantial, top it with grilled shrimp or chicken breasts.

8   anchovy fillets
4   garlic cloves
¼   cup lemon juice
2   tablespoons Dijon mustard
½   cup extra-virgin olive oil
3   medium heads of romaine
      lettuce, tough outer
      leaves discarded,
      remaining leaves
      separated

¾   cup grated Parmesan cheese
      Salt and freshly ground
      pepper
3   cups Garlic Croutons
      (recipe follows)

1. Combine anchovy fillets and garlic in a food processor or blender. Mince together. Add lemon juice and mustard. With machine on, gradually drizzle in oil. If not using within 2 hours, cover and refrigerate. Bring to room temperature before using.

2. In a large bowl, combine lettuce and ¼ cup cheese. Drizzle with dressing and toss until well blended. If needed, season with salt and pepper to taste. Divide among 6 plates and sprinkle with remaining ½ cup cheese and croutons. Serve at once.

2   GARLIC CROUTONS
Prep: 10 minutes   Cook: 25 minutes   Makes: 3 cups

To ensure that the garlic doesn't burn, these croutons are baked at a low temperature. They can be sautéed on the stove until golden as well, but baking them in the oven is less labor-intensive.

4   tablespoons butter, melted,
      or ¼ cup olive oil
3   garlic cloves, minced

3   cups (¾-inch) cubes French
      or Italian bread

1. Preheat oven to 325°F. In a large bowl, combine butter and garlic. Add bread and toss quickly until well blended. Transfer to a large baking sheet and arrange in a single layer.

2. Bake, stirring occasionally, until crisp and golden, about 25 minutes. Transfer to paper towels and let cool. If not using within 2 hours, store airtight for up to 3 days.

3 CHEF'S SALAD WITH THOUSAND ISLAND DRESSING
Prep: 25 minutes   Cook: none   Serves: 8 to 10

Any number of salad dressings, including light vinaigrettes and heavier mayonnaise-based ones, will complement this salad standard. The ingredients are especially eye-appealing arranged in a spoke or linear pattern, but if you prefer a more casual salad, toss them all together.

12 cups shredded iceberg or
    romaine lettuce
3 cups diced (½-inch) Swiss
    cheese (about 12 ounces)
3 cups diced (½-inch) cooked
    ham (about 12 ounces)
3 cups diced (½-inch) cooked
    turkey (about 12 ounces)

8 medium plum tomatoes,
    quartered lengthwise
8 hard-cooked eggs,
    quartered lengthwise
1½ cups Thousand Island
    Dressing (recipe follows)

Divide lettuce among 8 to 10 plates. Arrange cheese, ham, and turkey in a spoke pattern on top of lettuce. Arrange tomatoes and eggs around edges of salads and serve. Pass dressing at table.

4 THOUSAND ISLAND DRESSING
Prep: 10 minutes   Cook: none   Makes: about 1½ cups

An old-fashioned favorite, Thousand Island dressing is thick and creamy. It's always based on mayonnaise and chili sauce, and it variously contains stuffed green olives, peppers, pickles, onions, and hard-cooked eggs.

1 cup mayonnaise
¼ cup bottled chili sauce or
    ketchup
3 tablespoons minced red bell
    pepper
1 tablespoon minced green
    bell pepper

1 tablespoon minced chives
    or chopped scallion green
1 tablespoon minced parsley
2 teaspoons tarragon vinegar

In a small bowl, whisk together all ingredients until well blended. If not serving within an hour, cover and refrigerate.

5   OLD-FASHIONED CHICKEN SALAD
Prep: 10 minutes   Cook: 1 to 1¼ hours   Serves: 4

Old-fashioned chicken salad is mostly chicken. As our eating patterns have changed to include less meat, so has chicken salad. This traditional recipe is for those who want a taste of the past in their diet. Chopped fine, it can also be used as a sandwich filling. For variety, add capers, crushed pineapple, chopped scallions, chopped pickles, pickled jalapeño peppers, sliced water chestnuts, or chopped hard-cooked eggs. For an old-fashioned salad sampler, arrange one-third each chicken, tuna, and egg salads (recipes follow) on 4 lettuce-lined plates.

1 (3½- to 4-pound) chicken
2 celery ribs, thinly sliced
½ cup Handmade
    Mayonnaise or
    Machine-Made
    Mayonnaise (both
    page 15)

Salt and freshly ground
    pepper
Green leaf lettuce leaves
4 large plum tomatoes, sliced
    into thin wedges

1. Preheat oven to 375°F. Rinse chicken inside and out and pat dry. Place on a lightly greased baking pan. Roast chicken for 1 to 1¼ hours, or until thigh juices run clear when pierced with a sharp knife. When cool enough to handle, shred chicken. Discard skin and bones.

2. In a large bowl, combine chicken, celery, and mayonnaise until well blended. If needed, season with salt and pepper to taste. Divide among lettuce-lined plates and arrange tomato wedges around salad. Serve at once.

Variations

OLD-FASHIONED EGG SALAD
Substitute 4 cups chopped hard-cooked eggs for chicken.

OLD-FASHIONED TUNA FISH SALAD
Substitute 4 cups cooked fresh or drained canned tuna for chicken.

6 HANDMADE MAYONNAISE
Prep: 3 minutes   Cook: none   Makes: about ½ cup

Homemade mayonnaise is far superior to even the best commercial ones. It should be soft, but firm, and just hold its shape when lifted with a spoon. For a firmer mayonnaise, add a bit more oil; for a thinner one, add a bit more lemon juice or warm water. If you prefer, substitute vinegar for the lemon juice and peanut, corn, or other vegetable oil for the olive oil.

1 egg yolk (see Note,
   page 6)
¼ teaspoon salt
⅛ teaspoon white pepper

1 teaspoon lemon juice, at
   room temperature
½ cup mild-flavored olive oil

1. In a medium bowl, combine egg yolk, salt, and pepper. Whisk until yolks look slightly pale, about 1 minute. Add lemon juice and whisk until well blended.

2. While whisking, add oil drop by drop to begin with. When sauce begins to thicken, continue whisking, adding oil in a thin stream. If not using immediately, cover and refrigerate.

7 MACHINE-MADE MAYONNAISE
Prep: 2 minutes   Cook: none   Makes: 1 to 1½ cups

A food processor or blender takes the work out of making mayonnaise from scratch, and you can use an entire egg instead of just the yolk. It results in a firmer dressing that is not quite as rich.

1 egg (see Note, page 6)
2 teaspoons lemon juice, at
   room temperature

1 to 1½ cups mild-flavored
   olive oil
Salt and white pepper

Combine egg and lemon juice in a food processor or blender. Blend together. With machine on, drizzle in oil drop by drop. Once mayonnaise starts to thicken, add oil in a steady stream. Add lesser amount of oil for a soft mayonnaise; add larger amount for firmer one. If needed, add extra lemon juice and salt and pepper to taste.

8   CAPONATA WITH TUNA FISH

*Prep: 20 minutes   Stand: 30 minutes   Cook: 20 minutes
Marinate: 2 hours   Serves: 4*

Caponata is a Sicilian favorite that is traditionally served as a salad, relish, or side dish with fish. It's a sweet-and-sour stew of eggplant, tomatoes, celery, olives, onions, pine nuts, and capers. This version incorporates fish into the salad, making it an easy one-dish meal. Since it can be refrigerated for up to 2 days to give the flavors a chance to meld, it's also an easy do-ahead meal. For a special occasion, forgo the canned tuna and add your favorite grilled fish.

1 medium eggplant (about 1 pound), cut into ¾-inch cubes	½ cup pitted green olives
4 teaspoons salt	3 tablespoons balsamic vinegar
2 tablespoons olive oil	4 teaspoons capers, drained
1 small red onion, chopped	2 (6½-ounce) cans solid white tuna, drained and flaked
1 small zucchini, chopped	2 tablespoons pine nuts (pignoli), lightly toasted
2 celery ribs, thinly sliced	
1 (14½-ounce) can diced peeled tomatoes, in juice	

1. In a large colander, sprinkle eggplant with salt and toss until well blended. Let stand 30 minutes. Rinse eggplant, drain well, and pat dry with paper towels.

2. In a large skillet, heat oil over medium-high heat until it shimmers. Add eggplant, red onion, zucchini, and celery. Cook, stirring frequently, until vegetables are softened, about 5 minutes. Add tomatoes and their juice, olives, vinegar, and capers. Simmer 15 minutes, stirring occasionally. Remove to a large bowl. Cover and marinate in the refrigerator at least 2 hours and up to 24 hours.

3. When ready to serve, stir in tuna. Divide among 4 plates and sprinkle with pine nuts. Serve chilled or at cool room temperature.

9 CRAB LOUIS

Prep: 20 minutes   Cook: 2 to 3 minutes   Serves: 4

This beautiful, simple salad is supposed to have originated in San Francisco, where crab is a mainstay. If crab is unavailable, substitute cooked medium shrimp.

16 asparagus spears, woody
    ends removed
1 pound cooked or canned
    crabmeat, drained and
    picked over
¾ cup Louis Dressing (recipe
    follows)
    Green leaf lettuce leaves

6 cups shredded iceberg
    lettuce
4 hard-cooked eggs,
    quartered lengthwise
4 small plum tomatoes,
    quartered lengthwise
    Lemon wedges

1. In a large pot of lightly salted boiling water, cook asparagus until crisp-tender, 2 to 3 minutes, depending on thickness of stalks. Drain, run under cold water to cool, and drain again.

2. In a small bowl, blend crab with half of dressing. Line 4 plates with lettuce leaves and divide shredded lettuce among them. Place crab on top of shredded lettuce.

3. Arrange asparagus, eggs, tomatoes, and lemon wedges around crab. Pass extra dressing at table.

10 LOUIS DRESSING

Prep: 5 minutes   Cook: none   Makes: about ¾ cup

This dressing is similar to Thousand Island dressing in color, consistency, and flavor, since both are based on a blend of mayonnaise and chili sauce. However, Louis dressing is simpler with only the addition of parsley and scallion. Traditional Louis dressing calls for cream to thin it, but milk works equally well.

½ cup mayonnaise
2 tablespoons bottled chili
    sauce
2 tablespoons milk or heavy
    cream

1 tablespoon lemon juice
1 scallion, minced
1 tablespoon minced parsley
    Salt and freshly ground
    pepper

In a medium bowl, whisk together mayonnaise, chili sauce, milk or cream, lemon juice, scallion, and parsley until well blended. If needed, season with salt and pepper to taste. If not using immediately, cover and refrigerate.

11 PALACE COURT SALAD WITH GREEN GODDESS DRESSING

Prep: 15 minutes   Cook: 35 to 45 minutes   Stand: 1 hour
Chill: 30 minutes   Serves: 4

Although traditionally served with green goddess dressing, this salad featuring artichokes and crab can be served with Louis Dressing (page 17) or my favorite, Cajun Mayonnaise (page 86). If time is short, buy canned artichoke bottoms and eliminate steps 1 and 2. The salad's dressing enjoys far more familiarity than the salad itself, probably due to the commercialization of green goddess dressing.

¼ cup flour
2 tablespoons lemon juice
4 large artichokes
4 cups shredded iceberg lettuce
3 medium plum tomatoes, cut into ½-inch dice
3 hard-cooked eggs, chopped

¾ pound cooked or canned crabmeat, drained and picked over
3 scallions, thinly sliced
2 celery ribs, thinly sliced
¾ cup Green Goddess Dressing (recipe follows)

1. In a large saucepan, whisk together flour, lemon juice, and 4 cups water until well blended. Bring to a boil over medium heat and reduce heat to low. Do not allow to boil over.

2. Meanwhile, break or slice off artichoke stems close to base. Discard tough outer leaves. Snap off remaining leaves to expose inner cone. With a sharp knife, slice off inner cone of leaves. Trim bottom, removing all bits of green. As artichokes are trimmed, drop into simmering liquid. If needed, add more water to cover artichokes. Cover and simmer until tender when pierced with a knife, 35 to 45 minutes. Let cool 1 hour in liquid. Rinse under cold water. With a spoon, scrape off and discard hairy choke. Refrigerate at least 30 minutes.

3. Place an artichoke bottom on each of 4 plates. Arrange lettuce around artichokes and sprinkle tomatoes and eggs over lettuce. In a small bowl, blend together crab, scallions, celery, and dressing. Mound crab on artichoke bottoms. Serve chilled.

12 GREEN GODDESS DRESSING
Prep: 10 minutes   Cook: none   Makes: about ³/₄ cup

Sharp and thick, this creamy, tarragon-flavored dressing works best on sturdy greens. It was first served at San Francisco's Palace Hotel in the 1920s at the actor George Arliss's request. He was appearing in William Archer's play *Green Goddess.*

½ cup mayonnaise
2 tablespoons chopped chives
  or scallions
2 tablespoons chopped
  parsley

2 teaspoons lemon juice
2 teaspoons chopped fresh
  tarragon or 1 teaspoon
  dried
2 anchovy fillets, minced

In a small bowl, whisk together all ingredients until well blended. If not using at once, cover and refrigerate.

13 COBB SALAD
Prep: 25 minutes   Cook: 7 to 9 minutes   Serves: 4

Bob Cobb originated this hearty chef's salad in 1936 at the Brown Derby restaurant in Hollywood. This chopped version is packed with so many flavorful ingredients that it needs little dressing. For a more formal presentation, make a bed of chopped iceberg lettuce and top it with the individual ingredients arranged in a pattern.

8 slices of bacon
4 cups chopped iceberg
  lettuce
2 cups chopped leftover
  cooked turkey breast (8 to
  10 ounces)
1 cup crumbled blue cheese
4 hard-cooked eggs, chopped
2 medium plum tomatoes, cut
  into ½-inch dice

1 medium ripe avocado, cut
  into ½-inch dice
⅓ cup olive oil
2 tablespoons red wine
  vinegar
2 teaspoons Dijon mustard
2 garlic cloves, minced
  Salt and freshly ground
  pepper

1. In a large skillet, cook bacon over medium heat, turning until crisp, 7 to 9 minutes. Drain on paper towels. When cool enough to handle, crumble bacon.

2. In a large bowl, combine lettuce, turkey, cheese, eggs, tomatoes, avocado, and bacon.

3. In a small bowl, whisk together oil, vinegar, mustard, and garlic. Drizzle over salad and toss until well blended. Season with salt and pepper to taste.

14   CAPRESE

Prep: 20 minutes   Cook: none   Serves: 4

Traditionally served as a first course, this Italian classic is such a simple salad of so few ingredients that the quality of each of them is important. Use only vine-ripened tomatoes, tender fresh basil, and extra-virgin olive oil. Mozzarella di bufala is so superior to supermarket mozzarella that you may consider it a different cheese altogether. Usually kept in water, it is made from the milk of water buffaloes. It's well worth the effort to find it. Serve the salad with a loaf of rustic, crusty Italian bread.

1½ pounds vine-ripened
      tomatoes, cut into ¼-inch
      slices
8 ounces fresh mozzarella di
      bufala cheese, cut into
      ¼-inch slices
1 medium cucumber, cut into
      ¼-inch slices
16 to 20 fresh basil leaves

1 small red onion, thinly
      sliced and separated into
      rings
¼ cup extra-virgin olive oil
2 tablespoons balsamic
      vinegar
   Salt and freshly ground
      pepper

1. On a large platter or individual plates, alternately arrange slightly overlapping slices of tomato and cheese, forming a ring. Tuck cucumber and basil among tomato and cheese. Mound onion in center of ring.

2. In a small bowl, blend oil, vinegar, and salt and pepper to taste. Drizzle over salad. Serve at room temperature.

15   CHINESE CHICKEN SALAD

Prep: 20 minutes   Cook: 1 to 1¼ hours   Serves: 4

Nutty, hot, and slightly sweet flavors have made this crunchy salad a standard. Because rice sticks are so fragile, be sure to toss the salad immediately before serving it.

1 (3½- to 4-pound) chicken
¼ cup plus 2 tablespoons
      creamy peanut butter
3 tablespoons rice vinegar
3 tablespoons dry sherry
1 tablespoon sugar
1 tablespoon minced fresh
      ginger
1 teaspoon Chinese chili
      paste or Tabasco sauce

1 garlic clove, minced
   Vegetable oil for frying
1 ounce rice sticks, broken
      into pieces
6 cups shredded iceberg
      lettuce
4 scallions, thinly sliced
½ cup sliced almonds,
      preferably toasted

1. Preheat oven to 375°F. Rinse chicken inside and out and pat dry. Place in a lightly greased baking dish. Roast chicken until thigh juices run clear when pierced with a sharp knife, 1 to 1¼ hours. Meanwhile, prepare dressing and rice sticks.

2. In a large bowl, vigorously whisk together peanut butter, vinegar, sherry, sugar, ginger, chili paste, and garlic until well blended. Add just enough water to make dressing a pourable consistency, about 1 to 2 tablespoons.

3. In a large skillet or deep-fat fryer, heat at least 2 inches of oil to 375°F. Add rice sticks in batches and fry until puffed, 5 to 10 seconds per batch. Drain on paper towels.

4. When chicken is cool enough to handle, remove and discard skin and bones and shred meat. Add chicken, lettuce, scallions, and rice sticks to dressing. Toss until well blended. Divide among 4 plates and sprinkle with almonds. Serve at once.

16 ITALIAN CHOP-CHOP
Prep: 30 minutes   Cook: 12 to 14 minutes   Serves: 6 to 8

A restaurant favorite, this version of chef's salad is a pleasing blend of meats, cheeses, lettuce, and tomato that are all chopped about the same size. When on hand, use leftover roast chicken or turkey instead of raw chicken breasts.

2 chicken breast halves (about 1 pound)	1 cup diced (½-inch) fontina cheese
1 (14½-ounce) can reduced-sodium chicken broth	1 (8¾-ounce) can chickpeas, rinsed and drained
8 cups chopped iceberg lettuce	¼ cup chopped fresh basil
	2 scallions, thinly sliced
2 large tomatoes, cut into ½-inch dice	¼ cup red wine vinegar
	3 garlic cloves, minced
8 ounces salami, cut into ½-inch dice	1 tablespoon Dijon mustard
	1 tablespoon dried oregano
1 cup diced (½-inch) mozzarella cheese	½ cup extra-virgin olive oil

1. In a medium saucepan, place chicken breasts skin side down with chicken broth. Bring to a boil over medium-high heat. Reduce heat to low, cover, and cook until chicken is opaque in center but still moist, 12 to 14 minutes. Let cool in broth. When cool enough to handle, pull meat off bones and cut into ½-inch cubes. Discard skin and bones; reserve broth for another use.

2. In a large bowl, combine chicken, lettuce, tomatoes, salami, mozzarella cheese, fontina cheese, chickpeas, basil, and scallions.

3. In a small bowl, combine vinegar, garlic, mustard, and oregano. Gradually whisk in oil. Pour dressing over salad and toss until well blended. Divide among 6 to 8 plates and serve at once.

17   CLASSIC THREE-BEAN SALAD WITH HAM
Prep: 15 minutes   Marinate: 8 hours   Cook: none   Serves: 7 to 8

Made from canned beans, three-bean salad is as easy as they come. The dressing is sweet, so the addition of savory, slightly salty ham balances the flavors and rounds out the salad to make a delicious one-dish meal.

½ cup vegetable oil
½ cup cider vinegar
½ cup sugar
1 teaspoon salt
½ teaspoon black pepper
2 (14½-ounce) cans cut green
   beans, drained
2 (15-ounce) cans kidney
   beans, drained

2 (14½-ounce) cans yellow
   wax beans, drained
1 medium red onion, thinly
   sliced and separated into
   rings
4 cups diced cooked ham
   (about 1 pound)
Red leaf lettuce leaves

1. In a medium bowl, stir oil, vinegar, sugar, salt, and pepper until well blended. Add green beans, kidney beans, wax beans, and onion. Stir gently until well blended. Cover and marinate 8 to 24 hours refrigerated.

2. Stir in ham and divide among 7 or 8 lettuce-lined plates. Serve cold or at room temperature.

18   GADO-GADO
Prep: 30 minutes   Cook: 20 to 25 minutes   Serves: 6 to 8

Standard fare in Malaysia and Indonesia, gado-gado is a seasonal assortment of cooked and raw vegetables that are rarely mixed, but served separately with a coconut milk–peanut butter dressing. If carefully arranged, the salad resembles a wheel of vivid colors. Change the vegetables to suit the season or your taste. Although not authentic, strips of grilled chicken or steak would make a delicious addition to the vegetables.

3 medium red potatoes
8 ounces green beans,
   trimmed and cut into
   1-inch lengths
1 (14-ounce) package firm
   tofu
6 hard-cooked eggs, chopped
3 cups shredded cabbage
3 cups bean sprouts
2 medium carrots, peeled and
   thinly sliced

1 large cucumber, quartered
   lengthwise and thinly
   sliced crosswise
1 small red onion, thinly
   sliced and separated into
   rings
1 cup chopped roasted
   peanuts
1¾ cups Indonesian Coconut
   Milk Dressing (recipe
   follows)

1. In a large pot of boiling water, cook potatoes until just tender when pierced with a sharp knife, 20 to 25 minutes; drain. When cool enough to handle, cut into bite-size pieces.

2. Meanwhile, in a medium pot of lightly salted boiling water, cook green beans until crisp-tender, 3 to 5 minutes. With a slotted spatula, remove beans to a colander. Drain, run under cold water to cool, and drain again. Add tofu to water, reduce heat to low, and simmer 10 minutes. Drain and cut into 1-inch cubes.

3. On a large platter or on 6 to 8 individual plates, separately arrange potatoes, green beans, tofu, eggs, cabbage, bean sprouts, carrots, cucumber, and red onion in a linear or spoke pattern. Sprinkle with peanuts. Serve dressing separately warm or at room temperature.

---

19 INDONESIAN COCONUT MILK DRESSING
Prep: 10 minutes   Cook: 15 minutes   Makes: about 1³/₄ cups

This rich dressing is nutty and spicy, but its heat is easily adjusted by altering the amount of hot red pepper. Be sure to watch the mixture carefully while it cooks, since the milk boils over readily. The dressing should be served warm or at room temperature and should be a pourable consistency. If you like, make it a week ahead and refrigerate; warm it just before serving. For a party, the sauce can be served in a small fondue pot or in a trimmed, hulled-out vegetable such as a large bell pepper or a small head of cabbage.

1 tablespoon vegetable oil	1¼ cups canned coconut milk
¼ cup minced onion	½ cup peanut butter
1 to 2 teaspoons crushed hot red pepper	2 tablespoons firmly packed brown sugar
1 tablespoon minced fresh ginger	2 tablespoons soy sauce
2 garlic cloves, minced	1 tablespoon lemon juice

1. In a small saucepan, heat oil over medium-low heat. Add onion, hot pepper, ginger, and garlic. Cook, stirring occasionally, until softened, about 5 minutes.

2. Blend in coconut milk, peanut butter, brown sugar, soy sauce, and lemon juice. Bring to a boil over medium-high heat. Reduce heat to low and simmer, stirring occasionally, until thickened, about 10 minutes. Serve warm or at room temperature.

20   TABBOULEH
Prep: 15 minutes   Stand: 1 hour   Cook: 5 to 7 minutes   Serves: 6

Tabbouleh is a refreshing Middle Eastern bulgur salad that's usually served with whole romaine lettuce leaves, which can be used as scoops for eating. To make this a more substantial main course, serve with olives and chunks of feta cheese.

1 **cup cracked bulgur wheat**	1 **cup minced parsley**
2 **cups boiling water**	½ **cup extra-virgin olive oil**
½ **cup pine nuts (pignoli)**	½ **cup minced fresh mint**
4 **scallions, thinly sliced**	⅓ **cup lemon juice**
3 **medium tomatoes, chopped**	1½ **teaspoons salt**
2 **celery ribs, minced**	**Romaine lettuce leaves**

1. In a medium heatproof bowl, combine bulgur and boiling water. Let stand 1 to 2 hours to plump grains. Drain, then squeeze dry in a kitchen towel.

2. Meanwhile, preheat oven to 350°F. Spread out nuts in a small baking dish and toast until fragrant and lightly browned, 5 to 7 minutes.

3. In a large bowl, combine bulgur with remaining ingredients except lettuce. Toss until well blended. Divide among 6 lettuce-lined plates. Serve at room temperature or chilled.

21   LOBSTER SALAD À LA LORENZO
Prep: 20 minutes   Cook: 16 minutes   Serves: 4

This luxurious main course is actually a combination of two classics: Lobster à la Russe and New York restaurant "21" 's Lorenzo Dressing. Sauce à la Russe and the Lorenzo dressing are very similar, since both are a mayonnaise-base highlighted with freshly minced watercress. The Lorenzo Dressing also incorporates prepared chili sauce, which is frequently paired with shellfish. Some versions of Lobster à la Russe call for incorporating Beluga caviar into the dressing. If you want, sprinkle 1 tablespoon of caviar onto each salad.

2 **(1½-pound) live lobsters**	**Green leaf lettuce leaves**
2 **cups asparagus tips**	3 **tablespoons chopped**
2 **cups peeled baby carrots**	**chives**
2 **cups cauliflower florets**	
¾ **cup Lorenzo Dressing**	
(recipe follows)	

1. Plunge lobsters into a large pot of boiling water. Cook until bright red in color, about 10 minutes. Drain, run under cold water to cool, and drain again. When cool enough to handle, remove meat from shells and cut into 1-inch chunks.

2. In separate medium pots of lightly salted boiling water, cook asparagus, carrots, and cauliflower until crisp-tender, about 2 minutes each. Drain each separately, run under cold water to cool, and drain again.

3. In a medium bowl, blend together lobster and about 3 tablespoons of dressing. Divide among 4 lettuce-lined plates, arranging in a mound in center of each. Toss each vegetable separately with about 3 tablespoons of dressing to coat and arrange in mounds around lobster. Sprinkle with chives and serve at once.

22 LORENZO DRESSING

Prep: 5 minutes   Cook: 7 to 9 minutes   Makes: about ¾ cup

For decades, almost all of the salads at the famous "21" restaurant in New York City were upholstered with this creamy dressing, which was invented by one of the waiters, whose name was Lorenzo. For a lighter dressing with the same blend of flavors, dilute the mustard with ¼ cup of water.

3 slices of bacon
½ teaspoon dry mustard
¼ teaspoon salt
⅛ teaspoon pepper
2 tablespoons tarragon
    vinegar
⅓ cup olive oil
2 tablespoons bottled chili
    sauce
2 tablespoons minced
    watercress

1. In a large skillet, cook bacon over medium heat, turning, until crisp, 7 to 9 minutes. Drain on paper towels. When cool enough to handle, crumble bacon.

2. In a small bowl, blend together mustard with 1 tablespoon water. Transfer to a food processor or blender. Add salt and pepper. With machine on, pour in vinegar in a slow, steady stream. Then gradually drizzle in oil. Add chili sauce and blend together. If not using within an hour, cover and refrigerate. Just before serving, blend in watercress.

23   SALMAGUNDI

Prep: 25 minutes   Cook: 1 to 1¼ hours   Serves: 8

This odd-sounding salad, which first appeared in English print in 1674, is named for the French *salmigondis*, or hodgepodge. Traditionally this English chef's-type salad is composed of diced meats that are formally arranged and garnished with pickles, anchovies, and hard-cooked eggs. This version is simply dressed with a basic vinaigrette.

1   (3½- to 4-pound) chicken
1   pound medium red
      potatoes
8   ounces green beans,
      trimmed
12 cups shredded iceberg
      lettuce
4   cups shredded cooked ham
      (about 1 pound)
1   (16-ounce) jar
      sweet-and-sour red
      cabbage, drained

4   medium plum tomatoes, cut
      into ½-inch dice
4   hard-cooked eggs, chopped
2   (2-ounce) cans anchovy
      fillets, drained
½   cup capers, drained
1⅓ cups Classic Vinaigrette
      (recipe follows)

1. Preheat oven to 375°F. Rinse chicken inside and out and pat dry. Place in a lightly greased baking dish. Roast chicken until thigh juices run clear when pierced with a sharp knife, 1 to 1¼ hours. When cool enough to handle, remove skin and bones and shred meat.

2. Meanwhile, in a large pot of boiling water, cook potatoes until tender when pierced with a sharp knife, 20 to 25 minutes; drain. When cool enough to handle, peel and cut potatoes into ¼-inch slices.

3. In a medium pot of lightly salted boiling water, cook green beans until just tender, 5 to 7 minutes. Drain, rinse under cold water, and drain again.

4. Divide lettuce among 8 plates. In a spoke pattern on top of lettuce, arrange chicken, potatoes, green beans, ham, and cabbage. In center of spokes, place tomatoes and eggs. Top with anchovy fillets and capers. Drizzle with vinaigrette and serve at once.

24   CLASSIC VINAIGRETTE
Prep: 1 minute   Cook: none   Makes: 1⅓ cups

A traditional vinaigrette is a blend of 3 parts oil to 1 part vinegar, but the formula is only a basis for hundreds of variations. Adding herbs, spices, and condiments; altering the proportion and types of vinegars or other acidic ingredients and oils; and changing the technique of blending them will alter the outcome. A simple vinaigrette such as this is perfect for a complicated salad of many textures and flavors, such as Salmagundi.

1 cup olive oil	**Salt and freshly ground**
⅓ cup red wine vinegar	**pepper**

In a small bowl, blend together oil and vinegar. Season with salt and pepper to taste. If not using at once, blend together again just before using.

25   HOT GERMAN POTATO SALAD
Prep: 15 minutes   Cook: 29 to 34 minutes   Serves: 4

German potato salad, which is really an American classic, is credited to German immigrants who came to this country. The salad tends to be strong on vinegar, perhaps due to the German penchant for pickling foods of all kinds. It is hearty, hot, and delicious. Serve with pumpernickel or rye bread.

1½ pounds medium red	½ teaspoon celery seed
potatoes	6 medium mushrooms, sliced
8 slices of bacon	1 small onion, chopped
½ cup cider vinegar	1 celery rib, thinly sliced
¼ cup chicken broth	Salt and freshly ground
1 tablespoon flour	pepper
½ teaspoon sugar	Green leaf lettuce leaves

1. In a large pot of boiling water, cook potatoes until barely tender when pierced with a sharp knife, about 20 to 25 minutes; drain. When cool enough to handle, peel and cut into ¾-inch cubes.

2. Meanwhile, in a large skillet, cook bacon over medium heat until crisp, about 7 to 9 minutes. Transfer bacon to paper towels to drain and reserve pan drippings. When cool enough to handle, crumble bacon.

3. In a small bowl, whisk together vinegar, broth, flour, sugar, celery seed, and ¼ cup water until well blended.

4. Pour off all but 2 tablespoons bacon fat and place skillet over medium heat. Add mushrooms, onion, and celery. Cook, stirring occasionally, until vegetables are softened, about 4 minutes. Stir vinegar mixture again and add to skillet. Bring to a boil, stirring until smooth. Add potatoes. Cover and cook until heated through, about 5 minutes. Season with salt and pepper to taste. Divide among 4 lettuce-lined plates. Sprinkle with bacon and serve hot.

26 ALL-AMERICAN POTATO SALAD WITH BACON

Prep: 10 minutes   Cook: 20 to 25 minutes   Serves: 4 to 5

Instead of using the gobs of mayonnaise that have accompanied traditional potato salad, this up-to-date version is lightly dressed. If you prefer, substitute nonfat plain yogurt for half of the mayonnaise.

2 pounds medium red
   potatoes
8 slices of bacon
½ cup mayonnaise
¼ cup minced sweet pickle
1 tablespoon Dijon mustard

3 hard-cooked eggs, chopped
2 celery ribs, thinly sliced
Salt and freshly ground
   pepper
Green leaf lettuce leaves

1. In a large pot of boiling water, cook potatoes until tender when pierced with a sharp knife, about 20 to 25 minutes; drain. When cool enough to handle, peel, if desired, and cut into ¾-inch cubes.

2. Meanwhile, in a large skillet, cook bacon over medium heat until crisp, 7 to 9 minutes. Drain on paper towels. When cool enough to handle, crumble bacon.

3. In a large bowl, combine mayonnaise, pickle, and mustard. Whisk until well blended. Add potatoes, bacon, eggs, and celery. Toss until well blended. Season with salt and pepper to taste. Divide among 4 or 5 lettuce-lined plates and serve at room temperature or cover and refrigerate at least 2 hours to serve cold.

27 HERRING, BEET, AND APPLE SALAD

Prep: 15 minutes   Cook: 10 to 15 minutes   Serves: 4 to 6

Standard fare in Scandinavia and Russia, this rosy-pink salad makes a hearty main course or an attractive addition to a buffet. Serve with pumpernickel or rye bread.

8 baby red potatoes
1 cup sour cream
½ cup red wine vinegar
2 tablespoons sugar
1 tablespoon prepared white
   horseradish
1 tablespoon Dijon mustard
1 (12-ounce) jar rollmop
   herring, drained
1 (15-ounce) can julienne-cut
   beets, drained

2 hard-cooked eggs, chopped
1 large Granny Smith apple,
   cored and chopped
Green leaf lettuce leaves
½ small red onion, thinly
   sliced and separated into
   rings
1 tablespoon chopped fresh
   dill or 1 teaspoon dried

1. In a large pot of boiling water, cook potatoes until barely tender when pierced with a sharp knife, 10 to 15 minutes; drain. When cool enough to handle, cut potatoes into quarters.

2. In a large bowl, combine sour cream, vinegar, sugar, horseradish, and mustard. Whisk until smooth. Unroll herring and remove gherkins. Mince gherkins and blend into dressing. Remove and reserve ½ cup dressing.

3. Cut herring into bite-size chunks. Add potatoes, herring, beets, eggs, and apple to 1 cup dressing. Stir until well blended. Divide among 4 to 6 lettuce-lined plates and sprinkle red onion and dill on top. Serve at room temperature or cover and refrigerate at least 2 hours to serve cold. Pass reserved dressing on the side.

---

28 GREEK SALAD
Prep: 25 minutes   Cook: none   Serves: 8 to 10

With their pleasing balance of assertive and subtle flavors and colorful ingredients, Greek salads have been a popular restaurant offering for decades. This efficient version calls for making the dressing first in the bottom of a large bowl. The main ingredients go on top, and everything is tossed together for a delicious one-dish meal. Serve with a loaf of crusty bread.

¾ cup extra-virgin olive oil
¼ cup lemon juice
2 teaspoons red wine vinegar
3 garlic cloves, minced
2 teaspoons dried oregano
1 teaspoon salt
8 cups torn red leaf lettuce
8 cups torn romaine lettuce
5 plum tomatoes, cut into
   ¾-inch dice
1 large green bell pepper, cut
   into ¾-inch dice

1 medium cucumber,
   quartered lengthwise, cut
   crosswise into
   ¾-inch-thick slices
1 small red onion, thinly
   sliced and separated into
   rings
1½ cups pitted kalamata olives
1½ cups crumbled feta cheese
   (6 ounces)
Freshly ground pepper

In a large bowl, whisk together oil, lemon juice, vinegar, garlic, oregano, and salt. Add remaining ingredients except ground pepper. Toss until well blended. Divide among 8 to 10 plates and serve at once with freshly ground pepper.

29   TACO SALAD
Prep: 25 minutes   Cook: 20 to 25 minutes   Serves: 6

This version of the perennially popular taco salad uses a tortilla shell that is baked instead of fried, eliminating all of the calories and bother involved in deep-frying. If you prefer, substitute purchased taco salad shells, which are available in many supermarket bakeries.

6 (10-inch) flour tortillas
  Vegetable oil
1 pound lean ground beef
2 garlic cloves, minced
1 tablespoon chili powder
1 (10-ounce) jar enchilada
  sauce
1 (15-ounce) can pinto or
  kidney beans, rinsed and
  drained
6 cups shredded iceberg
  lettuce

2 large tomatoes, seeded and
  chopped
1½ cups bottled salsa, mild or
  hot to taste
1 (2.2-ounce) can sliced ripe
  olives, drained
3 scallions, thinly sliced
2 cups shredded Cheddar
  cheese (8 ounces)
1½ cups sour cream
1½ cups Quick Guacamole
  (recipe follows)

1. Preheat oven to 350°F. Lightly brush tortillas on both sides with oil. Press into 6 (6-inch) round ovenproof dishes. Place a loose ball of foil into each to help tortilla retain a bowl-like shape. Bake until golden and crisp, 15 to 20 minutes.

2. Meanwhile, in a medium nonstick skillet, cook ground beef, garlic, and chili powder over medium heat, stirring frequently, until beef is no longer pink, 8 to 10 minutes. Drain off all liquid and stir in enchilada sauce. Return to heat and simmer, stirring occasionally, until thickened, 12 to 15 minutes. Remove from heat and blend in beans.

3. Remove foil and tortilla shells from bowls. Set shells on 6 serving plates. In each shell, layer beef, lettuce, tomatoes, salsa, olives, scallions, and cheese. Top each with sour cream and guacamole. Serve at once.

30   QUICK GUACAMOLE
Prep: 5 minutes   Cook: none   Makes: about 1½ cups

Rich and buttery, guacamole is simple to make in a food processor or by hand. With both methods, be sure your avocados are soft and ripe. Hass avocados are the first choice for the tastiest guacamole; the Fuerte variety, second.

2 medium ripe avocados,
  halved, pitted, and
  peeled
¼ cup bottled salsa, mild or
  hot to taste

2 tablespoons lemon juice
  Salt and freshly ground
  pepper

Place avocados, salsa, and lemon juice in a food processor or blender. Mince until small chunks remain or until almost smooth. (Or mash with a fork in a bowl.) Season with salt and pepper to taste.

31 SALAD NIÇOISE WITH GRILLED FRESH TUNA

Prep: 25 minutes   Cook: 18 to 25 minutes   Serves: 6

Niçoise refers to dishes garnished with tomatoes, capers, black olives, lemon juice, and anchovies. Chefs from the Mediterranean city of Nice made the term famous, and the most recognized such dish is salad Niçoise, which traditionally includes potatoes, green beans, and tuna.

12 baby red potatoes
8 ounces green beans, trimmed and cut into 1-inch lengths
6 fresh tuna steaks (about 2 pounds total), cut 1 inch thick
½ cup plus 2 tablespoons extra-virgin olive oil
6 cups torn Boston lettuce
6 cups torn curly endive
2 tablespoons lemon juice or red wine vinegar

2 teaspoons Dijon mustard
Salt and freshly ground pepper
6 small plum tomatoes, quartered lengthwise
3 hard-cooked eggs, quartered lengthwise
½ cup kalamata or other oil-cured black olives
12 anchovy fillets
6 lemon wedges

1. In a large saucepan of boiling water, cook potatoes until just tender when pierced with a sharp knife, 10 to 15 minutes; drain. When cool enough to handle, quarter potatoes. Meanwhile, in a medium saucepan of lightly salted boiling water, cook green beans until just tender, 5 to 7 minutes. Drain, run under cold water to cool, and drain again.

2. Light a hot fire in a barbecue grill or preheat broiler. Brush tuna steaks on both sides with 2 tablespoons oil. Grill or broil 4 to 6 inches from heat, turning once, until tuna is browned outside and opaque throughout but still moist and juicy inside, about 4 to 5 minutes per side.

3. In a large bowl, combine lettuce, endive, potatoes, and green beans. In a small bowl, whisk together remaining ½ cup olive oil, lemon juice, and mustard. Season with salt and pepper to taste. Drizzle dressing over salad and toss until well coated.

4. Divide among 6 plates. Arrange tomatoes and eggs around each salad and garnish with olives, anchovy fillets, and lemon wedges. Place a tuna steak on each salad and serve at once.

Chapter 2

Chicken Salads, Etc.

Not too long ago, chicken salad was a predictable combination of leftover chicken, celery, and gobs of mayonnaise. It could be found at ladies' luncheons in hollowed-out tomatoes, in downtown delis, and at home sandwiched between two pieces of white bread. It was loaded with fat, and its only virtue was that it was consistent.

Today's chicken and other poultry salads have slimmed down and, thankfully, become anything but predictable. They're capable of taking on the attributes and exotic ingredients of regional and worldwide cuisines, and they're as comfortable with vinaigrettes and Asian-based dressings as with traditional mayonnaise. Their versatility makes them appealing whether the poultry is grilled, poached, broiled, stir-fried, sautéed, or left over.

In this chapter, you'll find everything from roast chicken shredded and casually tossed into a slaw to breasts poached and thinly sliced to retain their shape for a formal composed salad. You'll find chicken, turkey, duck, and quail paired with fruits and cheeses, pestos and salsas, and vegetables and herbs. You'll find salads with flavors from around the world served warm, room temperature, and cold.

In general, cooking methods for poultry salads can be interchanged with only slight variations in flavor. Poaching and microwaving produce the moistest, blandest results; roasting, sauteíng, and stir-frying deliver intensified flavor; grilling and broiling impart a dark color and deep, charred taste.

Unless a salad calls for marinating before cooking, leftover chicken, duck, or turkey works perfectly well. Count on about 1 cup of meat per pound of whole bird. For example, a 3½- to 4-pound chicken will yield 3½ to 4 cups of meat after it's been roasted, skinned, boned, and cut up. Three quarters of a pound of skinless, boneless chicken breast will yield about 2 cups of cooked chicken, diced or shredded.

Poultry invites creativity, so use these recipes as a base. You'll find familiar-sounding salads with a twist, such as Chicken Waldorf Salad with Apple Butter Mayonnaise, Chicken Tonnato, and Turkey Club Salad (based on traditional club sandwich ingredients). For the adventurous, there's a Thai-style Fire-and-Ice Orange-Chicken Salad and Hoisin-Scented Chicken-Napa Slaw. For a special dinner, try the Warm Orange-Duck Salad or the Pomegranate, Blue Cheese, and Watercress Salad with Grilled Chicken. Armed with these recipes and a sense of adventure, you'll realize that using poultry in salads is limited only by the cook's imagination.

32   CHICKEN AND ARTICHOKE SALAD
Prep: 15 minutes   Cook: 10 minutes   Serves: 4

Brightly colored radicchio and pale Boston lettuce highlight this lightly herbed, lemony salad of chicken breasts and artichoke hearts.

¼ cup plus 2 tablespoons extra-virgin olive oil
4 skinless, boneless chicken breast halves
4 teaspoons lemon juice
1 tablespoon Dijon mustard
1½ teaspoons minced fresh tarragon or ½ teaspoon dried

1½ teaspoons minced fresh oregano or ½ teaspoon dried
1 (14-ounce) can quartered artichoke hearts, drained
6 cups torn Boston lettuce
2 cups torn radicchio
¼ cup grated Parmesan cheese

1. In a large skillet, heat 2 tablespoons oil over medium-high heat until hot. Add chicken and cook, turning occasionally, until golden brown on both sides and white throughout but still moist, about 10 minutes. Transfer to a cutting board and let rest while preparing dressing.

2. In a large bowl, whisk together remaining ¼ cup olive oil, lemon juice, mustard, tarragon, and oregano. Cut chicken into ¾-inch cubes. Add chicken, artichoke hearts, lettuce, and radicchio to dressing. Toss until well blended. Divide all ingredients evenly among 4 plates. Sprinkle with Parmesan cheese and serve.

33   CHICKEN AND CHICKPEA SALAD
Prep: 20 minutes   Cook: 1 to 1¼ hours   Serves: 4 to 6

Fruits, chickpeas, nuts, and a bit of curry complement roast chicken in this well-balanced main course. Yogurt makes a fat-free base for a slightly sweet-and-hot creamy dressing, and olive oil gives it an appealing sheen.

1 (3½- to 4-pound) chicken
1 cup nonfat plain yogurt
2 tablespoons olive oil
1 tablespoon curry powder
1 tablespoon sugar
1 (15-ounce) can chickpeas, rinsed and drained
3 scallions, thinly sliced

1 cup seedless red grapes, cut in half
1 cup slivered almonds, lightly toasted
½ cup raisins
Salt and freshly ground pepper
Green leaf lettuce leaves

1. Preheat oven to 375°F. Rinse chicken inside and out and pat dry. Place in a lightly greased baking dish. Roast chicken until thigh juices run clear when pierced with a sharp knife, 1 to 1¼ hours. Remove to a cutting board and let cool. Meanwhile, prepare salad.

2. In a large bowl, blend together yogurt, oil, curry powder, and sugar until smooth. Add chickpeas, scallions, grapes, almonds, and raisins. Cover and refrigerate while chicken cooks.

3. When chicken is cool enough to handle, shred meat (discard skin and bones) and add to salad. Toss salad until well blended. Season with salt and pepper to taste. Divide among 4 to 6 lettuce-lined plates and serve at room temperature or cold.

34 CHIPOTLE CHICKEN SALAD WITH MANGOES
Prep: 30 minutes   Marinate: 20 minutes   Cook: 8 to 10 minutes
Serves: 8

Based on a popular offering at Zarela's, a Mexican restaurant in New York City, this salad includes smoky, spicy chicken that is briefly marinated in chipotle chiles and garlic. Cooling iceberg lettuce and refreshing mangoes provide the perfect contrast. The chicken can be grilled or broiled, as it is here, or quickly pan-fried.

1 (7-ounce) can chipotle chiles in adobo sauce
½ cup plus 2 tablespoons olive oil
4 garlic cloves, minced
8 skinless, boneless chicken breast halves
2 tablespoons red wine vinegar

2 teaspoons dried oregano
12 cups shredded iceberg lettuce
6 scallions, thinly sliced
Salt and freshly ground pepper
3 large ripe mangoes, peeled, pitted, and thinly sliced

1. Light a medium-hot fire in a barbecue grill or preheat broiler. Mince 4 chipotle chiles and set aside. In a large baking dish, combine remaining chipotle chiles with sauce from can, 2 tablespoons oil, and 3 garlic cloves. Add chicken and turn once to coat. Marinate 20 to 30 minutes at room temperature.

2. Lift chicken from marinade; reserve marinade. Grill on an oiled grill 4 to 6 inches from coals or broil, turning once and basting occasionally with marinade, until white throughout but still moist, about 8 to 10 minutes. Transfer chicken to a cutting board and let rest while preparing salad.

3. In a large bowl, combine 4 minced chiles, remaining ½ cup oil, remaining garlic clove, vinegar, and oregano. Add lettuce and scallions and toss until well blended. If needed, season with salt and pepper to taste. Divide among 8 plates. Slice chicken thinly crosswise on diagonal, retaining shape of breasts. Top each salad with a sliced chicken breast. Divide mango slices among salads, arranging in slightly overlapping slices alongside chicken. Serve warm or at room temperature.

35   CUMIN-SCENTED CHICKEN SALAD WITH MANGO AND CASHEWS

Prep: 15 minutes   Cook: 10 minutes   Serves: 2 to 3

Buttery cashews and mangoes transform chicken salad into a luxurious meal. If you like, use leftover dark or light cooked chicken or turkey for this mildly spiced main course.

1 **tablespoon vegetable oil**
2 **skinless, boneless chicken breast halves**
¼ **cup mayonnaise**
2 **tablespoons bottled lime juice**
½ **teaspoon ground cumin**
1 **large mango, peeled, pitted, and cut into ¾-inch dice**

½ **cup chopped cashews**
3 **scallions, thinly sliced**
1 **celery rib, thinly sliced**
Salt and freshly ground pepper
Red leaf lettuce leaves

1. In a medium nonstick skillet, heat oil over medium-high heat until it shimmers. Add chicken and cook, turning occasionally, until golden brown on both sides and opaque throughout but still moist, about 10 minutes. Remove to a cutting board. Let rest 5 to 10 minutes. Cut into ¾-inch cubes.

2. In a large bowl, whisk together mayonnaise, lime juice, and cumin until well blended. Add chicken, mango, cashews, scallions, and celery. Toss until well blended. Season with salt and pepper to taste. Divide among 2 or 3 lettuce-lined plates and serve at room temperature.

36   DRIED CHERRY AND CHICKEN SALAD

Prep: 15 minutes   Cook: 1 to 1¼ hours   Serves: 4

Since fresh cherries enjoy such a short season, dried ones supply that special fruity flavor and chewy texture all year long. Here they are paired with walnuts, roasted chicken, and a colorful blend of lettuces.

1 **(3½- to 4-pound) chicken**
½ **cup fresh mint, chopped**
⅓ **cup walnut oil**
2 **tablespoons raspberry vinegar**
1 **tablespoon Dijon mustard**
4 **cups torn curly endive**

½ **cup shredded radicchio**
4 **scallions, chopped**
½ **cup dried cherries**
½ **cup chopped walnuts**
Salt and freshly ground pepper

1. Preheat oven to 375°F. Rinse chicken inside and out and pat dry. Roast until thigh juices run clear when pierced with a sharp knife, 1 to 1¼ hours. When chicken is cool enough to handle, remove and discard skin and bones and shred meat.

2. In a large bowl, whisk together mint, oil, vinegar, and mustard until well blended. Add chicken, endive, radicchio, scallions, dried cherries, and walnuts. Toss until well blended and season with salt and pepper to taste. Divide among 4 plates and serve at room temperature.

---

37   MAHOGANY HOT-AND-SWEET CHICKEN SALAD

Prep: 20 minutes   Marinate: 30 minutes   Cook: 3 minutes
Serves: 4

Warm in temperature and flavor, the chicken for this salad is marinated in soy sauce and mirin, a sweet Japanese wine made from glutinous rice. It takes on a lovely deep brown color while cooking. A bed of shredded iceberg lettuce provides a pleasant, cool contrast. Be sure not to eat the dried red chiles, since they are intolerably hot.

½ cup mirin or sweet sherry
¼ cup plus 2 tablespoons soy sauce
1 tablespoon Asian sesame oil
4 skinless, boneless chicken breast halves, sliced crosswise into ½-inch strips
¼ cup vegetable oil
3 tablespoons ketchup
2 tablespoons lemon juice

1 tablespoon sugar
1 (1-inch) piece of fresh ginger, peeled and minced
8 cups shredded iceberg or romaine lettuce
2 tablespoons peanut oil
16 dried small red chiles
8 scallions, sliced into 1-inch lengths
¼ cup dry-roasted peanuts
¼ cup cilantro leaves

1. In a shallow nonreactive dish, combine mirin, 2 tablespoons soy sauce, and sesame oil. Add chicken and toss until well blended. Cover and marinate at room temperature 30 minutes or refrigerate 1 to 2 hours.

2. In a small bowl, blend remaining ¼ cup soy sauce, vegetable oil, ketchup, lemon juice, sugar, ginger, and ¼ cup water; set sauce aside. Divide lettuce among 4 large plates.

3. In a large wok over high heat, swirl peanut oil around pan. When hot, drain chicken and add to pan with chiles and scallions. Cook, stirring constantly, until chicken is just white in center but still moist, about 3 minutes. While warm, divide chicken among lettuce-lined plates. Sprinkle with peanuts and cilantro. Drizzle with dressing and serve warm.

38   SWEET AND HOT CURRIED CHICKEN SALAD

Prep: 15 minutes   Cook: 12 to 14 minutes   Serves: 2

This flavor- and texture-packed salad is practically instant if you use left-over chicken or buy deli-cooked or rotisserie chicken.

2   chicken breast halves (about 1 pound)
1   (14½-ounce) can reduced-sodium chicken broth
¼   cup mayonnaise
1   teaspoon curry powder
½   red-skinned apple, cored and cut into ¾-inch dice
¼   cup chopped pecans
3   tablespoons currants
1   celery rib, thinly sliced
1   scallion, thinly sliced
    Salt and freshly ground pepper

1. In a medium saucepan, place chicken breasts skin side down with chicken broth. Bring to a boil over medium-high heat. Reduce heat to low, cover, and cook until chicken is white in center but still moist, 12 to 14 minutes. Let cool in broth. When cool enough to handle, pull meat off bones and shred. Discard skin and bones.

2. In a medium bowl, blend together mayonnaise and curry powder until smooth. Add chicken, apple, pecans, currants, celery, and scallion. Stir until well blended. Season with salt and pepper to taste. Serve at room temperature or chilled.

39   GRAND MARNIER CHICKEN SALAD WITH ROQUEFORT CROUTONS

Prep: 15 minutes   Cook: 14 to 17 minutes   Serves: 4

2   tablespoons vegetable oil
4   skinless, boneless chicken breast halves (about 5 ounces each)
8   large slices of French or Italian bread, cut ½ inch thick
½   cup crumbled Roquefort cheese, at room temperature
6   cups torn assorted baby lettuces
½   cup chopped walnuts
½   cup Grand Marnier Vinaigrette (recipe follows)

1. In a large nonstick skillet, heat oil over medium-high heat until it shimmers. Add chicken and cook, turning occasionally, until golden brown on both sides and white throughout but still moist, about 10 minutes. Remove to a cutting board and let rest while preparing croutons and salad.

2. Preheat a broiler. On a large baking sheet, arrange bread in a single layer. Broil 4 to 6 inches from heat, turning once, until golden brown on both sides, about 3 to 5 minutes total. Spread cheese evenly on bread and place under broiler. Cook until cheese is heated through, 1 to 2 minutes.

3. In a large bowl, combine lettuces, walnuts, and vinaigrette. Toss until well blended. Divide among 4 plates. Cut chicken into thin slices, retaining shape of breast. Top each salad with a sliced chicken breast and garnish with 2 croutons. Serve warm or at room temperature.

---

40 GRAND MARNIER VINAIGRETTE
Prep: 8 minutes   Cook: 3 minutes   Makes: about ½ cup

Mahogany in color, deep and rich in flavor, this slightly sweet dressing also makes a delicious companion to fruit salads. Other orange-flavored liqueurs, such as Triple Sec or Strega, can be substituted for the Grand Marnier.

¼ cup Grand Marnier
2 tablespoons balsamic
    vinegar
2 tablespoons orange juice
1 large shallot, minced
1 garlic clove, minced

1 tablespoon lemon juice
2 teaspoons Dijon mustard
¼ cup extra-virgin olive oil
2 tablespoons walnut oil
    Salt and freshly ground
    pepper

1. In a small nonreactive saucepan, combine Grand Marnier, vinegar, orange juice, shallot, and garlic. Boil over high heat, stirring occasionally, until syrupy and reduced to 2 tablespoons, about 3 minutes. Transfer to a small bowl and let cool to room temperature.

2. Whisk in lemon juice and mustard. Gradually whisk in olive oil and walnut oil in a thin stream. If needed, season with salt and pepper to taste. If not using within an hour, cover and refrigerate. Let return to room temperature before using.

41 CHARRED CHICKEN AND TOMATO SALAD WITH HERBED ROQUEFORT VINAIGRETTE

Prep: 15 minutes   Cook: 8 to 10 minutes   Serves: 8

Blue cheese, charcoal-grilled chicken, ripe tomatoes, and buttery avocados are a favorite flavor combination of mine. The tomatoes, avocados, and chicken are arranged in slightly overlapping slices to create a beautiful but simple composed salad.

 8 skinless, boneless chicken
    breast halves
 ¼ cup vegetable oil
16 large red or green leaf
    lettuce leaves
 8 small plum tomatoes, thinly
    sliced

 4 medium ripe avocados,
    thinly sliced
 1 cup Herbed Roquefort
    Vinaigrette (recipe
    follows)

1. Light a medium-hot fire in a grill or preheat broiler. Brush chicken breasts on both sides with oil. Grill on a lightly oiled rack set 4 to 6 inches from heat or broil, turning once, until opaque throughout but still moist, about 8 to 10 minutes. Slice chicken crosswise into thin slices, retaining shape of breasts.

2. Line 8 plates with lettuce and top each with a sliced chicken breast. Arrange tomatoes and avocados in slightly overlapping slices alongside chicken. Drizzle dressing over salads and serve at room temperature.

42 HERBED ROQUEFORT VINAIGRETTE

Prep: 10 minutes   Cook: none   Makes: about 1 cup

Fragrant with extra-virgin olive oil, garlic, and fresh herbs, this nicely balanced dressing is so packed with flavors that a little goes a long way.

2 tablespoons minced fresh
   basil
2 tablespoons minced parsley
2 tablespoons red wine
   vinegar
1 teaspoon lemon juice
1 teaspoon Dijon mustard

¾ teaspoon sugar
 1 garlic clove, minced
 ½ cup extra-virgin olive oil
 ⅓ cup crumbled Roquefort
   cheese

In a small bowl, blend together basil, parsley, vinegar, lemon juice, mustard, sugar, and garlic. Gradually whisk in oil. Blend in cheese. If not using within an hour, cover and refrigerate. Let return to room temperature before serving.

43 ROQUEFORT-CHICKEN SALAD WITH BELGIAN ENDIVE AND PEARS

Prep: 30 minutes   Cook: 12 to 14 minutes   Serves: 4 to 6

4 chicken breast halves (about 2 pounds)

1 (14½-ounce) can reduced-sodium chicken broth

3 large Belgian endive spears, sliced

2 large Bartlett pears, preferably red, cored—1 cut into ¾-inch dice, 1 thinly sliced

8 cups torn escarole

4 scallions, thinly sliced

1 cup crumbled Roquefort cheese

1 cup chopped walnuts

3 tablespoons red wine vinegar

3 anchovy fillets, drained and minced

1 tablespoon Dijon mustard

1 teaspoon dried tarragon

¼ cup extra-virgin olive oil

Salt and freshly ground pepper

1. In a large saucepan or flameproof casserole that will just hold chicken in a single layer, place breasts skin side down with chicken broth. Bring to a boil over medium-high heat. Reduce heat to low, cover, and cook until chicken is opaque in center but still moist, 12 to 14 minutes. Let cool in broth. When cool enough to handle, pull meat off bones and shred. Discard skin and bones.

2. In a large bowl, combine chicken, sliced endive, diced pear, escarole, scallions, Roquefort, and walnuts.

3. In a small bowl, combine vinegar, anchovy fillets, mustard, and tarragon. Gradually whisk in oil. Drizzle dressing over salad and toss until well coated. Season with salt and pepper to taste. Divide among 4 to 6 plates. Garnish with slightly overlapping slices of remaining pear. Serve at once.

44 MAPLE-GLAZED ROAST CHICKEN, APPLE, AND WALNUT SALAD

Prep: 15 minutes   Cook: 1 to 1¼ hours   Serves: 4

This lightly dressed salad exudes the colors and flavors of fall. When available, use reddish-brown oak leaf lettuce to mimic the colors of maple syrup and balsamic vinegar. Tart, crisp apples provide a balance to the sweetness of the dressing.

1 (3½- to 4-pound) chicken
3 tablespoons maple syrup
3 tablespoons balsamic
   vinegar
1 tablespoon Dijon mustard
¼ teaspoon salt
¼ teaspoon pepper
¼ cup walnut oil

2 medium tart apples,
   quartered, cored, and cut
   into ¾-inch dice
2 celery ribs, thinly sliced
½ cup chopped walnuts
6 cups torn assorted salad
   greens

1. Preheat oven to 375°F. Rinse chicken inside and out and pat dry. Place in a lightly greased baking dish. Roast chicken for 1 to 1¼ hours, or until thigh juices run clear when pierced with a sharp knife. When cool enough to handle, shred chicken. Discard skin and bones.

2. In a large bowl, combine maple syrup, vinegar, mustard, salt, and pepper. Gradually whisk in oil. Add chicken, apples, celery, and walnuts. Toss until well blended. Divide salad greens among 4 plates and top with chicken mixture. Serve at room temperature.

45 FIRE-AND-ICE ORANGE-CHICKEN SALAD

Prep: 20 minutes   Cook: 8 minutes   Serves: 4 to 6

This Thai-style main course is quickly stir-fried and served warm on a bed of cooling shredded iceberg lettuce.

¼ cup Asian fish sauce
¼ cup firmly packed brown
   sugar
4 navel oranges
6 cups shredded iceberg
   lettuce
2 tablespoons peanut oil
4 skinless, boneless chicken
   breast halves, thinly
   sliced

3 jalapeño peppers, seeded
   and minced
1 medium onion, chopped
2 garlic cloves, minced
¼ cup dry-roasted peanuts
½ cup cilantro leaves

1. In a small bowl, blend fish sauce, brown sugar, and ½ cup water. Stir to dissolve sugar. Remove zest from 2 oranges. Mince and blend into fish sauce. Cut ends off all oranges and cut away skin and white pith. Cut into segments and reserve. Divide shredded lettuce among 4 to 6 plates.

2. In a large skillet or wok, heat 1 tablespoon oil over high heat until hot. Add chicken and cook, stirring constantly, until just white throughout but still moist, about 3 minutes. Remove to a plate.

3. Return skillet to heat and add remaining 1 tablespoon oil. When hot, add jalapeño peppers, onion, garlic, and peanuts and cook, stirring constantly, about 2 minutes. Blend in fish sauce mixture and bring to a boil, stirring constantly. Return chicken and any accumulated juices to pan. Toss to coat evenly. Divide chicken among lettuce-lined plates. Sprinkle with cilantro and arrange orange segments alongside salad. Serve warm or at room temperature.

---

46 FRESH CORN AND TOMATILLO SALSA SALAD WITH SHREDDED CHICKEN

Prep: 25 minutes   Cook: 1 to 1¼ hours   Serves: 4 to 5

This crunchy, slightly sweet, and mildly smoky salad is mostly salsa. If you prefer more heat, add up to another tablespoon of chipotle chiles. The salsa can be covered and refrigerated 2 days before using.

1 (3½- to 4-pound) chicken
2 ears of fresh corn, husked
8 medium fresh tomatillos (about 10 ounces), husked, rinsed, and chopped
2 large plum tomatoes, cut into ½-inch dice
1 small jicama (10 ounces), peeled and cut into ½-inch dice

1 small red onion, cut into ½-inch dice
1 cup chopped cilantro
¼ cup fresh lime juice
2 tablespoons vegetable oil
1 tablespoon canned chipotle chiles in adobo sauce, minced
Salt and freshly ground pepper
Green leaf lettuce leaves

1. Preheat oven to 375°F. Rinse chicken inside and out and pat dry. Place in a lightly greased baking dish. Roast chicken for 1 to 1¼ hours, or until thigh juices run clear when pierced with a sharp knife. When cool enough to handle, shred chicken; discard skin and bones.

2. Meanwhile, in a large pot of lightly salted boiling water, cook corn 2 minutes. Drain, run under cold water to cool, and drain again. Cut kernels from cob. In a large bowl, combine corn, tomatillos, tomatoes, jicama, onion, cilantro, lime juice, oil, and chipotle chiles. Toss until well blended. Season with salt and pepper to taste. If not using within 2 hours, cover and refrigerate.

3. Arrange chicken down center of lettuce-lined plates. Arrange salsa along both sides of chicken. Serve at room temperature.

47   CHICKEN WALDORF SALAD WITH APPLE BUTTER MAYONNAISE

Prep: 15 minutes   Cook: 12 to 14 minutes   Serves: 4 to 6

A simple blend of mayonnaise and apple butter makes a delicious dressing for classic Waldorf salad ingredients. With the addition of chicken, the famous side-dish salad becomes a full, satisfying meal. Grilled and sautéed chicken work equally as well as poached in this recipe.

4 chicken breast halves (about 2 pounds)
1 (14½-ounce) can reduced-sodium chicken broth
½ cup mayonnaise
⅓ cup apple butter
1 tablespoon lemon juice

2 medium red-skinned apples, cored and cut into ¾-inch dice
4 celery ribs, thinly sliced
½ cup chopped pecans
½ cup raisins or pitted chopped dates
Green leaf lettuce leaves

1. In a large saucepan or flameproof casserole that will just hold chicken in a single layer, place breasts skin side down with chicken broth. Bring to a boil over medium-high heat. Reduce heat to low, cover, and cook until chicken is white in center but still moist, 12 to 14 minutes. Let cool in broth. When cool enough to handle, pull meat off bones and cut into ¾-inch dice. Discard skin and bones.

2. In a large bowl, whisk together mayonnaise, apple butter, and lemon juice until well blended. Add chicken, apples, celery, pecans, and raisins. Toss until well blended and divide among 4 to 6 lettuce-lined plates. Serve at room temperature or chilled.

48   CHICKEN-NOODLE SALAD SZECHUAN

Prep: 15 minutes   Cook: 1 to 1¼ hours   Serves: 4

This spicy noodle salad can be served at room temperature or cold. After dressing the salad, cover and refrigerate it for up to 24 hours. The spinach will wilt slightly but will still be appealing.

1 (3½- to 4-pound) chicken
5 ounces fresh Chinese egg noodles or capellini
¼ cup rice wine vinegar
2 tablespoons soy sauce
1 teaspoon Asian sesame oil
¼ teaspoon hot chili oil or crushed hot red pepper

1 tablespoon minced fresh ginger
1 garlic clove, minced
2 cups shredded spinach
2 scallions, thinly sliced
1 small red bell pepper, cut into slivers

1. Preheat oven to 375°F. Rinse chicken inside and out and pat dry. Place in a lightly greased baking dish. Roast chicken for 1 to 1¼ hours, or until thigh juices run clear when pierced with a sharp knife. When cool enough to handle, shred chicken; discard skin and bones.

2. In a large pot of lightly salted boiling water, cook noodles until just tender, about 2 minutes. Drain, run under cold water, and drain again. In a large bowl, combine vinegar, soy sauce, sesame oil, chili oil, ginger, and garlic. Add noodles and toss until well coated.

3. Add chicken, spinach, scallions, and bell pepper to noodles. Toss again to mix. Divide among 4 plates. Serve at room temperature or cover and refrigerate at least 2 hours to serve cold.

49 PEACH MELBA CHICKEN SALAD
Prep: 20 minutes   Cook: 10 minutes   Serves: 4

Peach Melba is a dessert created for a popular Australian opera singer by the famous French chef Auguste Escoffier. It combines two fragile summer fruits, peaches and raspberries, whose seasons happily coincide. In this aromatic salad, both fruits complement just-cooked chicken breasts.

¼ cup plus 2 tablespoons extra-virgin olive oil
4 skinless, boneless chicken breast halves
4 teaspoons raspberry vinegar
1 teaspoon honey
½ teaspoon grated nutmeg
1 garlic clove, minced
6 cups torn assorted salad greens

Salt and freshly ground pepper
4 small peaches, peeled and thinly sliced
½ cup fresh raspberries
2 tablespoons pine nuts (pignoli) or slivered almonds

1. In a large nonstick skillet, heat 2 tablespoons oil over medium-high heat until hot. Add chicken and cook, turning occasionally, until golden brown on both sides and white throughout but still moist, about 10 minutes. Transfer to a cutting board and let rest while preparing salad.

2. In a large bowl, whisk together remaining ¼ cup olive oil, vinegar, honey, nutmeg, and garlic until well blended. Add greens and toss until well coated. Season with salt and pepper to taste. Divide among 4 plates.

3. Cut chicken into thin slices, retaining shape of breast. Top each salad with a sliced chicken breast half. Divide peaches among 4 plates, arranging in slightly overlapping slices alongside chicken. Sprinkle with raspberries and pine nuts. Serve warm or at room temperature.

50   POMEGRANATE, BLUE CHEESE, AND WATERCRESS SALAD WITH GRILLED CHICKEN

Prep: 25 minutes   Cook: 8 to 10 minutes   Serves: 4

Sparkling crimson pomegranate seeds always dress up a dish. If pomegranates are unavailable for this festive-looking fall salad, substitute red-skinned apples or red Bartlett pears, cut into ½-inch dice.

4 skinless, boneless chicken
  breast halves
¼ cup plus 2 tablespoons
  extra-virgin olive oil
2 tablespoons port
1 tablespoon balsamic
  vinegar
1 tablespoon orange juice
2 teaspoons Dijon mustard

2 Belgian endive spears,
  sliced
6 cups watercress, tough
  stems removed
¾ cup pomegranate seeds
⅓ cup crumbled blue cheese
⅓ cup chopped walnuts
  Salt and freshly ground
  pepper

1. Light a medium-hot fire in a barbecue grill or preheat broiler. Brush chicken breasts with 2 tablespoons oil. Grill on a lightly oiled rack set 4 to 6 inches from heat or broil, turning once, until white throughout but still moist, about 8 to 10 minutes. Remove chicken to a cutting board and let rest while preparing salad.

2. In a large bowl, combine port, vinegar, orange juice, and mustard. Gradually whisk in remaining ¼ cup olive oil. Add endive to dressing with watercress, pomegranate seeds, cheese, and walnuts. Toss until well blended. Season with salt and pepper to taste. Divide among 4 plates.

3. Slice chicken thinly crosswise on diagonal, retaining shape of breasts. Divide chicken among salads and serve.

51 CHICKEN-CURRY COLESLAW
Prep: 25 minutes   Cook: 12 to 14 minutes   Serves: 4

Slightly sweet and hot, this creamy, lightly curried dish elevates humble cabbage to center stage. Deep green spinach leaves provide beautiful contrast to the salad's pale yellow color. If you have leftover cooked chicken or turkey, use it in this recipe and eliminate step 1.

2 chicken breast halves (about 1 pound)
1 (14½-ounce) can reduced-sodium chicken broth
4 slices of bacon
½ cup mayonnaise
½ cup nonfat plain yogurt
2 tablespoons lemon juice

2 teaspoons sugar
2 teaspoons curry powder
6 cups finely shredded cabbage
3 scallions, thinly sliced
½ cup raisins
½ cup dry-roasted peanuts
   Large spinach leaves, tough stems removed

1. In a medium saucepan, place chicken breasts skin side down with chicken broth. Bring to a boil over medium-high heat. Reduce heat to low, cover, and cook until chicken is white in center but still moist, 12 to 14 minutes. Let cool in broth. When chicken is cool, pull meat off bones and shred. Discard skin and bones.

2. Meanwhile, in a large skillet, cook bacon over medium heat until crisp, 7 to 9 minutes. Drain on paper towels. When cool enough to handle, crumble bacon.

3. In a large bowl, whisk together mayonnaise, yogurt, lemon juice, sugar, and curry powder until smooth. Add chicken, bacon, cabbage, scallions, raisins, and peanuts. Toss until well blended. Divide among spinach-lined plates. Serve at room temperature or chilled.

52   SHREDDED CHICKEN ON EAST-WEST CABBAGE SLAW

Prep: 25 minutes   Cook: 1 to 1¼ hours   Serves: 4 to 6

Thai red curry paste, available in specialty shops and many supermarkets, gives food a rounded spiciness and heat. It's combined in this Napa-based slaw with cooling vegetables and roasted chicken.

1   (3½- to 4-pound) chicken
⅓   cup vegetable oil
1   tablespoon Asian sesame oil
¼   cup fresh lime juice
1   tablespoon soy sauce
1   tablespoon firmly packed brown sugar
2   teaspoons Thai red curry paste
2   garlic cloves, minced

1   jalapeño pepper, seeded and minced
4   cups shredded Chinese (Napa) cabbage
2   carrots, peeled and shredded
1   large red bell pepper, cut into ¼-inch-wide strips
½   cup dry-roasted peanuts
½   cup cilantro leaves

1. Preheat oven to 375°F. Rinse chicken inside and out and pat dry. Place in a lightly greased baking dish. Roast chicken for 1 to 1¼ hours, or until thigh juices run clear when pierced with a sharp knife. When cool enough to handle, remove and discard skin and bones from chicken and shred meat.

2. In a large bowl, whisk together vegetable oil, sesame oil, lime juice, soy sauce, brown sugar, curry paste, garlic, and jalapeño pepper until well blended. Add cabbage, carrots, and bell pepper. Toss until well blended and divide among 4 to 6 plates. Top slaw with chicken and sprinkle with peanuts and cilantro. Serve warm or at room temperature.

53 CHICKEN TONNATO
Prep: 20 minutes   Cook: 10 minutes   Serves: 8 to 10

Vitello tonnato, a famous Italian cold-meat dish of sliced veal enrobed in a boldly flavored tuna and anchovy mayonnaise, provides the inspiration for this colorful chicken salad. If necessary, cook the chicken in 2 batches or substitute 8 cups slivered leftover turkey breast.

2 tablespoons vegetable oil
8 skinless, boneless chicken
   breast halves
1 medium red bell pepper,
   cut into slivers
1 medium green bell pepper,
   cut into slivers
1 small red onion, thinly
   sliced and separated into
   rings

1¾ cups Tuna-Caper
   Mayonnaise (recipe
   follows)
6 cups torn red leaf lettuce
6 cups torn curly endive

1. In a large skillet, preferably nonstick, heat oil over medium-high heat until it shimmers. Add chicken and cook, turning occasionally, until golden brown on both sides and white throughout but still moist inside, about 10 minutes. Remove to a cutting board and let rest 5 to 10 minutes. Cut chicken into thin strips.

2. In a large bowl, combine red and green bell peppers, red onion, and Tuna-Caper Mayonnaise. Toss until well blended. Divide lettuce and endive among 8 to 10 plates. Top with pepper mixture and chicken and serve.

54 TUNA-CAPER MAYONNAISE
Prep: 5 minutes   Cook: none   Makes: about 1¾ cups

Bold, creamy, and rich, this dressing also makes a delicious spread for turkey and fish sandwiches or hamburgers. Use either tuna packed in water or in oil, but be sure to include the liquid from the can. If you're calorie-conscious, reduced-fat or no-fat mayonnaise make passable substitutes for the real thing here, since the stronger flavors of tuna and anchovies dominate the dressing.

2 garlic cloves
2 anchovy fillets
1 (6½-ounce) can solid white
   tuna, water or oil
   reserved

1 cup mayonnaise
2 tablespoons lemon juice
2 tablespoons capers, drained
   Salt and freshly ground
   pepper

Combine garlic and anchovy fillets in a food processor or blender. Mince together. Add tuna with its liquid, mayonnaise, and lemon juice. Blend together until smooth. Blend in capers and salt and pepper to taste. If not using immediately, cover and refrigerate.

55   HOISIN-SCENTED CHICKEN-NAPA SLAW

Prep: 20 minutes   Cook: 1 to 1¼ hours   Serves: 4 to 5

Crunchy and colorful, sweet and spicy, this salad owes its aroma to soybean-based hoisin sauce, which is available in jars and cans in specialty stores and most large supermarkets. Although white, frilly Napa cabbage provides a beautiful backdrop for red bell pepper and cilantro, iceberg lettuce makes a reliable substitute.

1 **(3½- to 4-pound) chicken**	6 **cups shredded Chinese**
¼ **cup hoisin sauce**	**(Napa) cabbage**
¼ **cup creamy peanut butter**	6 **scallions, thinly sliced**
¼ **cup rice vinegar**	1 **medium red bell pepper,**
1 **tablespoon soy sauce**	**cut into slivers**
1 **tablespoon sugar**	1 **cup cilantro leaves**
1 **teaspoon Asian sesame oil**	½ **cup dry-roasted peanuts**
¼ **teaspoon hot chili oil or**	
crushed hot red pepper	

1. Preheat oven to 375°F. Rinse chicken inside and out and pat dry. Place in a lightly greased baking dish. Roast chicken for 1 to 1¼ hours, or until thigh juices run clear when pierced with a sharp knife. When cool enough to handle, shred chicken. Discard skin and bones.

2. In a large bowl, combine hoisin sauce, peanut butter, vinegar, soy sauce, sugar, sesame oil, and chili oil. Whisk vigorously until smooth.

3. Add chicken, cabbage, scallions, bell pepper, cilantro, and peanuts. Toss until well mixed. Divide among 4 or 5 plates and serve at room temperature.

56   TURKEY CLUB SALAD

Prep: 25 minutes   Cook: 14 to 18 minutes   Serves: 12

This salad combines all the tastes of the ever-popular club sandwich, even down to croutons that mimic the 3 layers of toast that enclose the main ingredients. If you don't have leftover turkey on hand, substitute shredded cooked chicken.

18 **slices of bacon**	8 **large plum tomatoes, cut**
1½ **cups mayonnaise**	**into ½-inch dice**
3 **tablespoons lemon juice**	4 **cups croutons**
12 **cups shredded iceberg**	**Salt and freshly ground**
lettuce	**pepper**
10 **to 12 cups shredded leftover**	**Red leaf lettuce leaves**
cooked turkey breast	
(about 2½ to 3 pounds)	

1. In a large skillet, cook bacon in 2 batches over medium heat, turning until crisp, 7 to 9 minutes per batch. Drain on paper towels. When cool enough to handle, crumble bacon.

2. In a large bowl, whisk mayonnaise and lemon juice until well blended. Add lettuce, turkey, tomatoes, croutons, and bacon. Toss until well blended. If needed, season with salt and pepper to taste. Divide among 12 lettuce-lined plates and serve at room temperature.

57   TURKEY, CRANBERRY, AND GOAT CHEESE SALAD

Prep: 15 minutes   Cook: 10 to 12 minutes   Serves: 4

Vivid greens, deep burgundy dressing, and white goat cheese make this festive salad remarkable to look at and marvelous to eat. To enjoy it all year long, stock up on bags of cranberries in the fall and store them in the freezer. To prepare the salad with leftovers, substitute 4 cups cooked, diced turkey or chicken and eliminate step 1.

⅓ **cup plus 2 tablespoons extra-virgin olive oil**
4 **slices uncooked turkey breast, about ½ inch thick (1 to 1¼ pounds)**
⅓ **cup orange-flavored liqueur**
⅓ **cup red wine vinegar**
¼ **cup plus 2 tablespoons sugar**

1½ **cups fresh cranberries**
4 **cups torn Boston lettuce**
2 **cups torn arugula**
2 **cups torn radicchio**
   Salt and freshly ground pepper
½ **cup crumbled mild goat cheese, such as Montrachet**

1. In a large skillet, heat 2 tablespoons olive oil over medium-high heat until it shimmers. Add turkey and cook, turning once, until white throughout but still moist, about 2 minutes per side. Transfer to a cutting board and let rest while preparing dressing.

2. In a small saucepan, combine liqueur, vinegar, and 3 tablespoons sugar. Stir over medium heat until sugar dissolves, about 1 minute. Add cranberries and simmer, stirring occasionally, until skins just begin to pop, 5 to 7 minutes. Strain cooking liquid into a small bowl and place cranberries in a large bowl. While hot, stir remaining 3 tablespoons sugar into cranberries. Let cooking liquid and cranberries cool at least 10 minutes.

3. Cut turkey into ¾-inch cubes and add to cranberries along with lettuce, arugula, and radicchio. Whisk remaining ⅓ cup olive oil into cooking liquid and drizzle over salad. Toss until well blended, breaking up cranberries and distributing them evenly throughout. Season with salt and pepper to taste. Divide salad among 4 plates and sprinkle cheese on top. Serve at once.

58 CAULIFLOWER, CARROT, AND SMOKED TURKEY SALAD
Prep: 10 minutes   Cook: none   Chill: 8 hours   Serves: 6

Raisins add a pleasant surprise to this creamy, colorful salad. Since it needs to marinate overnight and requires no last-minute fussing, it makes an easy potluck or buffet dish.

1 cup mayonnaise
1 cup sour cream
1 (.6-ounce) package Good Seasons Zesty Italian dressing mix
1 tablespoon sugar
6 cups cauliflower florets (1 small head)

6 scallions, thinly sliced
3 cups shredded smoked turkey (about 12 ounces)
2 medium carrots, peeled and cut into ½-inch slices
1 small bunch of radishes, thinly sliced
1 cup raisins

In a large bowl, blend together mayonnaise, sour cream, dressing mix, and sugar. Add cauliflower, scallions, turkey, carrots, radishes, and raisins. Toss until well blended. Cover and refrigerate 8 hours or overnight. Serve chilled or at room temperature.

59 DAY-AFTER-THANKSGIVING SALAD
Prep: 20 minutes   Cook: none   Serves: 6 to 8

This perky salad transforms turkey-day leftovers, including gravy, cranberry sauce, and turkey, into a totally different but delicious form. It can all be assembled ahead, and it's fine cold or at room temperature, so the salad can be pulled from the refrigerator with no more fussing before serving.

¾ cup leftover turkey gravy
⅓ cup mayonnaise
8 cups diced leftover cooked turkey (about 2 pounds)
6 celery ribs, thinly sliced
6 scallions, thinly sliced

4 cups seedless red grapes, halved
Red leaf lettuce leaves
1½ cups Cranberry Dressing (recipe follows)

1. In a large bowl, whisk together gravy and mayonnaise until smooth. Add turkey, celery, scallions, and grapes and toss until well mixed.

2. Line a platter or 6 to 8 individual plates with lettuce. Mound salad on top. Serve cold or at room temperature. Pass Cranberry Dressing at table.

60   CRANBERRY DRESSING
Prep: 3 minutes   Cook: none   Makes: about 1½ cups

Chutneylike in texture, this sweet-and-tart dressing gets its body from canned cranberry sauce that may be freshly opened or left over from a big turkey dinner. It's delicious on most salads containing bits of fruit.

1¼ cups jellied cranberry sauce
    or 1 (8-ounce) can
½ cup vegetable oil

¼ cup red wine vinegar
1½ tablespoons Dijon mustard

In a medium bowl, vigorously whisk all ingredients together until smooth. If not using within 2 hours, cover and refrigerate. Let return to room temperature before serving.

61   WARM ORANGE-DUCK SALAD
Prep: 15 minutes   Cook: 1 hour 20 minutes to 1 hour 30 minutes
Serves: 4 to 5

Soy sauce provides a hint of Asian flavor to the time-honored combination of oranges and rich duck in this easy-to-prepare salad. If you can buy precooked duck, available in many full-service Asian markets, skip to step 2, in which case the salad makes a practically instant main course.

1 (4½- to 5-pound) duck
2 large navel oranges
⅓ cup vegetable oil
¼ cup red wine vinegar
3 tablespoons soy sauce
3 tablespoons orange
    marmalade

2 teaspoons Dijon mustard
1 teaspoon pepper
6 cups torn red leaf lettuce
3 cups torn curly endive

1. Preheat oven to 400°F. With a sharp fork, prick duck skin all over without piercing meat. Place duck, breast side-up, on a lightly oiled rack in a roasting pan. Roast 30 minutes, basting with juices and pouring off excess fat occasionally. Reduce heat to 350° and roast, continuing to baste, until skin is crisp and golden and thigh juices run clear when pierced with a sharp knife, 50 to 60 minutes longer.

2. Meanwhile, strip zest from oranges and mince finely. In a large bowl, combine orange zest, oil, vinegar, soy sauce, marmalade, mustard, and pepper. Whisk together until well blended. Cut ends off oranges and cut away skin and white pith. Cut oranges into segments and reserve.

3. Slice skin and meat from duck and cut into bite-size pieces. Discard bones. While warm, add duck to dressing and toss until well blended. Divide lettuce and endive among 4 or 5 plates. Top with duck. Arrange orange sections alongside duck and serve warm or at room temperature.

62 DUCK AND RASPBERRIES ON WATERCRESS WITH POPPY SEED VINAIGRETTE
Prep: 15 minutes   Cook: 11 to 13 minutes   Serves: 6

A sweet-and-sour dressing and peppery watercress complement the richness of duck in this vividly colored salad. If your raspberries are especially fragile, do not toss them. Sprinkle them over the salad as a last step.

6 small skinless, boneless
   duck breast halves (about
   3 pounds total)
4 cups watercress, tough
   stems removed
4 cups torn Boston lettuce

1 pint raspberries
1 cup chopped pecans
6 scallions, thinly sliced
⅔ cup Poppy Seed Vinaigrette
   (recipe follows)

1. In a dry, large heavy skillet set over medium heat, place duck breasts skin side down and cook, shaking pan occasionally, until they release some fat, about 5 minutes. Increase heat to high and cook, turning once, until golden outside but still pink and juicy inside, 3 to 4 minutes per side. Transfer to a cutting board and let rest while preparing salad.

2. In a large bowl, combine watercress, lettuce, raspberries, pecans, and scallions. Drizzle with vinaigrette and toss gently until well coated. Divide among 6 plates.

3. Slice duck crosswise into thin slices, retaining shape of breasts. Top each salad with a sliced duck breast and serve.

63 POPPY SEED VINAIGRETTE
Prep: 3 minutes   Cook: none   Makes: about ⅔ cup

The delicate crunch of poppy seeds highlights this classic sweet-and-sour combination. For a creamy dressing, combine all the ingredients except the oil in a blender or food processor and gradually drizzle in the oil.

2 tablespoons raspberry
   vinegar
1 tablespoon mild honey
1 tablespoon Dijon mustard

1 tablespoon poppy seeds
¼ teaspoon salt
⅛ teaspoon pepper
½ cup extra-virgin olive oil

In a small bowl, whisk together vinegar, honey, mustard, poppy seeds, salt, and pepper until well blended. Gradually whisk in oil until thickened and smooth. If not using within 1 hour, cover and refrigerate. Let return to room temperature before serving.

64 QUAIL SALAD WITH PAPAYA AND AVOCADO

Prep: 25 minutes   Marinate: 2 hours   Cook: 9 to 12 minutes
Serves: 8

You can find partially boned quail, in which the breastbone and backbone have been removed, in the frozen food section of many groceries and in specialty food stores. These small, dark-meat birds cook quickly and should be removed from the heat as soon as the breast meat runs slightly pink when pierced with a sharp knife.

½ cup minced fresh mint
¼ cup plus 3 tablespoons
     raspberry vinegar
2 small shallots, minced
½ teaspoon pepper
8 partially boned quail (1½ to
     2 pounds total)
¼ cup orange juice

1 tablespoon honey
½ cup nonfat plain yogurt
¼ cup walnut oil
12 cups assorted baby lettuces
2 large ripe avocados, thinly
     sliced
2 large papaya, thinly sliced

1. In shallow bowl, combine ¼ cup mint, ¼ cup vinegar, 1 shallot, and pepper. Add quail and turn to coat. Cover and refrigerate 2 to 6 hours, turning at least once.

2. Prepare a hot fire in a grill. Remove quail from marinade and reserve marinade. Place birds on a well-oiled grill set 6 inches over coals. Cook, turning occasionally and basting with reserved marinade, until skin is browned and breast meat is just pink in center, about 8 to 10 minutes.

3. In a small nonreactive saucepan, combine remaining ¼ cup mint, 3 tablespoons vinegar, 1 shallot, orange juice, and honey. Place over medium-low heat and stir until honey dissolves, 1 to 2 minutes. Transfer to a medium bowl and let cool to room temperature. Add yogurt and oil and whisk vigorously until well blended.

4. Divide lettuces among 8 plates. Top each salad with 1 quail and arrange avocados and papaya in slightly overlapping slices alongside quail. Drizzle dressing over salads and serve warm or at room temperature.

Chapter 3

Meaty Salad Meals

Let's face it. Americans love meat: thick, juicy steaks, hamburgers, and hot dogs. However, food, just like fashion, changes as trends come and go.

As we have become concerned with fat intake, we have sought a number of ways to eat leaner, including adding more vegetables and other complex carbohydrates to our diet, becoming part-time vegetarians, and choosing only the leanest of meats to consume in small amounts.

Main-course salads are the ideal way to find this proper balance of foods. Since their meat content is relatively low, salads offer a reasonable balance of meat when combined with pastas, beans, grains, and fresh vegetables and fruits. By eating main-course salads, we can enjoy the taste of the meat we love, but we can stretch that taste by combining it with other healthier ingredients.

This chapter includes recipes for salads that contain beef, lamb, and pork. Many of them make ingenious use of leftovers, although the recipes include cooking instructions in case leftovers are not on hand.

Whether grilling, broiling, or pan-frying, always trim excess fat from meat. Aside from the obvious health benefits, trimming fat helps prevent flare-ups during cooking. Since meats continue to cook for a few minutes after they've been removed from the heat, most of the recipes call for cooking the meat first and letting it rest so that the juices return to the center of the meat. This allows just about enough time to prepare a dressing and the remaining salad ingredients. Once the rest of the salad is ready, the meat will be at its prime time to slice to retain as much as possible of its juice.

This chapter includes salads that incorporate ingredients and flavors from around the world. For international flavor, try Mongolian Lamb Salad with Thai Curry Paste, Chinese Sausage and Asian Pear Salad, Thai-Style Pork in Lettuce Cups with Snow Peas and Mandarin Oranges, Italian Sausage and Cannellini Salad with Tomato-Fennel Vinaigrette, or a Festive Mexican Grilled Pork and Vegetable Salad. For a stunning presentation combining two American favorite foods, try the Marinated Steak Salad in Potato Baskets.

65   LAMB AND GRAPE SALAD WITH CURRY-CHUTNEY VINAIGRETTE

Prep: 30 minutes   Cook: 3 minutes   Serves: 8 to 12

This versatile meat and fruit salad is beautiful enough for the best of company. The purple tones of red grapes, red onion, and radicchio complement each other, and green leaf lettuce provides colorful contrast. If you prefer, substitute chicken for the lamb.

2 tablespoons vegetable oil
2 pounds boneless leg of
     lamb, cut into thin strips
     about 2 x ½ inch
12 cups torn leaf lettuce
4 cups torn radicchio
1 medium red onion, thinly
     sliced and separated into
     rings

3 cups seedless red grapes,
     halved
1 cup walnut halves
1 cup chopped fresh mint
1 cup Curry-Chutney
     Vinaigrette (recipe
     follows)

1. In a large wok or skillet, heat oil over high heat until it shimmers. Add lamb, stirring frequently, until brown on outside but still pink and juicy inside, about 3 minutes.

2. In a large bowl, combine lamb, lettuce, radicchio, red onion, grapes, walnuts, and mint. Drizzle with vinaigrette and toss until well blended. Divide among 8 to 12 plates and serve at once.

66   CURRY-CHUTNEY VINAIGRETTE

Prep: 5 minutes   Cook: none   Makes: about 1 cup

Curry and chutney have long been paired for good reason. The heat, sweetness, and acidity they provide make a pleasing roundness of flavor on the tongue. This versatile dressing complements salads made with fruit, poultry, or shrimp. If you like, make lots to keep on hand; it will keep refrigerated for up to 2 months.

¼ cup bottled or homemade
     chutney
1 garlic clove
2 tablespoons red wine
     vinegar

4 teaspoons Dijon mustard
1 teaspoon curry powder
½ cup olive oil
     Salt and freshly ground
     pepper

1. Place chutney and garlic in a food processor or blender. Mince together. Add vinegar, mustard, and curry powder and blend together.

2. With machine on, slowly drizzle in oil. Season with salt and freshly ground pepper to taste. If not using within 2 hours, cover and refrigerate. Let return to room temperature before using.

67 COUSCOUS AND LAMB SALAD WITH MINT–RED CURRANT VINAIGRETTE

Prep: 25 minutes   Cook: 3 minutes   Serves: 4 to 5

2 cups chicken stock or
  reduced-sodium canned
  chicken broth
2 tablespoons olive oil
2 garlic cloves, minced
2 cups couscous
1 pound boneless leg of lamb,
  cut into ¾-inch dice
1 (15-ounce) can chickpeas,
  rinsed and drained

¾ cup Mint–Red Currant
  Vinaigrette (recipe
  follows)
Salt and freshly ground
  pepper
Green leaf lettuce leaves
2 cups cherry tomatoes,
  quartered
4 or 5 sprigs of fresh mint

1. In a medium saucepan, combine stock, 1 tablespoon oil, and garlic. Bring to a boil and stir in couscous. Remove from heat, cover, and let stand until couscous is tender and all liquid is absorbed, about 5 minutes. Transfer to a large bowl and fluff with a fork to separate grains. Let cool at least 5 minutes.

2. In a large skillet or wok, heat remaining 1 tablespoon oil over medium-high heat until it shimmers. Add lamb and cook, stirring constantly, until brown on outside but still pink and juicy inside, about 3 minutes.

3. Add lamb, chickpeas, and vinaigrette to couscous. Toss until well blended. Season with salt and pepper to taste. Divide among 4 or 5 lettuce-lined plates. Sprinkle with tomatoes and garnish with mint. Serve at room temperature or cover and refrigerate at least 2 hours to serve chilled.

68 MINT–RED CURRANT VINAIGRETTE

Prep: 5 minutes   Cook: none   Makes: ¾ cup

2 tablespoons raspberry
  vinegar
2 tablespoons red currant
  jelly, melted
¼ cup fresh mint, minced

1 garlic clove, minced
½ cup extra-virgin olive oil
Salt and freshly ground
  pepper

In a medium bowl, whisk vinegar, jelly, mint, and garlic until well blended. While whisking, gradually drizzle in oil. Season with salt and pepper to taste. If not using within 2 hours, cover and refrigerate. Let return to room temperature before serving.

69 MONGOLIAN LAMB SALAD WITH THAI CURRY PASTE

Prep: 25 minutes   Marinate: 1 hour   Cook: 3 minutes   Serves: 4

This substantial, quickly stir-fried salad gets its heat from Thai curry paste, crushed hot red pepper, and fresh ginger. Since the marinade is packed with flavor, the meat is best left refrigerated for the full 12 hours, if possible. Cucumber and mint provide welcome cooling balance to the lamb.

½ cup plus 1 tablespoon soy sauce
¼ cup mirin or sweet sherry
1½ tablespoons minced fresh ginger
2 garlic cloves, minced
½ teaspoon crushed hot red pepper
1 pound boneless leg of lamb, cut into ¾-inch cubes

6 cups torn romaine lettuce
1 cucumber, thinly sliced
¼ cup minced fresh mint
¼ cup plus 2 tablespoons vegetable oil
2 tablespoons red wine vinegar
1 teaspoon Thai red curry paste

1. In a shallow dish, blend ½ cup soy sauce, mirin, ginger, garlic, and hot pepper. Add lamb and toss until well coated. Cover and marinate 1 hour at room temperature or refrigerate up to 12 hours.

2. In a large bowl, toss lettuce, cucumber, and mint. Divide among 4 plates. In a small bowl, stir together ¼ cup oil, remaining 1 tablespoon soy sauce, vinegar, and curry paste.

3. In a large wok or skillet, heat remaining 2 tablespoons oil over high heat until shimmering. Drain lamb and add it to pan. Cook, stirring constantly, until brown outside but still pink and juicy inside, about 3 minutes. Remove pan from heat and transfer lamb to a plate. Add curry paste mixture to pan and whisk until smooth. Return lamb and any accumulated juice to pan. Toss until well blended. Arrange on top of salads and serve.

70 MINTED LAMB SALAD WITH CITRUS FRUITS AND ALMONDS

Prep: 30 minutes   Marinate: 1 hour   Cook: 3 minutes
Serves: 4 to 5

½ cup extra-virgin olive oil
¼ cup orange juice
¼ cup lemon juice
2 teaspoons grated orange zest
3 garlic cloves, minced
½ teaspoon salt
¼ teaspoon black pepper
1 pound boneless leg of lamb, cut into 1 x 3-inch thin strips
2 large oranges
2 small pink grapefruit

4 cups torn Boston lettuce
3 cups watercress, tough stems removed
1 cup torn radicchio
2 tablespoons chopped fresh mint
2 tablespoons peanut oil
1 small red onion, thinly sliced and separated into rings
½ cup slivered almonds, preferably lightly toasted

1. In a small bowl, combine olive oil, orange juice, lemon juice, orange zest, garlic, salt, and pepper. Transfer ½ cup of dressing to a shallow dish. Add lamb and toss until well coated. Cover and marinate 1 hour at room temperature or cover and refrigerate overnight. Cover and refrigerate remaining dressing.

2. Using a sharp knife, cut off ends of oranges and grapefruit. Peel them and discard all bitter white pith. Cut between membranes to release sections and cut into ¾-inch dice.

3. In a large bowl, toss lettuce, watercress, radicchio, and mint. Divide among 4 or 5 plates.

4. In a large wok or skillet, heat peanut oil over high heat until it shimmers. Drain lamb and add to pan. Cook, stirring constantly, until brown on outside but still pink and juicy inside, about 3 minutes. Transfer to a large bowl. Add oranges, grapefruit, red onion, and almonds. Drizzle on reserved dressing and toss until well blended. Top salads with lamb and fruit mixture and serve.

71   BEEF, BEET, AND DAIKON RADISH SALAD
Prep: 15 minutes   Cook: 10 minutes   Serves: 4 to 6

Shreds of burgundy beets and crisp bright white daikon radish nest alongside just-cooked beef tenderloin in this entree, making it festive looking as well as delicious. If you have leftover cooked roast beef, substitute it for the tenderloin and eliminate step 1.

1 pound beef tenderloin steaks, cut 1 inch thick	1 (15-ounce) can julienne-cut beets, drained
8 cups torn assorted salad greens	2 cups shredded, peeled daikon radish (about 8 ounces)
⅔ cup Horseradish-Red Currant Dressing (recipe follows)	

1. Prepare a hot fire in a grill. Place steaks on an oiled rack set 4 to 6 inches from coals. Grill, turning once, until well browned outside but still pink and juicy inside, about 5 minutes per side for medium-rare. Remove to a cutting board and let rest while preparing salad.

2. In a large bowl, combine greens with dressing and toss until well blended. Divide among 4 to 6 plates. Slice steaks thinly and arrange in slightly overlapping slices over center of greens.

3. Divide beets and radish among salads, arranging each separately alongside steaks. Serve at once.

72   HORSERADISH–RED CURRANT DRESSING
Prep: 5 minutes   Cook: none   Makes: about ⅔ cup

Mildly sweet and hot, this creamy dressing also makes a delicious accompaniment to roast duck or chicken.

¼ cup vegetable oil	1 tablespoon cider vinegar
2 tablespoons sour cream	Salt and freshly ground pepper
2 tablespoons prepared white horseradish	
2 tablespoons red currant jelly, melted	

In a small bowl, whisk together oil, sour cream, horseradish, jelly, and vinegar until mixture is smooth and thick. If needed, season with salt and pepper to taste. If not serving at once, cover and refrigerate. Let return to room temperature before serving.

73 SIZZLING SOUTHWEST STEAK SALAD
Prep: 30 minutes   Marinate: 2 hours   Cook: 10 minutes   Serves: 8

This warm salad is lightly dressed but packed with flavor. Chiles in adobo sauce are canned dried, smoked red jalapeños that are stewed with tomatoes, spices, and vinegar. They provide smokiness and heat. Mangoes, jicama, and avocado here offer cooling contrast.

3 tablespoons fresh lime juice
2 tablespoons minced
    chipotle chiles in adobo
    sauce
1½ tablespoons ground cumin
2 pounds beef tenderloin
    steaks, cut 1 inch thick
2 ripe avocados, cut into
    ¾-inch dice
2 mangoes, cut into ¾-inch
    dice

1 small jicama, peeled and cut
    into ¾-inch dice (about
    2 cups)
1 small red onion, thinly
    sliced and separated into
    rings
16 cups torn curly endive
1¼ cups Spicy Lime-Cilantro
    Dressing (recipe follows)

1. In a shallow dish, blend lime juice, chiles, and cumin. Add steaks and turn to coat. Cover and refrigerate 2 to 8 hours.

2. Prepare a hot fire in a grill. Lift meat from marinade and place on an oiled rack set 4 to 6 inches from coals. Grill, turning once, until well browned outside but still pink and juicy inside, about 5 minutes per side for medium-rare. Transfer to a cutting board to rest while preparing salad.

3. In a large bowl, combine avocados, mangoes, jicama, red onion, and endive. Drizzle with dressing and toss until well blended. Divide among 8 plates. Slice steaks thinly against grain and arrange in slightly overlapping slices on salads. Serve warm or at room temperature.

74 SPICY LIME-CILANTRO DRESSING
Prep: 10 minutes   Cook: none   Makes: about 1¼ cups

This is a mildly spicy dressing balanced with tart lime juice and fresh-tasting cilantro.

⅓ cup fresh lime juice
¼ cup minced cilantro
1½ tablespoons minced
    chipotle chiles in adobo
    sauce

2 garlic cloves, minced
1 teaspoon salt
¾ cup vegetable oil

In a medium bowl, blend together lime juice, cilantro, chiles, garlic, and salt. Gradually whisk in oil. If not using within 2 hours, cover and refrigerate. Let return to room temperature before using.

75 MARINATED STEAK SALAD IN POTATO BASKETS

Prep: 20 minutes   Marinate: 1 hour   Cook: 8 to 12 minutes
Serves: 4

Soy sauce adds depth of flavor to a vinaigrette that serves as both marinade and dressing in this hearty salad with a distinctive presentation. The
potatoes, first cooked like a pancake and then baked into a basket shape,
make a dramatic appearance, cradling the entire salad.

½   **cup olive oil**
⅓   **cup red wine vinegar**
3   **tablespoons soy sauce**
1   **tablespoon Dijon mustard**
2   **garlic cloves, minced**
½   **teaspoon Tabasco sauce**
12   **ounces flank steak**
4   **Potato Baskets (recipe**
     follows)

6   **cups shredded iceberg**
     lettuce
2   **cups thinly sliced**
     mushrooms (about
     4 ounces)
2   **cups cherry tomatoes (about**
     16), sliced in half

1. In a small bowl, blend together oil, vinegar, soy sauce, mustard, garlic,
and Tabasco sauce. Transfer ¼ cup of dressing to a shallow dish. Add steak
and turn once to coat. Cover and refrigerate meat and remaining dressing
separately for 1 to 3 hours.

2. Light a hot fire in a barbecue grill or preheat broiler. Grill steak on an
oiled rack or broil 4 to 6 inches from heat, turning once, until browned outside and still pink and juicy inside, 4 to 6 minutes per side. Transfer steak to
a cutting board and let rest at least 5 minutes. Slice thinly against grain. Turn
and cut strips into 1-inch lengths.

3. Place a potato basket on each of 4 plates. Divide lettuce and then mushrooms among baskets. Arrange steak over mushrooms. Sprinkle tomatoes
on top and drizzle dressing over salads. Serve at room temperature.

76 POTATO BASKETS

Prep: 10 minutes   Cook: 49 to 54 minutes   Makes: 4

Crunchy and lacy, these potato baskets are actually potato pancakes that
are baked in a basket shape until crisp.

1¼   **pounds russet potatoes,**
       peeled and grated

1   **teaspoon salt**
¼   **cup oil**

1. Preheat oven to 350°F. Spray underside of 4 (6-inch) ovenproof bowls
with nonstick vegetable cooking spray and place them underside up on a
baking sheet. In a large bowl, mix potatoes and salt until well blended.

2. In a large nonstick skillet, heat 1 tablespoon oil over medium-high heat. Swirl oil to coat pan. Add one-fourth of potato mixture, spreading and flattening it out to form a 7- to 8-inch round. Cook until golden underneath, about 3 minutes. Turn carefully and cook until second side is golden, about 3 minutes. With a wide spatula, transfer cooked potatoes to underside of a bowl. If needed, press edges of potatoes onto dish to form basket shape. Repeat with remaining potato mixture.

3. Bake until baskets are firm and golden brown, about 25 to 30 minutes. Let cool on bowls at least 10 minutes and remove each carefully just before serving. Use within an hour or cover and refrigerate overnight. Recrisp over bowls in a 350° oven 10 to 15 minutes.

77 GRILLED STEAK AND MIXED GREEN SALAD WITH CRANBERRY-HORSERADISH VINAIGRETTE

Prep: 20 minutes   Cook: 8 to 12 minutes   Serves: 8

Beautiful shades of red and green make this salad a stunning dish. Although it's delicious with steak just off the grill, this recipe also makes clever use of leftovers. When available, substitute leftover cooked roast beef, duck, or chicken for the flank steak and eliminate step 1.

2 pounds flank steak
8 cups torn Boston lettuce
4 cups torn watercress or
   spinach, tough stems
   removed
2 cups torn radicchio
2 large red-skinned apples,
   cored and cut into ½-inch
   dice

1 small red onion, thinly
   sliced and separated into
   rings
1¼ cups Cranberry-
   Horseradish Vinaigrette
   (recipe follows)

1. Light a hot fire in a barbecue grill or preheat broiler. Grill steak on an oiled rack set 4 to 6 inches from heat or broil, turning once, until browned outside and still pink and juicy inside, 4 to 6 minutes per side. Transfer steak to a cutting board and let rest while preparing salad.

2. In a large bowl, combine lettuce, watercress, radicchio, apples, and red onion. Cut steak lengthwise into 2-inch-wide lengths. Turn and thinly slice crosswise. Add to salad, drizzle with vinaigrette, and toss until well mixed. Divide among 8 plates and serve at once.

78   CRANBERRY-HORSERADISH VINAIGRETTE

Prep: 5 minutes   Cook: 5 minutes   Makes: about 1¼ cups

The tartness of cranberries cuts through the heaviness of rich meats, such as beef, lamb, and duck. When cranberries are available in the fall, buy a couple of extra bags to stash in the freezer and enjoy them all year long.

¾ **cup fresh or frozen cranberries**
⅓ **cup sugar**
¼ **cup orange juice**
⅓ **cup cider vinegar**
2 **teaspoons prepared white horseradish**

1 **teaspoon Dijon mustard**
⅔ **cup vegetable oil**
Salt and freshly ground pepper

1. In a small nonreactive saucepan, combine cranberries, sugar, and orange juice. Bring to a boil over medium-high heat, stirring constantly until sugar dissolves. Reduce heat to medium-low and cook, stirring, until cranberries start to pop, about 5 minutes. Remove from heat; let cool to room temperature.

2. Combine cranberry mixture, vinegar, horseradish, and mustard in a food processor or blender. Blend together. With machine on, gradually drizzle in oil. If needed, season with salt and pepper to taste. If not serving within an hour, cover and refrigerate. Let return to room temperature before serving.

79   CARPACCIO WITH SHAVED PARMESAN CHEESE ON BABY LETTUCES

Prep: 10 minutes   Freeze: 30 to 40 minutes   Cook: none   Serves: 4

This salad featuring Italian carpaccio, a simple treatment of paper-thin raw beef, requires the very best of its few ingredients. Use prime, fresh beef; if you're a regular customer of a butcher, ask him to prepare the meat for you. If you prefer not to eat raw meat, sauté or grill it 30 seconds per side.

8 **ounces beef tenderloin**
¼ **cup extra-virgin olive oil**
2 **tablespoons lemon juice**
1 **garlic clove, minced**
   Salt and freshly ground pepper

8 **cups assorted baby lettuces**
4 **teaspoons capers, drained**
1 **(2-ounce) chunk of Parmesan cheese, preferably imported**

1. Freeze beef until firm but not quite frozen, about 30 to 40 minutes. With a sharp knife, cut against grain as thinly as possible. Place meat in a single layer on a cutting board and cover with plastic wrap. With a meat pounder or flat side of a cleaver, pound meat until evenly paper-thin.

2. In a small bowl, blend together oil, lemon juice, and garlic. Season with salt and pepper to taste. Divide lettuce among 4 plates. Arrange beef over lettuce. Drizzle on dressing and sprinkle with capers. Using a swivel-bladed vegetable peeler, shave Parmesan cheese into wafer-thin slices and scatter over each salad. Serve at once.

80 FESTIVE MEXICAN GRILLED PORK AND VEGETABLE SALAD
Prep: 25 minutes   Cook: 8 to 10 minutes   Serves: 4

12 ounces center-cut boneless pork loin
4 cups shredded romaine lettuce
2 small ripe avocados, cut into ³/₄-inch dice
1 small jicama, peeled and cut into ³/₄-inch dice

1 red bell pepper, cut into ³/₄-inch dice
1 small red onion, thinly sliced and separated into rings
1 cup Honey-Cumin Vinaigrette (recipe follows)

1. Prepare a hot fire in a barbecue grill. Slice pork lengthwise into long slabs about ¹/₂ inch thick. Grill on an oiled rack 4 to 6 inches from heat 4 to 5 minutes on each side, or until white throughout but still juicy. Transfer to a cutting board and let rest 5 to 10 minutes. Slice crosswise into thin strips.

2. In a large bowl, combine pork, lettuce, avocados, jicama, bell pepper, and red onion. Drizzle on vinaigrette and toss until well blended. Divide among 4 plates and serve at once.

81 HONEY-CUMIN VINAIGRETTE
Prep: 10 minutes   Cook: none   Makes: about 1 cup

This spicy, hot, and sweet dressing also complements chicken or fruit salads.

¹/₃ cup fresh lime juice
2 tablespoons minced cilantro
2 tablespoons honey
4 teaspoons ground cumin
1 jalapeño pepper, seeded and minced

2 garlic cloves, minced
1 teaspoon salt
¹/₂ cup vegetable oil

In a small bowl, combine lime juice, cilantro, honey, cumin, jalapeño pepper, garlic, and salt. Gradually whisk in oil. If not using within 1 hour, cover and refrigerate. Let return to room temperature before serving.

82 ASIAN PEAR AND BEET SALAD WITH PORK TENDERLOIN

Prep: 15 minutes   Cook: 1 hour 10 minutes to 1 hour 13 minutes
Serves: 4

Slightly sweet beets and crunchy Asian pear complement roasted pork in this beautiful, lightly dressed salad. If you don't have time to bake the beets, use cut canned beets.

4   medium beets (about
      1 pound total), tops and
      roots trimmed
¼   cup plus 1 tablespoon olive
      oil
1   pork tenderloin (about
      12 ounces)
2   tablespoons mint jelly or
      mild jalapeño jelly,
      melted

2   tablespoons chicken broth
1   tablespoon cider vinegar
2   teaspoons Dijon mustard
1   large Asian pear, peeled,
      cored, and cut into thin
      wedges
      Salt and freshly ground
      pepper
6   cups torn red leaf lettuce

1. Preheat oven to 350°F. Wrap beets in foil and bake until tender when pierced with a sharp knife, about 1 hour. When cool enough to handle, peel beets, cut in half, and slice into thin wedges.

2. Increase oven heat to 400°. In a large ovenproof skillet, heat 1 tablespoon oil over medium-high heat until it shimmers. Add pork tenderloin and cook, turning frequently, until browned all over, about 2 to 3 minutes. Transfer to oven and roast until just cooked through with no trace of pink in center, 8 to 10 minutes. Meat should register 160° to 165°F on an instant-reading thermometer. Transfer meat to a cutting board and let rest while making salad.

3. In a large bowl, blend together jelly, broth, vinegar, and mustard until smooth. Slowly whisk in remaining ¼ cup oil. Add beets and pear; toss until well blended. Season with salt and pepper to taste.

4. Divide lettuce among 4 plates. Top with beets and Asian pear, placing just off-center. Slice pork thinly and arrange alongside beets and pear. Serve warm or at room temperature.

83 ORANGE-PORK SALAD WITH FIERY GREEN CHILE DRESSING

Prep: 20 minutes   Cook: 15 to 20 minutes   Serves: 4 to 6

Oranges and avocado provide cooling relief from the double dose of chiles in the dressing of this lovely composed salad.

1 pork tenderloin (about 12 ounces)
½ teaspoon salt
½ teaspoon black pepper
3 large oranges
1 small jalapeño pepper, seeded
1 garlic clove
2 teaspoons sugar
1 (4-ounce) can mild green chiles

⅓ cup fresh lime juice
½ cup sour cream
8 cups torn red leaf lettuce
1 medium ripe avocado, thinly sliced
1 small red onion, thinly sliced and separated into rings

1. Prepare a hot fire in a barbecue grill. Trim fat and silver membrane off pork and rub with salt and pepper. Grill pork on an oiled rack set 4 to 6 inches from heat, turning occasionally, until just cooked through with no trace of pink in center, about 15 to 20 minutes. Meat should register 160° to 165°F on an instant-reading thermometer. Transfer meat to a cutting board and let rest while making dressing.

2. Strip zest from oranges and place in a food processor or blender with jalapeño pepper, garlic, and sugar. Mince together. Add chiles and lime juice and blend together. Add sour cream and blend again. Working over dressing to catch juices, cut ends off oranges and cut away skin and white pith. Release segments into a small bowl.

3. Divide lettuce among 4 to 6 plates. Cut pork into thin rounds and arrange in slightly overlapping slices on lettuce. Arrange orange segments and avocado slices alongside of pork. Scatter red onion rings over salads and drizzle on half of dressing. Serve at once, passing remaining dressing at table.

84   THAI-STYLE PORK IN LETTUCE CUPS WITH SNOW PEAS AND MANDARIN ORANGES

Prep: 25 minutes   Cook: 12 to 16 minutes   Serves: 3

This unusual, meaty salad can be completely assembled and refrigerated a few hours ahead of time. Just let it return to room temperature before serving.

1¼   cups chopped trimmed snow peas (about 3 ounces)
½   cup flaked sweetened coconut
1   tablespoon vegetable oil
1   pound lean ground pork
¼   cup minced fresh ginger
4   garlic cloves, minced
1   (11-ounce) can mandarin oranges, drained

¼   cup fresh lime juice
2   tablespoons chopped fresh mint
2   tablespoons Asian fish sauce
1   jalapeño pepper, seeded and minced
9   to 12 large iceberg lettuce leaves

1. In a small saucepan of boiling water, cook snow peas until crisp-tender, about 1 minute. Drain, run under cold water, and drain again.

2. In a large nonstick skillet, cook coconut over medium heat, stirring frequently, until golden and fragrant, 6 to 8 minutes. Transfer to a plate. In same pan, heat oil over medium-high heat until it shimmers. Add pork, ginger, and garlic. Cook, stirring frequently, until meat has no trace of pink, 5 to 7 minutes. Remove from heat and drain off fat.

3. Stir snow peas, mandarin oranges, lime juice, mint, fish sauce, jalapeño pepper, and half of coconut into pork. Arrange 3 to 4 lettuce leaves to form a large cup on each of 3 plates. Spoon in warm pork mixture. Sprinkle remaining coconut on top and serve warm or at room temperature.

85   HONEY AND BOURBON–GLAZED HAM ON WATERCRESS

Prep: 20 minutes   Cook: none   Serves: 4

1   large pink grapefruit
2   tablespoons honey
2   tablespoons bourbon
2   tablespoons mayonnaise
6   cups watercress leaves, tough stems removed

3   cups shredded cooked ham (about 12 ounces)
1   cup shredded radicchio
2   scallions, thinly sliced
    Salt and freshly ground pepper

1. Working over a large bowl to catch juices, cut ends off grapefruit and cut away skin and white pith. Release segments and slice into ¾-inch pieces.

2. Add honey, bourbon, and mayonnaise to grapefruit juice. Whisk until well blended. Add watercress, ham, radicchio, scallions, and grapefruit. Toss until well blended. Season with salt and pepper to taste. Divide among 4 plates and serve at once.

---

86 ORANGE-HAM SALAD WITH WATERCRESS AND ENDIVE
Prep: 20 minutes   Cook: none   Serves: 4

4 small Belgian endive spears
4 small navel oranges
2 tablespoons balsamic
  vinegar
2 tablespoons Dijon mustard
¼ cup extra-virgin olive oil

3 cups shredded baked ham
  (about 12 ounces)
6 cups watercress, tough
  stems removed
Salt and freshly ground
  pepper

1. Remove and reserve 12 of largest outer leaves of Belgian endive. Cut remaining endive crosswise into ¼-inch-wide rounds.

2. Remove zest from oranges and mince. In a large bowl, combine orange zest, vinegar, and mustard. Gradually whisk in oil.

3. Cut ends off oranges. Working over dressing bowl to catch any juices, cut away skin and white pith. Release segments and add to dressing. Add ham, watercress, and sliced endive. Toss until well blended. Season with salt and pepper to taste. Arrange 3 endive spears pointing outward on each of 4 plates. Mound salad in center and serve at once.

---

87 HAM AND BEAN SALAD WITH TOMATOES AND MINT
Prep: 15 minutes   Cook: 1½ to 2 hours   Serves: 4

1⅓ cups dried white beans
  (about 8 ounces)
1½ cups diced cooked ham
  (about 6 ounces)
2 large plum tomatoes, cut
  into ½-inch dice

¾ cup chopped mint
¼ cup olive oil
2 tablespoons red wine
  vinegar
½ teaspoon salt
Green leaf lettuce leaves

1. Rinse beans and pick over to remove any grit. Place in a large saucepan and add enough water to cover by 2 to 3 inches. Bring to a boil over medium-high heat. Reduce heat to low, cover, and simmer until just tender, 1½ to 2 hours. Drain, run under cold water, and drain again well. Transfer to a large bowl.

2. Add ham, tomatoes, mint, oil, vinegar, and salt to beans. Toss until well blended. Divide among 4 lettuce-lined plates. Serve at room temperature.

88 SPICY-HOT SPINACH, HAM, AND KUMQUAT SALAD

Prep: 35 minutes   Cook: none   Serves: 8 to 10

This gorgeous deep green, orange, white, and pink salad is scorching with heat, but balanced with sweet and tart kumquats, lime juice, and honey. The dressing can be made by hand or by machine, but the machine creates a thicker, creamier dressing.

16 cups torn spinach
 4 cups shredded cooked ham
     (about 1 pound)
 4 Belgian endive, thinly
     sliced crosswise
20 kumquats (7 to 8 ounces
     total), thinly sliced and
     seeded

 3 garlic cloves
 1 jalapeño pepper, seeded
 ¼ cup fresh lime juice
 2 tablespoons honey
 ¾ cup olive oil
     Salt and freshly ground
     pepper

1. In a large bowl, combine spinach, ham, endive, and kumquats. Toss lightly to mix.

2. In a food processor or blender, mince together garlic and jalapeño pepper. Add lime juice and honey. With machine on, gradually drizzle in oil.

3. Drizzle dressing over salad and toss until well blended. Season with salt and pepper to taste. Divide among 8 to 10 plates and serve at once.

89 HAM AND PINEAPPLE COLESLAW

Prep: 25 minutes   Cook: none   Serves: 2 to 3

Most traditional coleslaws include heavy-handed amounts of mayonnaise, making them laden with fat and calories. This slimmed-down version is made with lean buttermilk and just a little sour cream.

 ¼ cup buttermilk
 ¼ cup sour cream
 1 tablespoon cider vinegar
 2 teaspoons sugar
 ½ teaspoon celery seed
 ½ teaspoon salt
 ¼ teaspoon pepper
 2 cups finely shredded green
     cabbage

 1 cup finely shredded red
     cabbage
1½ cups diced cooked ham
     (about 6 ounces)
 1 (8-ounce) can unsweetened
     pineapple chunks,
     drained
 4 scallions, thinly sliced

1. In a large bowl, combine buttermilk, sour cream, vinegar, sugar, celery seed, salt, and pepper. Whisk until well blended.

2. Add green cabbage, red cabbage, ham, pineapple, and scallions. Toss to mix well and serve.

90 CANADIAN BACON, CELERY ROOT, AND APPLE SALAD WITH HONEY-RICE VINAIGRETTE

Prep: 25 minutes   Cook: 1 minute   Serves: 8

2 tablespoons lemon juice
1 large celery root
   (about 1 pound)
6 Belgian endive spears
4 cups cubed (¾-inch)
   Canadian bacon
   (about 1 pound)
3 medium red-skinned
   apples, cut into ¾-inch
   dice

1 cup chopped walnuts
1¼ cups Honey-Rice
   Vinaigrette (recipe
   follows)
6 cups watercress leaves,
   tough stems removed
6 cups torn Boston lettuce

1. Stir lemon juice into a large bowl of water. Peel celery root and cut into ¾-inch cubes. As soon as it is cubed, add to acidulated water to keep it from turning brown. Bring a medium pot of water to a boil. Drain celery root, add to boiling water, and boil 1 minute. Drain, rinse under cold running water, and drain again. Transfer to a large bowl.

2. Remove 24 of largest outer endive leaves and arrange 3 pointing outward on each of 8 plates. Slice remaining endive crosswise into thin slices and add to celery root. Add Canadian bacon, apples, and walnuts. Drizzle on vinaigrette and toss until well mixed.

3. In a large bowl, toss watercress and lettuce and divide among plates. Top with celery root salad and serve at once.

91 HONEY-RICE VINAIGRETTE

Prep: 5 minutes   Cook: none   Makes: about 1¼ cups

Slightly sweet and garlicky, this winning dressing is a staple in my house. I make it in large quantities, store it in the refrigerator, and let it stand at room temperature before serving. It's especially good with salads containing fruit.

¼ cup rice vinegar
¼ cup honey
2 tablespoons lemon juice
2 garlic cloves, minced
½ teaspoon dry mustard

½ teaspoon paprika
½ cup vegetable oil
Salt and freshly ground
   pepper

In a small bowl, whisk together vinegar, honey, lemon juice, garlic, mustard, and paprika until well blended. Gradually whisk in oil. Season with salt and pepper to taste. If not using within 2 hours, cover and refrigerate. Let return to room temperature before using.

92   GERMAN SAUSAGE, SAUERKRAUT, AND APPLE SALAD

Prep: 25 minutes   Cook: 10 minutes   Serves: 8

1 pound German-style link
  sausage, such as
  bratwurst
1 cup vegetable oil
⅓ cup cider vinegar
¼ cup Dijon mustard
4 teaspoons sugar
4 teaspoons caraway seed
2 pounds sauerkraut, rinsed
  and squeezed dry

2 medium red-skinned
  apples, cut into ¾-inch
  dice
2 green bell peppers, cut into
  slivers
6 scallions, thinly sliced
  Salt and freshly ground
  pepper

1. Preheat broiler. Prick sausages evenly with a fork and broil 4 inches from heat, turning occasionally, until evenly browned, about 10 minutes. Remove to a cutting board and let rest while preparing dressing.

2. In a large bowl, whisk together oil, vinegar, mustard, sugar, and caraway seed until smooth and thickened. Slice sausage into ¼-inch rounds. Add sausage, sauerkraut, apples, bell peppers, and scallions to dressing. Toss until well mixed. Season with salt and pepper to taste. Serve at room temperature.

93   CHINESE SAUSAGE AND ASIAN PEAR SALAD

Prep: 20 minutes   Stand: 30 minutes   Cook: 9 minutes
Serves: 4 to 5

Sweet and crunchy Asian pear makes the perfect foil for savory stir-fried sausage and vegetables in this stunning, colorful entree. If you substitute Italian sausage, the flavor will not be the same, but the salad will still be delicious.

¾ ounce dried shiitake
  mushrooms
3 tablespoons vegetable oil
2 teaspoons Asian sesame oil
2 tablespoons soy sauce
2 tablespoons rice vinegar
4 medium Chinese sausages
  or 3 sweet Italian
  sausages (about 7 ounces
  total), thinly sliced

1 medium onion, chopped
1 small red bell pepper, cut
  into slivers
8 cups torn spinach
1 large Asian pear, peeled,
  cored, and thinly sliced

1. In a medium bowl, cover mushrooms with warm water. Let stand 30 minutes; drain well. Discard tough stems and slice caps into thin strips.

2. In a small bowl, combine vegetable oil, sesame oil, soy sauce, and vinegar. In a large skillet, cook sausages over medium-high heat, stirring frequently, until lightly browned, about 6 minutes. Transfer sausages to paper towels and discard all but 1 tablespoon fat in skillet. Add shiitakes, onion, and bell pepper. Cook, stirring constantly, until onion and pepper are crisp-tender, about 3 minutes. Remove from heat. Add sausages and sesame oil mixture. Toss until well blended.

3. Divide spinach among 4 or 5 plates and top with sausages and vegetables. Arrange slightly overlapping slices of pear alongside salad. Serve warm or at room temperature.

---

94 ITALIAN SAUSAGE AND CANNELLINI SALAD WITH TOMATO-FENNEL VINAIGRETTE
Prep: 20 minutes   Cook: 8 to 10 minutes   Serves: 4 to 5

Both fresh fennel and dried fennel seed lend their aniselike aroma to this main course. It's substantial in flavor and body, and it's festive with bright colors, so it also makes an attractive salad for parties. Serve it with crusty Italian bread with olive oil and balsamic vinegar.

12 ounces hot or mild Italian link sausage, sliced into ¼-inch rounds

1 (15-ounce) can cannellini or white kidney beans, rinsed and drained

1 small zucchini, cut into ½-inch dice

1 red bell pepper, cut into ½-inch dice

1 small bulb fennel, trimmed and thinly sliced

1 cup pitted kalamata or ripe olives

¾ cup Tomato-Fennel Vinaigrette (recipe follows)

¼ cup grated Parmesan cheese

1. In a large nonstick skillet, cook sausage over medium heat, stirring frequently, until cooked through with no trace of pink, 8 to 10 minutes. Drain on paper towels.

2. In a large bowl, combine sausage, beans, zucchini, bell pepper, fennel, and olives. Drizzle on vinaigrette and toss until well blended. Divide among 4 or 5 plates and sprinkle cheese on top. Serve at room temperature.

95 TOMATO-FENNEL VINAIGRETTE

Prep: 3 minutes   Cook: none   Makes: about ¾ cup

Most of the body and flavor of this brightly colored vinaigrette comes from fresh tomatoes. Garlic, fennel seed, and extra-virgin olive oil give it a decidedly Italian aroma. Try it as well over pasta salads.

2 garlic cloves
1 teaspoon salt
½ teaspoon sugar
3 small ripe plum tomatoes, quartered

¼ cup extra-virgin olive oil
2 tablespoons red wine vinegar
1 teaspoon fennel seed

Combine garlic, salt, and sugar in a blender. Mince together. Add tomatoes, oil, and vinegar. Blend together until smooth. Stir in fennel seed. If not using within an hour, cover and refrigerate. Let return to room temperature before serving.

Chapter 4

Fishing for Salads

For those of us in search of healthier eating, fish and shellfish salads provide the perfect marriage of ingredients. Seafood in general is high in protein, vitamins, and minerals, but very low in total fat. Most fish are low in cholesterol. When paired with fresh greens, fruits, and vegetables and lightly dressed with an olive oil–based vinaigrette, fish salads provide an ideal, healthful meal.

Thanks to food and transportation technology, the abundant array of seafood from fresh and salt waters is consistently, if seasonally, available across the country. The most important factor in choosing fish is freshness. If the fish you buy isn't impeccably fresh, the result will be poor no matter how you cook it. Instead of limiting your choices to a particular kind of fish, choose one that is fresh and that resembles what you desire in fat content, texture, and intensity of flavor. Firm-fleshed fish, such as swordfish, halibut, and fresh tuna, are best for salads since they will retain body when cooked and chilled. Delicate fish, such as sole and whiting, tend to fall apart when cooked.

When buying whole fish, look for glistening skin, firm flesh, bright red gills, and full, clear eyes. The entire fish should be free of slime or residue, and it should smell fresh. Fillets and steaks should be firm in texture, moist in appearance, and practically odorless.

No food is more sensitive to timing than fish. A minute of extra cooking can rob fish of its moisture and turn it tough. All fish and shellfish should be cooked until just opaque throughout and not a moment longer, so that it remains moist and tender. Steaks or fillets that are one inch thick or less make an ideal size for cooking, since the exterior will not be overcooked when the center is done.

Clams, mussels, and oysters are cooked when their shells open. Any that do not open should be discarded. Shrimp, crab, and lobster are cooked when their shells turn bright pinkish-red and their meat turns opaque. Overcooking makes them tough and dry, so keep a close eye.

If your idea of fish salad is mayonnaise-laden, old-fashioned tuna-fish-from-a-can salad, you're in for a treat. In this chapter, you'll find luxurious, tropical Cantaloupe, Macadamia, and Crab Salad; Swordfish and Chips Salad Caribe, which includes oven-baked plantain and sweet potato chips; and Bagel, Cream Cheese, and Lox-Lover's Salad, made of smoked salmon and Boston lettuce with a lemony cream cheese dressing.

96   SOY-BRAISED HALIBUT ON BOSTON LETTUCE

Prep: 20 minutes   Cook: 2 to 3 minutes   Serves: 4

Firm, white-fleshed halibut takes on a mahogany color in this quickly cooked salad. Creamy Boston lettuce provides a beautiful contrast in color, dramatizing the fish.

12 **ounces skinless, boneless halibut, cut into ¾-inch dice**
3 **tablespoons soy sauce**
2 **tablespoons minced fresh ginger**
2 **teaspoons sugar**

8 **cups torn Boston lettuce**
¼ **cup vegetable oil**
2 **tablespoons rice vinegar**
2 **large plum tomatoes, thinly sliced**
1 **medium cucumber, thinly sliced**

1. In a medium nonstick skillet, combine halibut, soy sauce, ginger, and sugar. Place skillet over medium heat and cook, stirring constantly, until all liquid is absorbed and fish is opaque throughout, about 2 to 3 minutes. Transfer to a large bowl.

2. Add lettuce and drizzle with oil and vinegar. Toss until well blended, then divide among 4 plates. Arrange tomato and cucumber slices on salads, overlapping slightly alongside lettuce. Serve at room temperature.

97   *HALIBUT SALAD WITH AVOCADOS AND SUN-DRIED TOMATOES*

Prep: 25 minutes   Marinate: 30 minutes   Cook: 10 minutes Serves: 8 to 10

In this substantial entree, tart lime juice, sweet sun-dried tomatoes, and buttery avocados lend color and flavor to warm, just-cooked halibut. If you prefer, cover and refrigerate the fish and dressing separately at least 2 hours in advance to serve the salad cold. The recipe also works well with fresh tuna or swordfish.

1 **cup olive oil**
½ **cup fresh lime juice**
1 **teaspoon Tabasco sauce**
1 **teaspoon salt**
2 **pounds halibut steaks, cut 1 inch thick**
1 **cup sun-dried tomatoes packed in oil, drained and thinly sliced**

4 **scallions, thinly sliced**
2 **ripe avocados, cut into ½-inch dice**
16 **cups torn red leaf lettuce**

1. In a small bowl, combine oil, lime juice, Tabasco sauce, and salt. Pour ½ cup of this mixture into a large baking pan; reserve remaining dressing. Add halibut to baking pan in a single layer and turn to coat. Marinate at room temperature 30 minutes.

2. Preheat oven to 400°F. Bake fish until just opaque throughout, about 10 minutes. When cool enough to handle, remove skin and bones and discard. Cut or flake fish into bite-size pieces and transfer to a large bowl.

3. Add sun-dried tomatoes, scallions, avocados, and remaining dressing. Toss gently to mix. Divide lettuce among 8 to 10 plates. Mound salad on top. Serve at room temperature.

---

98 GRILLED BLUEFISH ON BRUSCHETTA WITH ARUGULA

Prep: 15 minutes   Cook: 10 to 11 minutes   Serves: 4

4 plum tomatoes, cut lengthwise into thin wedges
½ cup extra-virgin olive oil
2 tablespoons balsamic vinegar
2 tablespoons thinly sliced fresh basil
1 pound bluefish fillets (½ to ¾ inch thick), cut into 4 equal pieces

Salt and freshly ground pepper
4 large slices Italian or other crusty bread, cut ¾ inch thick
1 garlic clove, halved
6 cups torn arugula or spinach
Lemon wedges

1. Prepare a medium-hot fire in a covered barbecue grill. In a medium bowl, blend together tomatoes, ¼ cup olive oil, vinegar, and basil. Set aside while cooking fish.

2. Brush both sides of fish with 2 tablespoons oil and sprinkle lightly with salt and pepper. Place bluefish, skin side down, on a lightly oiled rack set 4 to 6 inches from heat. Cover grill, leaving vents open, and cook until just opaque throughout but still moist and tender, about 8 minutes. Meanwhile, prepare bruschetta.

3. Rub both sides of bread with cut side of garlic. Brush lightly with remaining 2 tablespoons oil. When fish is cooked, transfer to a large platter and discard skin. Place bread on grill and cook, turning at least once, until golden on both sides, about 2 to 3 minutes.

4. Line 4 plates with arugula. Top with a slice of grilled bread. Set a bluefish fillet on each brushchetta. With a slotted spoon, remove tomatoes from dressing and arrange around bread. Drizzle dressing over arugula. Serve at once with lemon wedges.

99   OVEN-ROASTED SALMON SALAD

Prep: 15 minutes   Cook: 4 to 5 minutes   Serves: 4

2 tablespoons balsamic
   vinegar
1 tablespoon Dijon mustard
1 small shallot, minced
3 tablespoons walnut oil
2 tablespoons minced Italian
   parsley

Salt and freshly ground
   pepper
1 pound salmon fillet, cut
   crosswise on an angle
   into ¼-inch-thick slices
6 to 8 cups torn spinach

1. Preheat oven to 450°F. In a small bowl, blend together vinegar, mustard, and shallot. Gradually whisk in oil. Stir in parsley and season with salt and pepper to taste. If not using within an hour, cover and refrigerate. Return to room temperature before using.

2. Place salmon in a single layer on a lightly greased baking sheet. Sprinkle lightly with salt and pepper. Bake without turning until just opaque in center but still moist, 4 to 5 minutes.

3. Divide spinach among 4 plates. Top with salmon and drizzle dressing over each fillet. Serve at once while salmon is warm.

100   SWORDFISH AND CHIPS SALAD CARIBE

Prep: 25 minutes   Cook: 33 to 40 minutes   Serves: 6

Any firm-fleshed white fish will work in this slightly hot, slightly sweet salad. The chips in the title refer to two Caribbean favorites, plantain and sweet potato. They are oven-fried, using very little oil in the process. Since the chips are addictive, be sure to make extra for snacking. If plantains are not available, use 2 sweet potatoes.

1 long, thin sweet potato,
   peeled and sliced into
   ⅛-inch-thick rounds
¼ cup vegetable oil
1 large ripe plantain, peeled
   and sliced into
   ⅛-inch-thick rounds
3 swordfish steaks (6 to 8
   ounces each), cut ¾ inch
   thick

¼ cup fresh lime juice
¼ cup olive oil
2 garlic cloves, minced
2 jalapeño peppers, seeded
   and minced
9 cups assorted salad greens
4 scallions, thinly sliced
Salt and freshly ground
   pepper
Lime wedges

1. Preheat oven to 400°F. On a large baking sheet, toss sweet potato rounds with 1 tablespoon of oil. Arrange in a single layer and bake until tender and crisp, 18 to 20 minutes. Set aside.

2. Toss plantain slices with 1 tablespoon oil on baking sheet. Arrange in a single layer and bake until tender and lightly browned, about 7 to 12 minutes. Set aside.

3. Brush swordfish with remaining 2 tablespoons oil, set on baking sheet, and bake until just opaque in center but still moist, about 8 minutes. Cut each swordfish steak in half.

4. In a large bowl, combine lime juice, olive oil, garlic, and jalapeño peppers. Add salad greens and scallions and toss until well coated. Season with salt and pepper to taste. Divide among 6 plates. Top with a piece of swordfish. Arrange chips alongside fish and serve at once with lime wedges.

101   BAGEL, CREAM CHEESE, AND LOX-LOVER'S SALAD
Prep: 15 minutes   Cook: none   Serves: 4

For those of us who love bagels, cream cheese, and lox, this beautiful salad answers all of those cravings. Delicate Boston lettuce lets smoked salmon star in this delicious main-course salad, complete with all the trimmings—piquant capers and red onion. Serve with toasted bagels or bagel chips on the side.

8 cups torn Boston lettuce	3 tablespoons capers, drained
6 ounces lox or smoked salmon, cut into small dice	½ cup Cream Cheese and Lemon Dressing (recipe follows)
½ cup thinly sliced red onion	

In a large bowl, combine lettuce, lox, onion, and capers. Drizzle with dressing and toss until well blended. Divide among 4 plates and serve at once.

102   CREAM CHEESE AND LEMON DRESSING
Prep: 3 minutes   Cook: none   Makes: about ½ cup

1 (3-ounce) package cream cheese, at room temperature	½ teaspoon Dijon mustard
2 tablespoons lemon juice	⅓ cup olive oil
	Salt and freshly ground pepper

In a small bowl, combine cream cheese, lemon juice, and mustard. Beat with a hand-held electric mixer until well blended. Add oil and blend until smooth. Season with salt and pepper to taste. If not using within an hour, cover and refrigerate. Let return to room temperature before serving.

103 EAST-WEST TUNA FISH SALAD

Prep: 15 minutes   Cook: none   Serves: 4

Here's a tuna salad with a twist. Traditional mayonnaise is flavored with soy sauce and Asian sesame oil to produce a lightly dressed salad with a hint of the Far East. It's a delicious hodgepodge of colors, textures, and shapes. Freshly cooked or canned crab or shrimp can be substituted for the tuna. The salad can also be served over chow mein noodles or a bed of shredded iceberg lettuce.

½ cup mayonnaise
1 tablespoon soy sauce
1 teaspoon Asian sesame oil
2 (6½-ounce) cans solid white tuna, drained and flaked
1 (10-ounce) package frozen green peas, thawed
1 (7-ounce) can sliced water chestnuts, drained

1 (5½-ounce) can unsweetened pineapple chunks, drained
2 celery ribs, thinly sliced
2 scallions, thinly sliced
Green leaf lettuce leaves

In a large bowl, blend together mayonnaise, soy sauce, and sesame oil. Add tuna, peas, water chestnuts, pineapple, celery, and scallions. Toss until well blended. Serve at once on 4 lettuce-lined plates or cover and refrigerate at least 2 hours to serve cold.

104 BÉARNAISE-GLAZED SALMON WITH BROCCOLI

Prep: 25 minutes   Cook: 9 to 11 minutes   Chill: 2 hours   Serves: 8

This luxurious salad is rich with salmon and a creamy mayonnaise flavored like Béarnaise sauce with tarragon, shallots, lemon juice, and vermouth. It's special enough for your best company.

6 cups broccoli florets
2¼ pounds salmon steaks, cut ¾ inch thick
4 large plum tomatoes, cut into ½-inch dice
2 celery ribs, thinly sliced

1 (7-ounce) can sliced water chestnuts, drained
1 cup Béarnaise Mayonnaise (recipe follows)
Red leaf lettuce leaves

1. In a large pot of boiling salted water, cook broccoli until crisp-tender, 2 to 3 minutes. Drain, run under cold water, and drain again. Put in a bowl, cover, and refrigerate until chilled.

2. In a large skillet over medium heat, bring 2 cups lightly salted water to a boil. Reduce heat to low and place salmon in water. Simmer, uncovered, 4 minutes. With a slotted spatula, carefully turn salmon over and cook until opaque throughout but still moist, 3 to 4 minutes. Remove fish with slotted spatula and place on a platter. Blot excess water with a paper towel. Cover and refrigerate until cold, about 2 hours.

3. Remove skin and bones from salmon. Break meat into bite-size chunks and place in a large bowl. Add tomatoes, celery, water chestnuts, and half of mayonnaise. Toss gently until well blended. Divide among 8 lettuce-lined plates. Arrange broccoli florets on one side of salmon on each plate. Serve at once. Pass remaining mayonnaise on the side.

---

105   BÉARNAISE MAYONNAISE
Prep: 5 minutes   Cook: 2 minutes   Makes: about 2 cups

If you enjoy the classic French *sauce Béarnaise,* traditionally served warm with Chateaubriand, you'll love this homemade mayonnaise. They are both thick and creamy emulsified sauces, and they're both flavored with tarragon, shallots, and vinegar.

½ cup dry vermouth
¼ cup tarragon vinegar or
    white wine vinegar
2 medium shallots, minced
2 tablespoons plus
    2 teaspoons dried
    tarragon

2 eggs (see Note, page 6)
2 tablespoons lemon juice
1½ cups mild-flavored olive oil
    Salt and freshly ground
    pepper

1. In a small nonreactive saucepan, combine vermouth, vinegar, shallots, and 2 tablespoons tarragon. Bring to a boil, reduce heat to medium-low, and simmer until all but about 2 tablespoons liquid have evaporated. Strain mixture into a small bowl, pressing on solids to extract maximum flavor.

2. Combine eggs and lemon juice in a food processor or blender. With machine on, gradually drizzle in oil. Add reduced vermouth mixture and remaining 2 teaspoons tarragon. Blend together until slightly thickened and emulsified. Season with salt and pepper to taste. If not using immediately, cover and refrigerate.

106 NORI BASKETS WITH RICE AND SASHIMI

Prep: 15 minutes   Stand: 1 hour 5 minutes   Cook: 23 minutes
Serves: 4

In this stunning salad, crisscrossed sheets of dried seaweed form a basket similar to taco salad shells made of tortillas. If you don't have a reliable source of impeccably fresh fish, opt for lightly cooking it. Bright pink pickled ginger and black sesame seeds round out the dramatic presentation. All these Japanese ingredients can be found in the Asian foods section of your supermarket or in specialty food stores.

2 cups short-grain white rice
8 sheets of dried nori
¼ cup rice vinegar
1 tablespoon sugar
1 teaspoon salt
8 to 12 ounces raw fresh
   sushi-quality tuna, thinly
   sliced
1 medium ripe avocado,
   halved lengthwise and
   thinly sliced

3 tablespoons shredded
   pickled ginger, drained
2 teaspoons black sesame
   seeds
Soy-Wasabi Dipping Sauce
   (recipe follows)

1. Preheat oven to 350°F. Rinse rice until water runs clear. Cover rice with water and let stand 1 hour.

2. Meanwhile, arrange 4 sheets of nori on a flat surface. Top each with another sheet at a 45-degree angle to form a star pattern. Place each stack between 2 lightly oiled 6-inch ovenproof bowls and bake in middle of oven 5 minutes. (If you do not have enough bowls, bake in batches.) Let cool slightly and gently remove bowls from nori. Divide among 4 plates.

3. Drain rice well. In a medium saucepan, bring 2¼ cups water to a boil over medium-high heat. Add rice and stir briefly. Reduce heat to low, cover, and cook 18 minutes. Remove from heat and let stand 5 minutes. Meanwhile, in a large bowl, combine vinegar, sugar, and salt. While warm, add rice to vinegar mixture and toss until well blended. Set aside and let cool at least 5 minutes.

4. Divide rice among nori baskets. Arrange tuna and avocado in slightly overlapping slices on top of rice. Sprinkle pickled ginger and sesame seeds on top. Divide dipping sauce among 4 small serving dishes. Serve at once with dipping sauce alongside salad.

107   SOY-WASABI DIPPING SAUCE
Prep: 2 minutes   Cook: none   Makes: about ⅓ cup

¼ cup soy sauce
2 tablespoons mirin or sweet
  sherry

1 tablespoon brown sugar
⅛ teaspoon wasabi paste

In a small bowl, whisk together soy sauce, mirin, brown sugar, and wasabi paste until smooth. If desired, add more wasabi paste to taste.

108   SKEWERED SCALLOP SALAD
Prep: 20 minutes   Cook: 6 to 8 minutes   Serves: 12

A creamy, lemon-garlic dressing makes the perfect accompaniment for grilled sea scallops. Use this recipe for informal outdoor parties, where guests can grill their own scallops, or for a formal presentation, fan out the tomato and avocado on individual plates instead of tossing all together. If you prefer, substitute large shrimp or 1-inch chunks of firm-fleshed fish for the scallops.

1 large lemon
2 garlic cloves
2 eggs (see Note, page 6)
1½ tablespoons Dijon mustard
1 cup olive oil
  Salt and freshly ground
    pepper
1½ pounds asparagus, cut into
    1-inch lengths

3 pounds medium sea
    scallops
18 cups torn red leaf lettuce
4 large tomatoes, cut into
    ¾-inch dice
4 medium ripe avocados, cut
    into ¾-inch dice

1. If using bamboo skewers, soak them in water 30 minutes to prevent burning. Light a hot fire in a barbecue grill or preheat broiler. Remove zest from lemon and squeeze juice into a small bowl. Combine zest and garlic in a food processor or blender and mince together. Add lemon juice, eggs, and mustard. With machine on, gradually drizzle in oil. Season with salt and pepper to taste. If not using at once, cover and refrigerate.

2. In a large saucepan of boiling salted water, cook asparagus until crisp-tender, 2 to 3 minutes. Drain, run under cold water, and drain well.

3. Thread scallops on metal or bamboo skewers. Place on an oiled rack set 4 to 6 inches from coals or broil, turning once, until opaque throughout but still moist, about 4 to 5 minutes total. Transfer to a platter.

4. In a large bowl, combine lettuce, tomatoes, avocados, and asparagus. Drizzle with dressing and toss until well blended. Divide among 12 plates and top with skewered scallops. Serve while scallops are warm or at room temperature.

109   CAJUN-SPIKED SALMON ON GREENS
Prep: 15 minutes   Cook: 7 to 8 minutes   Chill: 2 hours   Serves: 6

This rich salad is a sophisticated version of old-fashioned canned tuna fish salad with celery and mayonnaise. Freshly cooked, buttery salmon is upholstered in a creamy, mildly spicy sauce. If fresh salmon is not available, substitute fresh tuna or shrimp.

1½ **pounds salmon steaks, cut**	¾ **cup Cajun Mayonnaise**
¾ inch thick	**(recipe follows)**
1 **pint cherry tomatoes, halved**	10 **to 12 cups torn assorted**
5 **scallions, thinly sliced**	**salad greens**
3 **celery ribs, thinly sliced**	

1. In a medium skillet, bring 2 cups lightly salted water to a boil over medium heat. Reduce heat to low and place salmon in water. Simmer, uncovered, 4 minutes. With a slotted spatula, carefully turn salmon over and cook until opaque throughout but still moist, 3 to 4 minutes. Remove fish with slotted spatula and place on a platter. Blot excess water with a paper towel. Cover and refrigerate until cold, about 2 hours.

2. Remove skin and bones from salmon. Break meat into bite-size chunks and place in a large bowl. Add tomatoes, scallions, celery, and mayonnaise. Toss until well blended. Divide greens among 6 plates. Top with salmon and serve cold or at room temperature.

110   CAJUN MAYONNAISE
Prep: 5 minutes   Cook: none   Makes: about ¾ cup

With its pleasing balance of garlic and spices, this mayonnaise is a staple in my house. Use it as a dip for raw vegetables or cooked ones, such as artichokes and asparagus. The mayonnaise keeps up to 2 months tightly covered and refrigerated.

½ **teaspoon dry mustard**	1 **garlic clove**
½ **teaspoon salt**	1 **egg (see Note, page 6)**
¼ **teaspoon pepper**	1 **tablespoon cider vinegar**
¼ **teaspoon ground cumin**	¾ **cup vegetable oil**
¼ **teaspoon cayenne**	

Place mustard, salt, pepper, cumin, cayenne, and garlic in a blender or small food processor. Mince together. Add egg and vinegar and blend well. With machine on, gradually drizzle in oil. Cover and refrigerate until ready to use.

111 TWO-ALARM FRESH TUNA SALAD

Prep: 25 minutes   Cook: 10 to 11 minutes   Serves: 8

Crisp croutons partially absorb the juices of freshly grilled tuna and the smoky, spicy flavors of the dressing in this unusual salad. The result is a pleasing blend of textures, temperatures, and flavors.

8 large slices of French or Italian bread, cut ½ inch thick

4 (8-ounce) fresh tuna steaks, cut ¾ inch thick

½ cup plus 2 tablespoons olive oil

Salt and freshly ground pepper

¼ cup fresh lime juice

2 tablespoons Dijon mustard

2 tablespoons finely chopped canned chipotle chiles

2 teaspoons sugar

8 cups torn curly endive

8 cups torn red leaf lettuce

⅓ cup coarsely chopped cilantro or parsley

Lime wedges

1. Prepare a medium-hot fire in a barbecue grill. Toast bread slices on a lightly oiled rack set 4 to 6 inches from heat, turning, until both sides are golden brown, 2 to 3 minutes. Brush both sides of fish with 2 tablespoons oil and sprinkle lightly with salt and pepper.

2. Place fish on grill and cook, turning once, until just barely opaque in center but still moist, about 4 minutes per side. Remove skin and bones from fish and cut each steak into 2 equal pieces.

3. In a large bowl, combine lime juice, mustard, chiles, and sugar. While whisking, gradually drizzle in remaining ½ cup oil. Add endive, lettuce, and cilantro and toss until well blended. Season with salt and pepper to taste.

4. Divide among 8 plates and top each with a slice of grilled bread. Set a fish fillet on each slice of bread and serve at once with lime wedges.

112   GRILLED SCALLOP SALAD WITH SHREDDED BEETS ON MÂCHE

Prep: 15 minutes   Cook: 4 to 5 minutes   Serves: 4

A bed of greens covered with burgundy beets topped with pearly white sea scallops makes this salad a stunning entree. Balsamic vinegar highlights the underlying sweetness of the scallops and beets.

1 **pound medium sea scallops**	**Salt and freshly ground**
⅓ **cup plus 2 tablespoons**	**pepper**
extra-virgin olive oil	1 **(15-ounce) can julienne**
4 **cups mâche**	**beets, drained**
4 **cups torn Boston lettuce**	**Lemon wedges**
2 **tablespoons balsamic**	
vinegar	

1. If using bamboo skewers, soak them in water 30 minutes to prevent burning. Light a hot fire in a barbecue grill or preheat broiler. Thread scallops onto metal or bamboo skewers and brush with 2 tablespoons oil. Place on an oiled grill set 4 to 6 inches from coals and grill or broil, turning once, until opaque but still moist, about 4 to 5 minutes total. Remove to a platter.

2. In a large bowl, combine mâche and lettuce. Drizzle on vinegar and remaining ⅓ cup olive oil and toss until well coated. Season with salt and pepper to taste. Divide greens among 4 plates.

3. Top each salad with about ½ cup beets, spreading them out to form a circle about 1 inch smaller than greens. Arrange scallops in center of salads and serve at once with lemon wedges.

113   WILD RICE WITH BAY SCALLOPS AND ORANGES

Prep: 15 minutes   Cook: 38 to 44 minutes   Serves: 6

This dramatic-looking, luxurious main course is composed of rings of bright green lettuce, brown wild rice, and pearly white scallops and oranges. It's well balanced and lightly dressed with a garlicky-orange dressing.

1½ **cups wild rice, rinsed**	**Salt and freshly ground**
½ **cup plus 1 tablespoon olive**	**pepper**
oil	3 **scallions, thinly sliced**
1¼ **pounds bay scallops**	1 **seedless cucumber, cut into**
3 **oranges**	**½-inch dice**
2 **garlic cloves**	**Green leaf lettuce leaves**
2 **tablespoons lemon juice**	

1. In a large saucepan, bring 4 cups of lightly salted water to a boil over medium-high heat. Add wild rice and stir briefly. Reduce heat to low, cover, and cook until just tender, 35 to 40 minutes. When rice is cooked, drain, run under cold water, and drain again well.

2. In a large nonstick skillet, heat 1 tablespoon oil over medium heat until hot. Add scallops and cook, stirring frequently, until opaque in center but still moist, 3 to 4 minutes. Transfer to a medium bowl to cool.

3. Remove zest from 2 oranges and mince together with garlic. Place in a medium bowl and add lemon juice. While whisking, drizzle in remaining ½ cup olive oil. Add salt and pepper to taste. Cut ends off oranges and cut away skin and white pith. Cut into segments. Add to scallops with scallions, cucumber, and dressing. Toss until well blended.

4. Divide wild rice among 6 lettuce-lined plates. Place scallops in center of rice. Serve at room temperature.

---

114 LEMON-GINGER SHRIMP CHINOIS
Prep: 20 minutes   Cook: 3 to 5 minutes   Serves: 4

Crisp, golden wonton strips mingled with shreds of iceberg lettuce provide a crunchy backdrop for plump, sweet shrimp in this delicious main course. Fresh ginger, honey, and lemon make the salad mildly tart, sweet, and spicy. To cut wonton skins quickly, leave them in their tidy stack as purchased and slice through the entire stack at once.

¼ cup lemon juice	½ teaspoon crushed hot red
Vegetable oil	pepper
2 tablespoons soy sauce	1 garlic clove, minced
2 tablespoons honey	1 pound large shrimp
2 tablespoons minced fresh	12 wonton skins
ginger	6 cups shredded iceberg
1 tablespoon minced lemon	lettuce
zest	3 scallions, thinly sliced

1. In a large bowl, whisk together lemon juice, 2 tablespoons vegetable oil, soy sauce, honey, fresh ginger, lemon zest, crushed hot pepper, and garlic. In a large saucepan of boiling water, cook shrimp until pink and loosely curled, 2 to 3 minutes. Drain, run under cold water, and drain again. When cool enough to handle, shell and devein shrimp and add to lemon juice mixture. Stir to blend well.

2. In a large skillet, heat at least 1 inch of vegetable oil to 375°F. Meanwhile, stack wonton skins, cut in half, and then into ¼-inch-wide strips. Separate wonton strips and deep-fry in batches until crisp and golden brown, about 15 to 20 seconds. As strips cook, drain on paper towels.

3. Add lettuce and scallions to shrimp and toss until well blended. Top with wonton strips and toss again. Divide among 4 plates and serve at once.

115   CRISPY ASIAN SHRIMP SLAW
Prep: 30 minutes   Cook: none   Serves: 4 to 6

Since it's made of sturdy, slivered vegetables that hold up well, this color-ful, practically fat-free salad makes great party fare. Leftover cooked steak, poultry, or firm-textured white fish can be used instead of the shrimp. To make the salad almost instant, use 5 cups of precut slaw mix instead of cut-ting your own vegetables.

1 cup matchstick-size strips
    peeled carrot (1 medium
    carrot)
1 cup matchstick-size strips
    trimmed snow peas
    (about 3 ounces)
1 cup matchstick-size strips
    red bell pepper (½ large
    bell pepper)

2 cups shredded Chinese
    (Napa) cabbage
1 pound cooked shelled and
    deveined bay (tiny)
    shrimp, thawed if frozen
⅓ cup Three-Flavor Asian
    Vinaigrette (recipe
    follows)
2 tablespoons sesame seeds

In a large bowl, combine carrot, snow peas, bell pepper, cabbage, and shrimp. Drizzle with vinaigrette and toss until well blended. Divide among 4 to 6 plates and sprinkle sesame seeds on top. Serve at room temperature.

116   THREE-FLAVOR ASIAN VINAIGRETTE
Prep: 10 minutes   Cook: none   Makes: about ⅓ cup

This hot, sweet, and salty dressing is assertive enough to accompany meats and poultry as well as more delicate fish.

2 tablespoons soy sauce
1 tablespoon mirin or sweet
    sherry
1 tablespoon rice vinegar
1 tablespoon fresh lime juice
2 teaspoons sugar

2 teaspoons minced fresh
    ginger
½ teaspoon hot chili oil or
    ¼ teaspoon cayenne
1 garlic clove, minced

In a small bowl, combine all ingredients. Stir until sugar dissolves. If not using within 1 hour, cover and refrigerate up to 4 days.

117 SHRIMP AND PAPAYA SALAD
Prep: 25 minutes   Cook: 2 to 3 minutes   Serves: 4 to 6

This Thai-inspired salad is lightly dressed and lightly spiced, so that the shrimp and papaya can be fully appreciated. Sturdy curly endive provides a slightly bitter flavor, and iceberg lettuce, cucumber, and almonds give the salad welcome crunch.

1 pound large shrimp, shelled
    and deveined
6 cups torn curly endive
2 cups shredded iceberg
    lettuce
1 large ripe papaya, cut into
    ¾-inch dice
2 scallions, thinly sliced
1 medium cucumber,
    quartered lengthwise and
    thinly sliced crosswise

½ cup slivered almonds,
    preferably lightly toasted
¼ cup cilantro or parsley
    leaves
½ cup Thai Ginger-Lime
    Dressing (recipe follows)

1. In a large saucepan of boiling water, cook shrimp until pink and loosely curled, 2 to 3 minutes. Drain and rinse under cold running water to cool.

2. In a large bowl, combine shrimp, endive, lettuce, papaya, scallions, cucumber, almonds, and cilantro. Drizzle with dressing and toss until well blended. Divide among 4 to 6 plates and serve at once.

118 THAI GINGER-LIME DRESSING
Prep: 10 minutes   Cook: none   Makes: about ½ cup

As is true of many Asian dishes, this dressing has a well-rounded balance of flavors. It's slightly sweet, salty, and tart all at once.

3 tablespoons vegetable oil
3 tablespoons fresh lime juice
2 tablespoons Asian fish
    sauce
2 tablespoons firmly packed
    brown sugar

4 teaspoons minced fresh
    ginger
1 garlic clove, minced
1½ teaspoons crushed hot red
    pepper

In a small bowl, whisk together all ingredients until well blended. If not using within 1 hour, cover and refrigerate.

119 GRILLED SHRIMP BROCHETTE SALAD WITH FENNEL AND PARMESAN CHEESE

Prep: 25 minutes   Cook: 4 to 6 minutes   Serves: 6

Tart lemon juice and anise-flavored fennel, time-honored complements to shrimp, team up here to round out a memorable main course.

24 to 30 medium shrimp,
    shelled and deveined
½ cup plus 2 tablespoons
    extra-virgin olive oil
¼ cup lemon juice
1 medium shallot, minced
½ teaspoon salt
½ teaspoon black pepper
6 small bulbs of fennel,
    trimmed and thinly
    sliced

3 cups watercress, tough
    stems removed
3 cups torn radicchio
1 (4- to 5-ounce) chunk of
    Parmesan cheese,
    preferably imported

1. If using bamboo skewers to thread shrimp, soak in water at least 30 minutes to prevent burning. Prepare a hot fire in a barbecue grill. Thread shrimp evenly on 6 skewers and brush with 2 tablespoons olive oil. Place on an oiled rack set 4 to 6 inches from coals. Grill, turning once, until shrimp turn pink and begin to curl, about 4 to 6 minutes.

2. In a large bowl, blend lemon juice, shallot, salt, and pepper. While whisking, slowly drizzle in remaining ½ cup olive oil. Add fennel, watercress, and radicchio and toss until well blended. Divide among 6 plates and top each salad with a skewer of shrimp. Using a vegetable peeler, shave Parmesan cheese into paper-thin slices and scatter over salads. Serve at once.

120 PRAWN, MANGO, AND AVOCADO SALAD WITH MANGO VINAIGRETTE

Prep: 20 minutes   Cook: 3 to 4 minutes   Serves: 4

In this luxurious salad, mango serves as both the basis for its fragrant dressing as well as a main ingredient.

16 prawns or jumbo shrimp,
    shelled and deveined
3 medium mangoes, peeled
    and pitted
1 garlic clove
¼ cup orange juice
2 tablespoons balsamic
    vinegar

½ teaspoon salt
¼ teaspoon white pepper
¼ cup extra-virgin olive oil
    Red leaf lettuce leaves
2 ripe avocados, halved
    lengthwise, pitted, and
    peeled

1. In a large saucepan of boiling water, cook shrimp until pink and loosely curled, 3 to 4 minutes. Drain, run under cold water until cool, and drain again.

2. Place 1 mango and garlic in a food processor or blender. Mince together. Add orange juice, vinegar, salt, and pepper. With machine on, slowly drizzle in oil and process until well blended.

3. Line 4 plates with lettuce. Cut remaining 2 mangoes and avocados lengthwise into ½-inch-thick slices. Arrange slices in a slightly overlapping pattern, alternating mango and avocado. Arrange shrimp alongside and drizzle dressing over salads. Serve at room temperature or slightly chilled.

---

121   CRAB CAKES ON MIXED GREENS
Prep: 15 minutes   Cook: 13 to 15 minutes   Serves: 4

Warm, delicate cakes brimming with crabmeat are featured in this wonderful salad. Because they contain so much crab and so little binding, they need to be handled carefully.

2 **tablespoons plus** 2 **teaspoons butter**	2 **eggs, lightly beaten**
1 **small red bell pepper,** **minced**	3 **tablespoons lemon juice**
2 **scallions, thinly sliced**	1 **tablespoon Worcestershire** **sauce**

1 **pound cooked or canned**
  crabmeat, preferably
  Dungeness, drained,
  picked over, and flaked
	6 **to 8 cups assorted baby**
	  lettuces

1½ **cups fresh white bread**
  crumbs
	¼ **cup extra-virgin olive oil**
	  Salt and freshly ground
	  pepper
	  Lemon wedges

1. In a large nonstick skillet, melt 2 teaspoons butter over medium-low heat. Add bell pepper and scallions. Cook, stirring occasionally, until softened, about 5 minutes. Transfer to a medium bowl. Add crab, bread crumbs, eggs, 1 tablespoon lemon juice, and Worcestershire. Stir gently until well blended. Form into patties about ½ inch thick.

2. In same skillet, melt remaining 2 tablespoons butter over medium heat. Cook crab cakes, turning carefully once, until lightly golden on both sides and just heated through, 4 to 5 minutes per side.

3. Place lettuces in a large bowl. Drizzle with oil and remaining 2 tablespoons lemon juice and toss until well blended. Season with salt and pepper to taste. Divide among 4 plates. Arrange warm crab cakes on top and serve at once with lemon wedges.

122   ISLAND SHRIMP SALAD WITH MACADAMIA NUTS AND COCONUT

Prep: 15 minutes   Cook: 2 to 3 minutes   Serves: 3 to 4

Sweet and hot, this tropical fruit and shrimp salad is beautiful enough to be shared with special company. It's particularly dramatic on a bed of dark green spinach leaves.

¾ **pound medium shrimp**
2 **celery ribs, thinly sliced**
1 **red bell pepper, cut into thin strips about 1½ inches long**
½ **cup chopped cilantro or parsley**
½ **cup macadamia nuts, or roasted cashews or peanuts**

½ **cup flaked coconut**
⅓ **cup Lime and Cumin Dressing (recipe follows)**
Salt and freshly ground pepper
Large spinach leaves
2 **bananas, sliced crosswise**

1. In a large saucepan of boiling water, cook shrimp until pink and loosely curled, 2 to 3 minutes. Drain and run under cold water. When cool enough to handle, shell and devein shrimp.

2. In a large bowl, combine shrimp, celery, bell pepper, cilantro, nuts, and coconut. Drizzle with dressing and toss until well blended. If needed, season with salt and pepper to taste.

3. Line 3 or 4 plates with spinach leaves. Mound shrimp salad on spinach and surround with banana slices. Serve at room temperature.

123   LIME AND CUMIN DRESSING

Prep: 5 minutes   Cook: none   Makes: about ⅓ cup

¼ **cup vegetable oil**
3 **tablespoons fresh lime juice**
2 **teaspoons firmly packed brown sugar**
1 **garlic clove, minced**

¾ **teaspoon ground cumin**
¼ **teaspoon Tabasco sauce**
½ **teaspoon salt**
Freshly ground pepper

In a small bowl, blend together oil, lime juice, brown sugar, garlic, cumin, and Tabasco sauce. Stir until sugar dissolves. Season with salt and pepper to taste. If not serving within 1 hour, cover and refrigerate.

124 TOMATO ASPIC WITH AVOCADO AND SHRIMP

Prep: 20 minutes   Cook: 3 minutes   Chill: 4 hours   Serves: 4

This molded, savory salad is speckled with tiny shrimp and avocado and enlivened with Tabasco sauce and lemon juice. Serve it with crusty bread or crisp crackers.

2 (¼-ounce) envelopes
  unflavored gelatin
3 cups tomato juice
1 teaspoon sugar
¼ cup lemon juice
½ teaspoon Tabasco sauce
½ teaspoon pepper
2 cups cooked shelled and
  deveined bay (tiny)
  shrimp (about 8 ounces)

½ cup minced celery
1 ripe avocado, cut into
  ½-inch dice
  Green leaf lettuce leaves
4 hard-cooked eggs,
  quartered lengthwise
½ cup mayonnaise

1. In a small bowl, blend together gelatin and ¼ cup cold water. Let stand until gelatin softens, about 5 minutes.

2. In a nonreactive medium saucepan, combine tomato juice and sugar. Place over medium heat and bring to a simmer, stirring until sugar dissolves, about 3 minutes. Remove from heat and blend in gelatin. Stir until gelatin dissolves. Stir in lemon juice, Tabasco sauce, pepper, shrimp, celery, and avocado. Pour into a 6-cup mold and refrigerate until set, at least 4 hours, preferably overnight.

3. When ready to serve, line a platter with lettuce. Run a knife around inside edge of mold. Dip mold into a large container of hot water almost up to its rim for 20 to 30 seconds. Invert salad onto lettuce. Surround aspic with wedges of eggs and serve chilled with mayonnaise.

125 CANTALOUPE, MACADAMIA, AND CRAB SALAD

Prep: 20 minutes   Cook: none   Serves: 5 to 6

This luxurious salad is a lovely blend of vivid colors and textures. It's simple and quick to prepare, but festive and delicious enough for the most discriminating diners.

6 cups torn red or green leaf lettuce
1 large cantaloupe, cut into ½-inch dice
1 large red bell pepper, cut into ½-inch dice
3 cups fresh cooked or canned crabmeat, drained and picked over

¾ cup chopped macadamia nuts
¼ cup extra-virgin olive oil
2 tablespoons balsamic vinegar
Salt and freshly ground pepper

In a large bowl, combine lettuce, cantaloupe, bell pepper, crab, and nuts. Drizzle with oil and vinegar and toss until well blended. Season with salt and pepper to taste. Divide among 5 or 6 plates and serve at once.

126 MARINATED CALAMARI SALAD

Prep: 25 minutes   Cook: 30 to 45 seconds
Marinate: 30 minutes   Serves: 4

This colorful salad is made simple by buying squid already cleaned. It requires less than a minute of cooking followed by a half hour of marinating.

¾ cup lemon juice
1 pound cleaned squid, cut into rings ½ inch thick; leave tentacles whole
½ cup olive oil
3 scallions, thinly sliced
1 garlic clove, minced
1 teaspoon dried tarragon
½ teaspoon Tabasco sauce
4 medium plum tomatoes, cut into ½-inch dice

1 large yellow or red bell pepper, cut into ½-inch dice
⅓ cup coarsely chopped pitted black olives
Salt and freshly ground pepper
6 cups torn red leaf lettuce

1. In a medium pot of lightly salted boiling water and ½ cup lemon juice, cook calamari until just opaque but still tender, 30 to 45 seconds. Do not overcook, or squid will be tough. Drain, run under cold water to cool, and drain again.

2. In a medium bowl, combine oil, remaining ¼ cup lemon juice, scallions, garlic, tarragon, and Tabasco sauce. Add calamari, tomatoes, bell pepper, and olives. Toss until well blended and marinate at room temperature 30 to 60 minutes or cover and refrigerate 2 to 3 hours.

3. Toss gently until well blended. Season with salt and pepper to taste. Divide lettuce among 4 plates. Mound salad on top and serve.

---

127 CRAB-STUFFED SHELLS WITH SAFFRON MAYONNAISE
Prep: 20 minutes   Cook: 15 to 18 minutes   Serves: 4

Large pasta shells packed with sweet crab and tomatoes grace this striking salad. If you prefer, substitute cooked salmon or small shrimp for the crab. For special occasions, place a tomato rose in the center of each salad. Be sure to cook the shells gently, since they may break in rapidly boiling water.

12 large pasta shells
 2 tablespoons olive oil
 2 tablespoons lemon juice
½ cup mayonnaise
⅛ teaspoon powdered saffron
12 ounces cooked or canned
    crabmeat, drained and
    picked over
 4 medium plum tomatoes, cut
    into ½-inch dice

 2 celery ribs, minced
   Salt and freshly ground
    pepper
   Green or red leaf lettuce
    leaves
 2 tablespoons chopped
    scallion
   Lemon wedges

1. In a large pot of lightly salted simmering water, cook pasta gently until just tender, 15 to 18 minutes. Drain well. While warm, transfer pasta to a large bowl. Drizzle with oil and 1 tablespoon lemon juice. Toss gently until coated evenly.

2. In a medium bowl, combine remaining 1 tablespoon lemon juice with mayonnaise and saffron. Whisk until smooth. Add crab, tomatoes, and celery. Toss gently until well blended. Season with salt and pepper to taste.

3. Stuff crab mixture into shells. Line 4 plates with lettuce leaves and arrange 3 shells on each plate. Sprinkle scallion on top, garnish with lemon wedges, and serve.

Chapter 5

Oodles of Noodles and Pasta Salads

Given the immense popularity of Italian pasta and Asian noodles in America—not to speak of their speed of preparation and easygoing versatility—it's not surprising that they've created a category of main-course salads all their own. Pasta's inherent blandness makes it easy to pair with a gamut of salad ingredients, including meats and fish, fresh vegetables and herbs, salsas and pestos, tart vinaigrettes and creamy dressings.

Some of the salads in this chapter, such as Puttanesca Salad, Pasta Salad Primavera, Macaroni and Mozzarella Salad, and Hay and Straw Salad, were inspired by classic warm pasta dishes. Others, such as East-Meets-Southwest Rigatoni and Chicken Salad and Slippery Noodle Salad with Grilled Pork Threads, reflect exciting new combinations of ingredients.

When choosing pasta for salads, it's usually best to opt for a commercially made dried pasta. It will cook to a firmer texture than fresh or homemade. Long, thin noodles, such as linguine and spaghetti, are best suited to light ingredients and liquid dressings, such as vinaigrettes. Chunkier shapes, such as bow tie and corkscrew, are well suited to trap heavier ingredients and thick, creamy dressings in their curls.

When cooking pasta, start testing for doneness after the shortest recommended cooking time. For salad, the pasta should be tender but still firm to the bite, or *al dente*. Tortellini, ravioli, and large pasta shells should be cooked gently since they may fall apart in rapidly boiling water.

As soon as the pasta is cooked, drain it in a waiting colander. Unless the pasta is to be dressed at once or eaten warm, run cold water over it to rinse off the surface starch, so the strands won't stick together. Shake the colander a few times up and down and sideways, to be sure of draining it well. Any remaining moisture will dilute dressings, and the flavor of the salad will suffer.

Most pasta salads taste best served at room temperature. Some of them hold up well when dressed and refrigerated for a day or two, which makes them ideal for buffets and picnics. Unless they contain delicate ingredients, such as lettuce, the salads can be made ahead and brought to room temperature before serving.

128 ASPARAGUS AND PENNE SALAD WITH FOUR CHEESES

Prep: 15 minutes   Cook: 8 to 10 minutes   Serves: 8 to 10

1 pound penne
1 pound asparagus, tough
    stems removed, sliced
    into 1-inch lengths
½ cup extra-virgin olive oil
¼ cup balsamic vinegar
¾ cup shredded mozzarella
    cheese

¾ cup shredded provolone
    cheese
¾ cup crumbled Gorgonzola
    cheese
¾ cup grated Parmesan cheese
    Salt and freshly ground
    pepper

1. In a large pot of lightly salted boiling water, cook penne until just tender, 8 to 10 minutes. At same time, in another large pot of lightly salted boiling water, cook asparagus until barely tender, 2 to 3 minutes, depending upon thickness of stalks. Drain pasta and asparagus separately, run under cold water, and drain again well.

2. In a large bowl, combine pasta and asparagus. Drizzle on oil and vinegar and toss until evenly coated. Add mozzarella, provolone, Gorgonzola, and Parmesan cheeses and toss gently until well blended. Season with salt and pepper to taste. Serve at room temperature.

129 CALAMARI SALAD WITH SPINACH FETTUCCINE

Prep: 20 minutes   Cook: 3 to 4 minutes   Serves: 4

Pearly white squares of squid dot a bed of green pasta in this garlicky, lemony salad. Buying frozen calamari steaks takes all the prep work out of cooking squid. They are cleaned and so thin that they will thaw quickly in a large bowl of cool water and cook within a minute.

1 (9-ounce) package fresh
    spinach fettuccine
⅓ cup plus 2 tablespoons
    extra-virgin olive oil
1 pound frozen calamari
    steaks, thawed and cut
    into ¾-inch dice
3 garlic cloves, minced
2 tablespoons lemon juice

Salt and freshly ground
    pepper
Large spinach leaves
8 sun-dried tomatoes, drained
    and chopped
1 (2.2-ounce) can sliced black
    olives, drained
2 tablespoons capers, drained

1. In a large pot of lightly salted boiling water, cook pasta until just tender, 2 to 3 minutes. Drain, run under cold water, and drain again well. Place in a large bowl.

2. In same pan, heat 2 tablespoons olive oil over medium heat until hot. Add calamari and garlic and cook, stirring constantly, until calamari is just opaque and barely cooked, about 1 minute. Add to pasta with remaining ⅓ cup olive oil and lemon juice. Toss until well blended. Season with salt and pepper to taste. Divide among 4 spinach-lined plates and sprinkle with tomatoes, olives, and capers. Serve warm or at room temperature.

---

130   GRILLED PORTOBELLO MUSHROOM AND RIGATONI SALAD WITH GOAT CHEESE
Prep: 10 minutes   Cook: 16 to 22 minutes   Serves: 4 to 6

Slightly sweet and chewy sun-dried tomatoes, mild goat cheese, and aged vinegar make a nice foil for beefy mushrooms in this main course.

12 ounces rigatoni
¾ cup Sun-Dried Tomato Vinaigrette (recipe follows)
4 large portobello mushroom caps (1 to 1½ pounds total)

1 tablespoon olive oil
8 cups shredded romaine lettuce
4 ounces mild goat cheese, such as Montrachet, crumbled

1. Prepare a medium-hot fire in a barbecue grill. In a large pot of lightly salted boiling water, cook rigatoni until just tender, 10 to 12 minutes. Drain, run under cold water, and drain again well. In a large bowl, combine rigatoni and vinaigrette. Toss until evenly coated.

2. Brush mushrooms with olive oil. Place on a lightly oiled rack set 4 to 6 inches from coals and cook until golden, turning once, 3 to 5 minutes per side. Cut into ½-inch-thick slices.

3. To serve, divide lettuce among 4 to 6 plates. Top with pasta and mushroom slices. Sprinkle with goat cheese and serve at room temperature.

---

131   SUN-DRIED TOMATO VINAIGRETTE
Prep: 8 minutes   Cook: none   Makes: about ¾ cup

8 sun-dried tomatoes packed in oil, drained and chopped
2 tablespoons balsamic vinegar

1 garlic clove, minced
1 teaspoon salt
½ cup extra-virgin olive oil

In a small bowl, blend together sun-dried tomatoes, vinegar, garlic, and salt. Gradually whisk in oil. If not using within 2 hours, cover and refrigerate. Let return to room temperature before serving.

132   TORTELLINI SALAD WITH ROASTED RED PEPPER VINAIGRETTE

Prep: 8 minutes   Cook: 7 to 8 minutes   Serves: 3

Stuffed tortellini are coated in a bright red, mildly peppery herbed dressing in this hearty entree. Without the lettuce, it's also delicious served hot.

9 ounces fresh cheese
  tortellini
2 cups sliced mushrooms
⅓ cup grated Parmesan cheese

1 cup Roasted Red Pepper
  Vinaigrette (recipe
  follows)
Green leaf lettuce leaves

1. In a large pot of lightly salted simmering water, cook tortellini gently until just tender, about 7 to 8 minutes. Drain, run under cold water, and drain again well.

2. In a large bowl, combine pasta, mushrooms, cheese, and vinaigrette. Toss until well blended. Divide among 3 lettuce-lined plates and serve at room temperature.

133   ROASTED RED PEPPER VINAIGRETTE

Prep: 5 minutes   Cook: 10 minutes   Makes: about 1 cup

Bell pepper and mustard give this smoky, bright red dressing lots of flavor and body with no fat.

1 large red bell pepper
2 tablespoons balsamic
  vinegar
2 tablespoons Dijon mustard
¼ teaspoon dried basil

¼ teaspoon dried oregano
¼ teaspoon dried thyme
Salt and freshly ground
  pepper

1. Preheat broiler. Cut bell pepper in half lengthwise. Scoop out seeds and cut out stems. Place pepper, skin side up, on a baking sheet and broil as close to heat as possible until skin is charred all over, about 10 minutes. Place pepper in a paper bag and let steam 10 to 15 minutes. Peel off blackened skin.

2. Combine roasted pepper, vinegar, mustard, basil, oregano, and thyme in a food processor or blender. Blend together until almost smooth and thickened, about 3 to 5 minutes. Season with salt and pepper to taste. If not using immediately, cover and refrigerate. Let return to room temperature before using.

134 ROTELLE AND GRILLED FRESH TUNA SALAD WITH TAPENADE

Prep: 15 minutes   Cook: 16 to 18 minutes   Serves: 6

Tapenade, a staple in Provence, is a thick paste of anchovies, ripe olives, capers, olive oil, and lemon juice that's used as a condiment alongside fish and meat. In this flavor-packed entree, it's used to dress curly pasta, which traps every bit of its richness. Freshly grilled tuna, shredded spinach, and ripe tomatoes round out this delicious salad.

6 cups rotelle
6 fresh tuna steaks, cut ½ inch thick (about 2 pounds total)
Salt and freshly ground pepper
3 cups shredded spinach

4 medium plum tomatoes, cut into ½-inch dice
¼ cup chopped fresh basil
¾ cup Tapenade (recipe follows)
Lemon wedges

1. Prepare a hot fire in a grill. In a large pot of lightly salted boiling water, cook rotelle until just tender, about 10 to 12 minutes. Drain, run under cold water, and drain again well.

2. Place tuna on a lightly oiled rack set 4 to 6 inches from heat and grill, turning once, until browned outside and just opaque throughout but still moist, about 3 minutes per side. Transfer to a platter and season with salt and pepper to taste.

3. In a large bowl, combine pasta, spinach, tomatoes, basil, and Tapenade. Toss until well blended and divide among 6 plates. Top each with a tuna steak and remove tuna skin. Serve while tuna is warm or at room temperature with lemon wedges.

135 TAPENADE

Prep: 10 minutes   Cook: none   Makes: about ¾ cup

Delicious over greens or pasta, this robust dressing is packed with the powerful flavors of Provence.

⅓ cup kalamata or other oil-cured black olives, pitted
3 oil-packed anchovy fillets, drained
2½ tablespoons lemon juice

2 garlic cloves
½ cup extra-virgin olive oil
1 tablespoon capers, drained
Salt and freshly ground pepper

Combine olives, anchovy fillets, lemon juice, and garlic in a food processor or blender. Mince together. With machine on, slowly drizzle in oil. Stir in capers. If needed, season with salt and pepper to taste. If not using within 2 hours, cover and refrigerate. Let return to room temperature before serving.

136   BOW-TIE PASTA WITH SMOKED CHICKEN AND PEPPER PUREE

Prep: 15 minutes   Cook: 10 minutes   Serves: 4 to 6

Red bell peppers make a flavorful, beautiful sauce for white pasta and smoked poultry against a bed of deep green spinach leaves. If smoked turkey or chicken is not available, use leftover cooked poultry.

12 ounces bow-tie pasta
      (farfalle)
2 medium red bell peppers,
      cut into large chunks
2 garlic cloves
½ cup mayonnaise
2 tablespoons Dijon mustard

2 cups chopped smoked
      chicken or turkey (about
      8 ounces)
   Large spinach leaves
½ cup kalamata or other
      oil-cured black olives
½ cup chopped fresh basil

1. In a large pot of lightly salted boiling water, cook pasta until just tender, about 10 minutes. Drain, run under cold water, and drain again well.

2. Place bell peppers and garlic in a food processor. Mince together. Add mayonnaise and mustard and blend until smooth. Transfer to a large bowl.

3. Add pasta and chicken and toss until well blended. Line a platter or 4 to 6 individual plates with spinach. Mound salad on spinach. Sprinkle olives and basil on top. Serve at room temperature.

137   ORZO AND SHREDDED CHICKEN WITH GREEN OLIVE SALSA

Prep: 10 minutes   Cook: 1 to 1¼ hours   Serves: 4

Robustly flavored with olives and garlic and brightly colored with flecks of parsley, a green olive salsa coats rice-shaped orzo pasta and roasted chicken in this unusual salad. Since it can be dressed and refrigerated ahead of time and will taste delicious at any temperature from cold to room temperature, it makes a convenient dish for a buffet or picnic.

1 (3½- to 4-pound) chicken
2 cups orzo (rice-shaped
      pasta)
1 cup parsley sprigs, tough
      stems removed
2 garlic cloves
¼ teaspoon salt
½ cup chopped pitted green
      olives

¼ cup white wine vinegar
1 teaspoon Dijon mustard
¼ cup extra-virgin olive oil
   Salt and freshly ground
      pepper
8 cherry tomatoes, quartered
   Red leaf lettuce leaves

1. Preheat oven to 375°F. Rinse chicken inside and out and pat dry. Place in a lightly greased baking dish. Roast chicken until thigh juices run clear when pierced with a sharp knife, 1 to 1¼ hours. Meanwhile, cook pasta and make salsa.

2. In a medium pot of lightly salted boiling water, cook orzo until just tender, about 8 minutes. Drain, run under cold water, and drain again.

3. Combine parsley, garlic, and salt in a food processor or blender. Mince together. Add olives, vinegar, and mustard. With machine on, slowly drizzle in oil. Season with salt and pepper to taste.

4. When cool enough to handle chicken, remove and discard skin and bones; shred meat. In a large bowl, combine chicken, pasta, tomatoes, and salsa. Toss until well blended and divide among 4 lettuce-lined plates. Serve at room temperature or chilled.

---

138   MACARONI AND MOZZARELLA SALAD
Prep: 15 minutes   Cook: 8 to 9 minutes   Serves: 8 to 10

A takeoff on ever-popular macaroni and cheese, this salad mimics the classic dish's creaminess, while tomatoes and fresh herbs lend it a fresh, sophisticated flavor.

1 **pound medium elbow pasta**
2 **cups shredded mozzarella**
    or Cheddar cheese
    (8 ounces)
8 **large plum tomatoes, cut**
    into ½-inch dice
1 **(3.8-ounce) can sliced ripe**
    olives, drained

2 **cups Creamy Herb and**
    Garlic Dressing (recipe
    follows)
    Salt and freshly ground
    pepper

1. In a large pot of lightly salted boiling water, cook pasta until just tender, 8 to 9 minutes. Drain, run under cold water, and drain again well.

2. In a large bowl, combine pasta, cheese, tomatoes, olives, and dressing. Toss until well mixed. Season with salt and pepper to taste. Serve at room temperature.

---

139   CREAMY HERB AND GARLIC DRESSING
Prep: 5 minutes   Cook: none   Makes: about 2 cups

1 **cup parsley sprigs**
1 **cup fresh basil leaves**
2 **garlic cloves**
1 **cup mayonnaise**

1 **cup nonfat plain yogurt**
1 **tablespoon lemon juice**
    Salt and freshly ground
    pepper

Combine parsley, basil, and garlic in a food processor or blender. Mince together. Add mayonnaise, yogurt, and lemon juice. Blend until smooth. Season with salt and pepper to taste. If not using immediately, cover and refrigerate. Let return to room temperature before using.

140 HAY AND STRAW SALAD

Prep: 10 minutes   Cook: 9 to 11 minutes   Serves: 4 to 6

Paglia e Fieno, loosely translated as Hay and Straw, is a classic pasta dish from Emilia-Romagna, the bread basket of Italy. It's named for the green and yellowish colors of spinach and plain fettuccine, which resemble straw and hay. This salad incorporates most of the same textures and flavors in warm Hay and Straw, including the 2 fettuccine, prosciutto, green peas, and a creamy, garlicky sauce.

6 ounces spinach fettuccine
6 ounces plain fettuccine
8 ounces medium mushrooms, thinly sliced
3 ounces thinly sliced prosciutto, cut into slivers

½ cup frozen green peas, thawed
¾ cup Parmesan-Parsley Dressing (recipe follows)

1. In a large pot of lightly salted boiling water, cook spinach and plain fettuccine until barely tender, 9 to 11 minutes. Drain, run under cold water, and drain again well.

2. In a large bowl, combine pasta, mushrooms, prosciutto, peas, and dressing. Toss until well mixed. Serve at room temperature.

141 PARMESAN-PARSLEY DRESSING

Prep: 3 minutes   Cook: none   Makes: about ¾ cup

This garlicky, pale green dressing is delicious over many pasta salads, especially with those that include fresh tomatoes.

¼ cup parsley sprigs
1 garlic clove
⅓ cup grated Parmesan cheese
2 tablespoons lemon juice

½ cup extra-virgin olive oil
Salt and freshly ground pepper

Combine parsley and garlic in a food processor or blender. Mince together. Add cheese and lemon juice. With machine on, gradually drizzle in oil. If needed, season with salt and pepper to taste. If not using immediately, cover and refrigerate. Let return to room temperature before using.

142 PASTA SALAD PRIMAVERA
Prep: 20 minutes   Cook: 12 to 15 minutes   Serves: 6

Fresh spring asparagus dressed in a creamy, mellow garlic vinaigrette is featured in this colorful version of pasta primavera. The original dish, served warm, was invented by Sirio Maccioni, the owner of New York's Le Cirque restaurant.

1 pound fettuccine
½ pound asparagus, tough
    ends removed, cut into
    1-inch pieces (about 2
    cups)
2 cups broccoli florets
1 cup frozen green peas,
    thawed

2 large tomatoes, cut into
    ½-inch dice
½ cup grated Parmesan cheese
1¼ cups Creamy Roasted Garlic
    Vinaigrette (recipe
    follows)

1. In a large pot of lightly salted boiling water, cook fettuccine until barely tender, 10 to 12 minutes. Drain, run under cold water, and drain again well.

2. In separate medium pots of lightly salted boiling water, cook asparagus and broccoli until crisp-tender, 2 to 3 minutes. Drain, run under cold water, and drain again.

3. In a large bowl, combine pasta, asparagus, broccoli, peas, tomatoes, cheese, and vinaigrette. Toss until well blended. Serve at room temperature.

143 CREAMY ROASTED GARLIC VINAIGRETTE
Prep: 10 minutes   Cook: 1 hour   Makes: about 1¼ cups

Slowly baked garlic provides nutty, mellow flavor and creaminess with no added fat. Dijon adds a decided spiciness; if using this dressing on a different salad that is especially delicate, eliminate the mustard.

4 heads of garlic, papery tips
    removed
¼ cup red wine vinegar
2 tablespoons Dijon mustard

½ cup extra-virgin olive oil
    Salt and freshly ground
    pepper

1. Preheat oven to 350°F. Place heads of garlic in a baking dish just large enough to hold them. Sprinkle with 1 tablespoon water and cover tightly. Bake until pulp is very tender when mashed with a fork, about 1 hour.

2. Squeeze garlic pulp into a food processor or blender. Add vinegar, mustard, and oil. Blend together until smooth. Season with salt and pepper to taste. If not using within 1 hour, cover and refrigerate. Let return to room temperature before serving.

144 MINTY COUSCOUS WITH TOMATOES, OLIVES, AND FETA CHEESE

Prep: 20 minutes   Cook: none   Serves: 6 to 7

⅓ cup plus 1 tablespoon
    extra-virgin olive oil
3 garlic cloves, minced
3 cups couscous
¾ cup crumbled feta cheese
½ cup chopped fresh mint

2 tablespoons lemon juice
  Salt and freshly ground
    pepper
18 cherry tomatoes, halved
1 (3.8-ounce) can sliced ripe
    olives, drained

1. In a large saucepan, combine 1 tablespoon oil, garlic, and 3 cups water. Bring to a boil. Stir in couscous, cover, and remove from heat. Let stand 5 minutes. Transfer to a large bowl and fluff with a fork to separate grains. Let cool at least 10 minutes.

2. Add feta cheese, mint, remaining ⅓ cup oil, and lemon juice to couscous. Toss to mix well. Season with salt and pepper to taste. Serve at room temperature, with tomatoes and olives sprinkled on top.

145 SALAMI, RIGATONI, AND FONTINA SALAD

Prep: 15 minutes   Cook: 10 to 12 minutes   Serves: 4

The flavor-packed ingredients in this colorful salad are cut to mimic the long, thin shape of rigatoni.

8 ounces rigatoni
¼ cup extra-virgin olive oil
¼ cup balsamic vinegar
½ teaspoon crushed hot red
    pepper
½ teaspoon salt
2 garlic cloves, minced
4 small plum tomatoes,
    seeded and cut into thin
    strips

4 ounces thinly sliced salami,
    cut into thin strips
4 ounces thinly sliced fontina
    cheese, cut into thin
    strips
1 cup fresh basil leaves,
    shredded
  Green or red leaf lettuce

1. In a large pot of lightly salted boiling water, cook rigatoni until just tender, 10 to 12 minutes. Drain, run under cold water, and drain again well. In a large bowl, combine oil, vinegar, hot pepper, salt, and garlic. Add pasta and toss until well blended.

2. Add tomatoes, salami, cheese, and basil to rigatoni. Toss until well blended. Divide among 4 lettuce-lined plates and serve at room temperature.

146   EAST-WEST ANGEL HAIR SALAD WITH GRILLED CHICKEN

Prep: 20 minutes   Cook: 12 minutes   Serves: 4 to 6

8 ounces angel hair pasta
2 teaspoons Asian sesame oil
6 ounces snow peas (about 3 cups), trimmed
1 medium red bell pepper, cut into thin strips about 1½ inches long

⅓ cup chopped cilantro
6 scallions, thinly sliced
¾ cup Nutty Rice Vinaigrette (recipe follows)
4 skinless, boneless chicken breast halves
2 tablespoons vegetable oil

1. Light a hot fire in a barbecue grill or preheat broiler. In a large pot of boiling water, cook pasta until just tender, about 3 minutes. Drain, run under cold water, and drain again well. Transfer to a large bowl, drizzle with sesame oil, and toss until lightly coated.

2. In a medium pot of lightly salted boiling water, cook snow peas until crisp-tender, about 1 minute. Drain, run under cold water, and drain again. Add snow peas, bell pepper, cilantro, and scallions to pasta. Pour on dressing and toss until well mixed. Divide among 4 to 6 plates.

3. Brush chicken on both sides with oil and place on a lightly oiled grill rack 4 to 6 inches from heat. Cook, turning once, until browned outside and white throughout but still moist, about 4 minutes per side. Slice crosswise into ½-inch strips and arrange over pasta. Serve at room temperature.

147   NUTTY RICE VINAIGRETTE

Prep: 5 minutes   Cook: none   Makes: about ¾ cup

I have a weakness for Asian peanut sauces, and this one is no exception. It's sweet, mildly hot, and smoky.

¼ cup creamy peanut butter
¼ cup rice vinegar
1 tablespoon soy sauce
1 tablespoon sugar

1 tablespoon Asian sesame oil
½ teaspoon hot chili oil or crushed hot red pepper

In a medium bowl, vigorously whisk together all ingredients and 3 to 4 tablespoons water until well blended. Dressing should be easily pourable. If not using within 2 hours, cover and refrigerate. Let return to room temperature before using. If dressing is too thick, whisk in additional water 1 tablespoon at a time.

148 PEPPERY FRESH RAVIOLI SALAD
Prep: 10 minutes   Cook: 5 to 6 minutes   Serves: 3 to 4

A jar of undrained marinated artichoke hearts provides the dressing for this quick-to-fix, flavor-packed salad.

1 (9-ounce) package fresh
   cheese ravioli
1 (6½-ounce) jar marinated
   artichoke hearts,
   undrained
1 (4-ounce) jar seasoned
   mushrooms, drained

1 (2.2-ounce) can sliced black
   olives, drained
   Salt and freshly ground
   pepper
1 large bunch of watercress,
   tough stems removed
⅓ cup grated Parmesan cheese

1. In a large pot of lightly salted simmering water, gently cook ravioli until just tender, 5 to 6 minutes. Drain, run under cold water, and drain again well.

2. In a large bowl, combine ravioli, artichoke hearts and their marinade, mushrooms, and olives. Toss gently until well mixed. Season with salt and pepper to taste.

3. Arrange watercress on 3 or 4 plates. Mound ravioli salad on top. Sprinkle with cheese and serve at room temperature.

149 WAGON WHEEL PASTA WITH TUNA AND BROCCOLI
Prep: 20 minutes   Cook: 7 to 8 minutes   Serves: 4 to 6

Whimsically shaped small wagon wheels of pasta make any dish seem out of the ordinary. Paired with shredded mozzarella cheese, red bell pepper, and broccoli florets, this well-balanced main course is satisfying and colorful.

8 ounces wagon wheel pasta
4 cups broccoli florets (about
   8 ounces)
⅓ cup olive oil
2 tablespoons red wine
   vinegar
2 garlic cloves, minced
1 teaspoon dried oregano
½ teaspoon dried thyme

2 (6½-ounce) cans solid white
   tuna, drained
2 cups shredded mozzarella
   cheese (8 ounces)
1 medium red bell pepper,
   cut into slivers
   Salt and freshly ground
   pepper

1. In a large pot of salted boiling water, cook pasta until just tender, 7 to 8 minutes. Meanwhile, in a medium pot of lightly salted boiling water, cook broccoli until crisp-tender, about 2 minutes. Drain pasta and broccoli separately, run under cold water, and drain again well.

2. In a large bowl, blend together olive oil, vinegar, garlic, oregano, and thyme. Add pasta, broccoli, tuna, cheese, and bell pepper. Toss until well mixed. Season with salt and pepper to taste. Serve at room temperature.

---

150   PUTTANESCA SALAD
Prep: 15 minutes   Cook: 10 to 12 minutes   Serves: 6 to 8

Transforming one of my favorite classic warm Italian dishes, pasta Puttanesca, into a salad was a pleasure. The robust, well-rounded flavors of the sauce enliven salad greens as well as pasta. The combination, which provides welcome crunch and substance, makes a satisfying meal with just a loaf of crusty Italian bread.

12 ounces rotelle
1 tablespoon red wine
   vinegar
4 garlic cloves, minced
1 tablespoon anchovy paste
1/3 cup extra-virgin olive oil
8 cups shredded romaine
   lettuce
3 (14½-ounce) cans stewed
   tomatoes, drained well
   and chopped

1½ cups kalamata or other
   oil-cured black olives,
   pitted and chopped
½ cup capers, drained
   Salt and freshly ground
   pepper

1. In a large pot of lightly salted boiling water, cook pasta until just tender, 10 to 12 minutes. Drain, run under cold water, and drain again well.

2. In a large bowl, whisk together vinegar, garlic, and anchovy paste until well blended. Gradually whisk in oil. Add pasta, lettuce, tomatoes, olives, and capers. Toss until well mixed. Season with salt and pepper to taste. Serve at room temperature.

151   CORKSCREW PASTA WITH PROSCIUTTO VINAIGRETTE

Prep: 30 minutes   Cook: 10 to 12 minutes   Serves: 5 to 6

The ingredients in this salad scream Italian in flavor and color. Corkscrew-shaped pasta traps bits of cheese and prosciutto in its curls, distributing their flavors evenly. Many specialty markets sell ends of prosciutto for less than thin slices. It's easier to mince prosciutto that's in a chunk, and you'll save money as well.

1 pound rotelle	4 medium plum tomatoes, cut
½ cup finely chopped	into ½-inch dice
prosciutto (about 3	⅓ cup grated Parmesan cheese
ounces)	⅓ cup chopped Italian flat-leaf
¼ cup extra-virgin olive oil	parsley
1 tablespoon lemon juice	Salt and freshly ground
2 garlic cloves, minced	pepper
4 cups shredded spinach	

1. In a large pot of lightly salted boiling water, cook rotelle until just tender, about 10 to 12 minutes. Drain, run under cold water, and drain again well.

2. In a large bowl, blend together prosciutto, oil, lemon juice, and garlic. Add pasta, spinach, tomatoes, cheese, and parsley. Toss until well blended and season with salt and pepper to taste. Divide among 5 or 6 plates and serve at room temperature or cover and refrigerate for up to 24 hours. Let return to room temperature before serving.

152   SLIPPERY NOODLE SALAD WITH GRILLED PORK THREADS

Prep: 20 minutes   Cook: 8 to 10 minutes   Serves: 6

6 ounces bean thread, or	3 tablespoons minced fresh
cellophane, noodles	ginger
1 to 1½ pounds boneless pork	3 garlic cloves, minced
loin, sliced about 1 inch	1 (8-ounce) can baby corn,
thick	drained
2 tablespoons vegetable oil	1 (8-ounce) can straw
⅓ cup soy sauce	mushrooms, drained
2 tablespoons rice vinegar	1 large red bell pepper, cut
1 tablespoon Asian sesame	into slivers
oil	4 scallions, thinly sliced

1. Preheat a hot fire in a barbecue grill or preheat broiler. Bring a large pot of water to a boil. Drop noodles into water and stir briefly to separate strands. Remove from heat and let stand until softened and tender, 15 to 20 minutes.

2. Meanwhile, brush pork with oil and grill on an oiled rack 4 to 6 inches from heat until browned outside and white in center, about 4 to 5 minutes per side. Remove to a cutting board and let rest about 5 minutes. Slice into 3 x 1/2-inch thin strips.

3. In a large bowl, combine soy sauce, vinegar, sesame oil, ginger, and garlic. Drain noodles well, add to dressing, and toss until well blended. Add pork strips, corn, mushrooms, bell pepper, and scallions. Toss gently to mix. Serve at room temperature or chilled.

153 ASIAN NOODLE SALAD WITH VEGETABLES

Prep: 20 minutes   Cook: 5 to 6 minutes   Serves: 5 to 6

In this lovely salad, bunches of colorful vegetables are nestled in a cushion of spicy, nutty noodles. For a dramatic presentation, serve it on a bed of large deep green spinach leaves.

1 pound angel hair pasta
3/4 pound asparagus, cut into
    1-inch lengths
1/2 cup creamy peanut butter
1/4 cup red wine vinegar
2 tablespoons soy sauce
1 tablespoon Asian sesame
    oil
1 teaspoon hot chili oil or
    crushed hot red pepper

1 teaspoon sugar
2 tablespoons minced fresh
    ginger
2 garlic cloves, minced
1 large red bell pepper, cut
    into thin strips about
    1 1/2 inches long
2 cups fresh bean sprouts
4 scallions, thinly sliced

1. In a large pot of boiling water, cook pasta until just tender, about 3 minutes. Drain, run under cold water, and drain again well.

2. In a medium saucepan of lightly salted boiling water, cook asparagus until crisp-tender, 2 to 3 minutes. Drain, run under cold water, and drain again.

3. In a large bowl, vigorously whisk together peanut butter, vinegar, soy sauce, sesame oil, chili oil, sugar, ginger, garlic, and 1/2 cup water until well blended. If needed, add extra water to make dressing easily pourable. Add pasta and toss until evenly coated. Divide among 5 or 6 plates.

4. Arrange little bunches of asparagus, bell pepper, and bean sprouts over pasta. Sprinkle scallions on top. Serve at room temperature.

154   MALAYSIAN PASTA AND SHRIMP SALAD

Prep: 20 minutes   Cook: 10 to 12 minutes   Serves: 6 to 7

Shrimp, rigatoni, and Napa cabbage are tossed together in a Malaysian peanut butter–based sauce that lightly coats all of the ingredients in this substantial salad.

12	ounces rigatoni or rotelle	4	cups shredded Chinese
1	pound medium shrimp,		(Napa) cabbage
	shelled and deveined	4	scallions, thinly sliced
½	cup soy sauce		Large spinach leaves
½	cup creamy peanut butter	6	large plum tomatoes, thinly
⅓	cup fresh lime juice		sliced crosswise
3	tablespoons sugar	2	medium cucumbers, thinly
½	teaspoon hot chili oil or		sliced
	crushed hot red pepper	½	cup coarsely chopped
3	garlic cloves, minced		cilantro
1½	tablespoons minced fresh		
	ginger		

1. In a large pot of lightly salted boiling water, cook pasta until just tender, 10 to 12 minutes. Drain, run under cold water, and drain again.

2. Meanwhile, in a medium saucepan of boiling water, cook shrimp until pink and loosely curled, 2 to 3 minutes. Drain, run under cold water, and drain again.

3. In a large bowl, vigorously whisk together soy sauce, peanut butter, lime juice, sugar, chili oil, garlic, and ginger until well blended. Add pasta, shrimp, cabbage, and scallions and toss until well mixed. If not serving at once, cover and refrigerate.

4. When ready to serve, line a large platter or 6 or 7 individual plates with spinach. Toss pasta again and mound onto spinach. Arrange tomatoes and cucumbers in slightly overlapping slices alongside pasta. Garnish with cilantro and serve at room temperature.

155 EAST-MEETS-SOUTHWEST RIGATONI AND CHICKEN SALAD

Prep: 20 minutes   Cook: 16 to 18 minutes   Serves: 5 to 6

Lightly cooked onions and bell peppers, crunchy iceberg lettuce, and soy sauce–flavored pasta make this just-cooked chicken salad memorable. Letting the pasta sit in the dressing while cooking the chicken gives it time to absorb the flavors.

8 ounces rigatoni
½ cup soy sauce
¼ cup plus 3 tablespoons
    vegetable oil
¼ cup rice vinegar
1 teaspoon sugar
3 garlic cloves, minced
1 jalapeño pepper, seeded
    and minced
4 skinless, boneless chicken
    breast halves, cut into
    ¾-inch cubes

1 medium green bell pepper,
    cut into slivers
1 medium red bell pepper,
    cut into slivers
4 scallions, thinly sliced
4 cups shredded iceberg
    lettuce

1. In a large pot of lightly salted boiling water, cook pasta until just tender, 10 to 12 minutes. Drain, run under cold water, and drain again well.

2. In a large bowl, blend together soy sauce, ¼ cup oil, vinegar, sugar, garlic, and jalapeño pepper. Add pasta and toss until well mixed.

3. In a wok or large nonstick skillet, heat 2 tablespoons oil over medium-high heat until it shimmers. Add chicken and cook, stirring constantly, until golden outside and just white but still juicy in center, about 3 minutes. Add to pasta.

4. Heat remaining 1 tablespoon oil in skillet. Add bell peppers and cook over high heat, stirring constantly, until crisp-tender, about 3 minutes. Add to pasta. Add scallions and lettuce and toss until well mixed. Divide among 5 or 6 plates and serve at once.

156   TORTELLINI SALAD WITH BLUE CHEESE PESTO

Prep: 10 minutes   Cook: 7 to 8 minutes   Serves: 4

This simple dish is a beautiful combination of flavors and colors. It's delicious with other filled or unfilled chunky shapes of pasta as well.

9 ounces fresh or frozen cheese tortellini	1 cup Blue Cheese Pesto (recipe follows)
1 pint cherry tomatoes, halved	Salt and freshly ground pepper
⅓ cup coarsely chopped walnuts	12 red leaf lettuce leaves

1. In a large pot of lightly salted simmering water, cook tortellini gently until just tender, about 7 to 8 minutes. Drain, run under cold water, and drain again well.

2. In a large bowl, combine tortellini, tomatoes, walnuts, and pesto. Toss gently until well mixed. Season with salt and pepper to taste. Line a platter or 4 plates with lettuce and mound tortellini on top. Serve at room temperature.

BLUE CHEESE PESTO

Prep: 5 minutes   Cook: none   Makes: about 1 cup

This untraditional pesto is pungent with garlic and sharp with blue cheese. Use it as you would traditional pesto on foods that will be complemented by a strongly flavored sauce.

1½ cups fresh basil leaves	½ cup crumbled blue cheese
2 garlic cloves, crushed	½ cup grated Parmesan cheese
½ cup extra-virgin olive oil	

Combine basil and garlic in a food processor or blender. Mince together. Add oil, blue cheese, and Parmesan cheese. Process until evenly blended. If not using immediately, cover and refrigerate. Let return to room temperature before using.

Chapter 6

Great Grains, Rice, and Beans

Grains and beans are, at long last, being elevated to their deserved status in our everyday diet. The rediscovery of the pleasure of healthy whole grains and hearty legumes is due in part to American cooks' concern with eating healthy. As we depend less on meat for protein, beans and grains provide a logical, economical, plentiful alternative. In many parts of the world where animal protein is expensive or scarce, beans and grains provide the bulk of the human diet. They are also a major source of complex carbohydrates, vitamins, and fiber.

A tremendous variety of grains and canned and dried beans are available in supermarkets. (The few that are more difficult to find, such as quinoa, can be located in health food or specialty stores.) Canned beans are a great convenience because with them, you don't need to plan ahead to allow time for soaking and cooking. And they have the same nutritional content as cooked dried beans. The biggest difference is that canned beans have a higher salt content, but rinsing them will eliminate much of their saltiness.

As America's interest in international cuisines has expanded, intriguing flavors have been added to our bean and grain repertoire, lending these ingredients interesting new treatments. In this chapter, discover lemony, garlicky, bulgur-based Shrimp Tabbouleh from the Middle East; Bulgur and Lentil Salad with Ham and Tomatoes from India; and Fava and Cannellini Bean Salad with Mediterranean accents. From Mexico, enjoy an unusual, stunning Black Bean and Cactus Salad.

The ancient Peruvian grain, quinoa, is incorporated into tempting salads such as Ham and Quinoa Salad with Spiced Dried Fruit and Smoky Chicken and Quinoa Salad with Oranges, Raisins, and Mint. Hearty barley appears German-style in Barley, Bratwurst, and Apple Salad and Italian-style in Barley and Wild Mushroom Salad with Shaved Parmesan Cheese.

Closer to home, you'll find Wheat Berry, Sour Cherry, and Ham Salad; Triple Bean and Cheese Salad Southwestern Style; Black-Eyed Pea and Bacon Salad; and Andouille Sausage, Rice, and Lentil Jumble.

157   BARLEY, BRATWURST, AND APPLE SALAD
Prep: 20 minutes   Cook: 35 to 40 minutes   Serves: 6

Hearty and well balanced, this beautiful salad needs only a loaf of crusty bread to be complete. The dressing, dosed with mustard and horseradish, is both slightly sharp and slightly sweet—the perfect complement to sausage and apples.

1⅓ cups pearl barley	12 ounces fully cooked
¼ cup cider vinegar	bratwurst sausage,
3 tablespoons Dijon mustard	quartered lengthwise and
2 tablespoons prepared white	thinly sliced crosswise
horseradish	1 (10-ounce) package frozen
2 tablespoons firmly packed	peas, thawed
brown sugar	3 medium apples, quartered,
1 teaspoon salt	cored, and thinly sliced
½ cup vegetable oil	4 scallions, thinly sliced

1. In a medium saucepan, bring 4 cups lightly salted water to a boil over medium-high heat. Add barley and stir briefly. Reduce heat to low, cover, and cook until just tender, about 35 to 40 minutes. Drain well.

2. Meanwhile, in a large bowl, blend together vinegar, mustard, horseradish, brown sugar, and salt. Slowly whisk in oil until well blended.

3. Add warm barley to dressing. Toss until well blended. Add sausage, peas, apples, and scallions and toss again. Serve at room temperature.

158   BARLEY AND WILD MUSHROOM SALAD WITH SHAVED PARMESAN CHEESE
Prep: 20 minutes   Cook: 35 to 40 minutes   Serves: 8

Earthy mushrooms and comforting barley make this salad a natural for fall and winter. A lemony dressing provides delightful contrast.

3 cups reduced-sodium	4 cups wild mushrooms, such
chicken broth	as shiitakes, chanterelles,
1½ cups pearl barley	or portobellos, thinly
½ cup olive oil	sliced
¼ cup lemon juice	16 cups torn curly endive
¼ cup minced Italian parsley	1 (4-ounce) chunk of
1 tablespoon minced fresh or	Parmesan cheese,
dried rosemary	preferably imported
1 teaspoon salt	

1. In a medium saucepan, bring chicken broth and 2 cups water to a boil. Stir in barley. Reduce heat to low, cover, and cook until tender, 35 to 40 minutes. Drain well.

2. In a large bowl, whisk together oil, lemon juice, parsley, rosemary, and salt. Add warm barley and mushrooms. Toss until well mixed.

3. Divide endive among 8 plates. Top with barley and mushroom mixture. Using a swivel-bladed vegetable peeler, shave Parmesan cheese into thin slices and scatter over each salad. Serve warm or at room temperature.

---

159 SMOKY CHICKEN AND QUINOA SALAD WITH ORANGES, RAISINS, AND MINT

Prep: 10 minutes   Cook: 25 to 27 minutes   Serves: 8

Light, protein-rich quinoa is as versatile as it is nutritious. Its tiny, bead-shaped grains take on whatever flavors they're paired with—in this case, smoky Asian sesame oil.

2 cups quinoa	4 scallions, thinly sliced
1 cup raisins	1 cup unsalted roasted
¼ cup Asian sesame oil	peanuts
2 tablespoons vegetable oil	¼ cup chopped fresh mint
4 skinless, boneless chicken	Salt and freshly ground
breast halves	pepper
4 navel oranges	Green leaf lettuce

1. In a large saucepan, bring 4 cups of water to a boil. Add quinoa and stir briefly. Reduce heat to low, cover, and cook 10 minutes. Stir in raisins and continue to cook until all liquid is absorbed, about 5 minutes. Transfer to a large bowl. Drizzle on sesame oil and toss until well blended.

2. In a large skillet, heat vegetable oil over medium-high heat until it shimmers. Add chicken and cook, turning occasionally, until golden brown on both sides and white in center but still moist, 10 to 12 minutes. Remove to a cutting board. Let stand 5 to 10 minutes, then cut into ¾-inch cubes.

3. Meanwhile, with a swivel-bladed vegetable peeler, remove zest from 2 oranges; mince fine. Working over quinoa to catch any juices, cut ends off oranges and cut away skin and white pith. Slice oranges into segments.

4. Add orange zest, chicken, scallions, peanuts, and mint to quinoa. Toss until well mixed. Season with salt and pepper to taste. Line a platter or 8 individual plates with lettuce leaves. Mound salad on lettuce. Top with slightly overlapping orange segments and serve at room temperature.

160 MOROCCAN-SPICED BULGUR, CURRANT, AND HAM SALAD

Prep: 20 minutes   Stand: 1 hour   Cook: none   Serves: 4

To lighten this salad considerably, substitute yogurt for the mayonnaise, use 95 percent fat-free ham, and eliminate the almonds.

1 cup cracked bulgur wheat	3 medium carrots, peeled and
¾ cup currants	shredded
2 cups boiling water	½ cup slivered almonds,
¼ cup mayonnaise	preferably toasted
1 tablespoon lemon juice	Salt and freshly ground
1 teaspoon honey	pepper
2 teaspoons ground cumin	½ cup cilantro or parsley
½ teaspoon cinnamon	leaves
¼ pound sliced baked ham,	
cut into slivers	

1. In a medium heatproof bowl, combine bulgur and currants. Add boiling water, stir briefly, and let stand 1 hour. Drain, then squeeze dry in a kitchen towel.

2. In a large bowl, blend together mayonnaise, lemon juice, honey, cumin, and cinnamon. Add bulgur mixture, ham, carrots, and almonds to mayonnaise. Toss until well blended. Season with salt and pepper to taste. Sprinkle cilantro on top. Serve at room temperature.

161 BULGUR AND LENTIL SALAD WITH HAM AND TOMATOES

Prep: 20 minutes   Cook: 24 to 28 minutes   Serves: 5 to 6

This satisfying salad gets plenty of heat from fresh jalapeño pepper and tartness from lemon juice, so it's flavor-packed entirely without oil. The salad remains tantalizing even after 2 days in the refrigerator, but be sure to serve it warm or at room temperature.

2 tablespoons butter	1 cup cracked bulgur wheat
1 medium onion, chopped	1½ cups shredded cooked ham
2 garlic cloves, minced	(about 6 ounces)
1 jalapeño pepper, seeded	4 large plum tomatoes, cut
and minced	into ½-inch dice
4 cups reduced-sodium	¾ cup chopped parsley
chicken broth	¼ cup lemon juice
1 cup lentils, rinsed and	Salt and freshly ground
picked over	pepper

1. In a large saucepan, melt butter over medium-low heat. Add onion and cook, stirring occasionally, until slightly softened, 3 to 5 minutes. Add garlic and jalapeño pepper. Cook, stirring occasionally, 3 minutes longer.

2. Add broth and 1 cup water. Bring to a boil over medium-high heat. Add lentils and bulgur and stir briefly. Reduce heat to low, cover, and cook until just tender, 18 to 20 minutes. Drain well and place in a large bowl.

3. Add ham, tomatoes, parsley, and lemon juice. Toss until well blended. Season with salt and pepper to taste. Serve warm or at room temperature.

---

162   ARTICHOKE, FONTINA, AND RICE SALAD
Prep: 20 minutes   Cook: 15 to 18 minutes   Serves: 4 to 5

Speckled with sweet, chewy sun-dried tomatoes, sliced black olives, and shreds of creamy fontina cheese, this rice salad is delicious and beautiful enough for entertaining. It can be refrigerated for up to 2 days and returned to room temperature shortly before serving.

1 cup long-grain white rice
1½ tablespoons lemon juice
½ teaspoon anchovy paste
½ teaspoon salt
2 garlic cloves, minced
¼ cup extra-virgin olive oil
1 (8¼-ounce) can quartered
   artichoke hearts, drained
8 sun-dried tomatoes packed
   in oil, drained and
   chopped

4 scallions, thinly sliced
1 cup shredded fontina
   cheese
1 (2.2-ounce) can sliced black
   olives, drained
Salt and freshly ground
   pepper

1. In a medium saucepan, bring 2 cups lightly salted water to a boil over medium-high heat. Add rice and stir briefly. Reduce heat to low, cover, and cook until liquid is absorbed and rice is tender, 15 to 18 minutes.

2. Meanwhile, in a large bowl, mix together lemon juice, anchovy paste, salt, and garlic. Slowly whisk in oil until well blended.

3. Add warm rice to dressing and toss until coated. Let cool at least 5 minutes. Add artichoke hearts, tomatoes, scallions, cheese, and olives. Toss until well mixed. Season with salt and pepper to taste. Serve at room temperature.

163   SHRIMP TABBOULEH
Prep: 20 minutes   Stand: 1 hour   Cook: none   Serves: 4

Garlic, lemon, and mint flavor nutritious bulgur in this Middle Eastern favorite, tabbouleh. Tiny cooked shrimp make it not quite traditional, but delicious nonetheless. Everything in the salad is quite small, so it can be picked up with romaine leaves and eaten without utensils. It's often served with a crisp bread, such as lavosh.

2 cups cracked bulgur wheat
4 cups boiling water
2 cups cooked shelled and
    deveined bay (tiny)
    shrimp
4 plum tomatoes, cut into
    ½-inch dice
⅓ cup chopped fresh mint

¼ cup extra-virgin olive oil
¼ cup lemon juice
⅓ cup pine nuts (pignoli),
    lightly toasted
3 garlic cloves, minced
1 teaspoon salt
    Romaine lettuce leaves

1. In a medium heatproof bowl, combine bulgur and boiling water. Let stand 1 hour. Drain, then squeeze dry in a kitchen towel.

2. In a large bowl, combine bulgur, shrimp, tomatoes, mint, oil, lemon juice, pine nuts, garlic, and salt. Toss until well blended. Divide among 4 lettuce-lined plates and serve at room temperature or cover and refrigerate at least 2 hours to serve cold.

164   HAM AND QUINOA SALAD WITH SPICED DRIED FRUIT
Prep: 15 minutes   Cook: 15 minutes   Serves: 6

1 cup quinoa
6 dried apricots, chopped
¾ cup currants
3 cups slivered cooked ham
    (about 12 ounces)
½ cup coarsely chopped
    pecans
4 scallions, thinly sliced

3 tablespoons minced fresh
    ginger
½ teaspoon cinnamon
½ teaspoon grated nutmeg
⅓ cup olive oil
3 tablespoons lemon juice
    Salt and freshly ground
    pepper

1. In a medium saucepan, bring 2 cups of lightly salted water to a boil. Add quinoa and stir briefly. Reduce heat to low, cover, and cook 10 minutes. Stir in apricots and currants and continue to cook until quinoa is tender and all liquid is absorbed, about 5 minutes. Transfer to a large bowl. Let cool at least 10 minutes.

2. Add ham, pecans, scallions, ginger, cinnamon, and nutmeg to quinoa. Drizzle on oil and lemon juice and toss until well blended. Season with salt and pepper to taste. Serve at room temperature.

165 WHEAT BERRY, SOUR CHERRY, AND HAM SALAD

Prep: 10 minutes   Cook: 1½ hours   Serves: 4

Crunchy apples, chewy sour cherries, and slightly resistant wheat berries lend this interesting salad many textures. It's surprisingly filling, and although it requires substantial cooking time, it's effortless cooking. The salad can be made a day ahead and tossed again just before serving.

1 **cup wheat berries (whole grain wheat)**	½ **cup dried sour cherries**
1 **small orange**	1 **cup diced (½-inch) cooked ham**
2 **medium red-skinned apples, cored and cut into ½-inch dice**	3 **tablespoons rice vinegar**
	Salt and freshly ground pepper

1. In a large pot of lightly salted simmering water, cook wheat berries, stirring occasionally, until tender, about 1½ hours. Drain, run under cold water, and drain again well.

2. With a swivel-bladed vegetable peeler, remove zest from orange and mince fine. Squeeze orange juice into a large bowl. Add zest, wheat berries, apples, cherries, ham, and vinegar. Toss until well mixed. Season with salt and pepper to taste. Serve at room temperature or chilled.

166 CRACKED WHEAT SALAD WITH SAUSAGES AND PEPPERS

Prep: 20 minutes   Cook: 10 minutes   Serves: 4

2 **cups reduced-sodium chicken broth**	½ **cup pitted kalamata olives**
1 **cup cracked bulgur wheat**	½ **cup minced parsley**
12 to 16 **ounces hot or mild Italian sausage**	¼ **cup capers, drained**
2 **small red bell peppers, cut into ½-inch dice**	¼ **cup extra-virgin olive oil**
4 **scallions, thinly sliced**	4 **teaspoons red wine vinegar**
	Salt and freshly ground pepper

1. Preheat broiler. In a medium saucepan, bring broth to a boil. Add bulgur and stir briefly. Reduce heat to low, cover, and cook until tender and broth is absorbed, 8 to 10 minutes.

2. Meanwhile, prick sausage evenly with a fork and broil 4 to 6 inches from heat, turning occasionally, until evenly browned, about 10 minutes. Remove to a cutting board and slice into ¼-inch rounds.

3. In a large bowl, combine bulgur, sausage, bell peppers, scallions, olives, parsley, and capers. Drizzle with olive oil and vinegar and toss until well blended. Season with salt and pepper to taste. Serve at room temperature.

167   FIERY CALYPSO SHRIMP SALAD
Prep: 25 minutes   Cook: 15 to 18 minutes   Serves: 5 to 6

This colorful salad provides a well-balanced one-dish meal that's loaded with flavor. It can be made a day ahead and served cold or at room temperature, which makes it perfect for parties or picnics.

2 cups reduced-sodium
  chicken broth
1 cup long-grain white rice
1 pound cooked shelled and
  deveined bay (tiny)
  shrimp
1 (15-ounce) can black beans,
  rinsed and well drained
4 scallions, thinly sliced
1 ripe papaya, peeled, seeded,
  and cut into ½-inch cubes
1 large red bell pepper, cut
  into ¼-inch dice

⅓ cup chopped cilantro or
  parsley
½ cup fresh lime juice
¼ cup olive oil
4 teaspoons molasses
2 teaspoons Tabasco or other
  hot pepper sauce
2 garlic cloves, minced
  Salt and freshly ground
  pepper

1. In a medium saucepan, bring broth to a boil over medium-high heat. Add rice and stir briefly. Reduce heat to low, cover, and cook until liquid is absorbed and rice is just tender, 15 to 18 minutes. Run under cold water to cool and separate grains. Drain well and transfer to a large bowl. Add shrimp, black beans, scallions, papaya, bell pepper, and cilantro.

2. In a small bowl, whisk together lime juice, olive oil, molasses, Tabasco sauce, and garlic. Drizzle over rice and toss until well blended. Season with salt and pepper to taste. Serve at room temperature.

168   GREEK SHRIMP AND RICE SALAD
Prep: 20 minutes   Cook: 17 to 21 minutes   Serves: 6 to 8

4 cups reduced-sodium
  chicken broth
2 cups long-grain white rice
1 pound medium shrimp
1 cucumber, quartered
  lengthwise, then cut
  crosswise into ½-inch
  slices
1 pint cherry tomatoes, halved

1 small red onion, chopped
1 cup crumbled feta cheese
¼ cup extra-virgin olive oil
¼ cup lemon juice
2 teaspoons dried oregano
2 teaspoons dried dill
  Salt and freshly ground
  pepper
  Green leaf lettuce leaves

1. In a medium saucepan, bring broth to a boil over medium-high heat. Add rice and stir briefly. Reduce heat to low, cover, and cook until liquid is absorbed and rice is just tender, 15 to 18 minutes. Transfer to a large bowl and let cool at least 10 minutes.

2. In a large saucepan of boiling water, cook shrimp until pink and loosely curled, 2 to 3 minutes. Drain and rinse under cold running water to cool. Shell and devein shrimp. Add shrimp, cucumber, tomatoes, onion, and cheese to rice.

3. In a small bowl, blend together oil, lemon juice, oregano, and dill. Drizzle over rice and toss until well blended. Season with salt and pepper to taste. Divide among 6 to 8 lettuce-lined plates. Serve at once or chilled.

169 GREEK COUSCOUS AND CHICKPEA SALAD

Prep: 20 minutes   Cook: none   Serves: 4 to 6

Since this salad is lightly dressed, the subtle, nutty flavor of garbanzo beans shines through. The salad can be made with or without fresh mint, and it can be kept up to 24 hours covered and refrigerated.

1½ **cups couscous**
2½ **cups boiling water**
1 **(15-ounce) can chickpeas, rinsed and drained**
4 **plum tomatoes, cut into ½-inch dice**
1 **small red onion, chopped**
1 **large green bell pepper, chopped**
1 **small cucumber, quartered lengthwise and thinly sliced crosswise**

1 **to 1½ cups crumbled feta cheese (4 to 6 ounces)**
½ **cup Greek black olives**
½ **cup chopped fresh mint (optional)**
⅓ **cup extra-virgin olive oil**
3 **tablespoons lemon juice**
Salt and freshly ground pepper

1. Place couscous in a large heatproof bowl. Pour in boiling water and stir briefly. Let stand 10 minutes, or until couscous is tender and water is absorbed. Fluff with a fork to separate grains; let cool at least 10 minutes.

2. Add chickpeas, tomatoes, onion, bell pepper, cucumber, cheese, olives, and mint to couscous. Drizzle on oil and lemon juice and toss until well blended. Season with salt and pepper to taste. Serve at room temperature or cover and refrigerate at least 2 hours to serve cold.

170   INDONESIAN RICE SALAD WITH PINEAPPLE AND CASHEWS

Prep: 25 minutes   Cook: 15 to 18 minutes   Serves: 4 to 5

Resembling tossed confetti, this colorful salad is festive and satisfying. Fruits, vegetables, nuts, and rice make it a nutritionally sound, meatless meal.

1 **cup long-grain white rice**
1 **cup fresh or drained canned unsweetened pineapple chunks** ·
¾ **cup dry-roasted cashews or peanuts, chopped**
½ **cup raisins**
2 **scallions, thinly sliced**
1 **small red bell pepper, cut into ½-inch dice**

1 **small green bell pepper, cut into ½-inch dice**
1 **celery rib, thinly sliced**
1 **cup fresh bean sprouts**
1¼ **cups Orange-Sesame Dressing (recipe follows)**
  Salt and freshly ground pepper

1. In a medium saucepan, bring 2 cups lightly salted water to a boil over medium-high heat. Add rice and stir briefly. Reduce heat to low, cover, and cook until liquid is absorbed and rice is tender, 15 to 18 minutes. Transfer rice to a large bowl and let cool at least 10 minutes.

2. Add pineapple, cashews, raisins, scallions, red bell pepper, green bell pepper, celery, and bean sprouts to rice. Drizzle dressing over salad and toss until well blended. Season with salt and pepper to taste. Serve at room temperature or chilled.

171   ORANGE-SESAME DRESSING

Prep: 10 minutes   Cook: none   Makes: about 1¼ cups

This nutty, fruity dressing is also a favorite over cooked Asian noodles and shrimp.

¾ **cup orange juice**
⅓ **cup vegetable oil**
2 **tablespoons soy sauce**
1 **teaspoon Asian sesame oil**
1 **tablespoon minced fresh ginger**

2 **teaspoons minced fresh orange zest**
1 **garlic clove, minced**
  Salt and freshly ground pepper

In a small bowl, blend together orange juice, vegetable oil, soy sauce, sesame oil, ginger, orange zest, and garlic. Season with salt and pepper to taste. If not using within 1 hour, cover and refrigerate. Let return to room temperature before serving.

172 HAM AND EGG FRIED RICE SALAD

Prep: 15 minutes   Cook: 17 to 18 minutes   Serves: 5 to 6

Although not truly fried, this salad is a takeoff on my favorite fried rice of Chinese food scholar and chef Barbara Tropp. It's lightly seasoned so that all of the trimmings can be individually savored.

2 cups short-grain white rice, rinsed	3 cups diced cooked ham (about 12 ounces)
1 tablespoon vegetable oil	4 scallions, thinly sliced
4 eggs, lightly beaten	¼ cup rice vinegar
1 (10-ounce) package frozen peas, thawed	¼ cup soy sauce

1. In a medium saucepan, bring 4 cups lightly salted water to a boil over medium-high heat. Add rice and stir briefly. Reduce heat to low, cover, and cook until just tender, about 15 minutes. Remove from heat and let stand 15 to 20 minutes. Transfer to a large bowl and fluff rice with a fork to separate grains. Let cool at least 5 minutes.

2. In a medium skillet, preferably nonstick, heat oil over medium heat until hot. Add eggs, stirring frequently, until large curds form and eggs are just cooked through but still moist, 2 to 3 minutes.

3. Add eggs, peas, ham, and scallions to rice. Drizzle with vinegar and soy sauce and toss until well blended. Serve at room temperature.

173 SCANDINAVIAN SMOKED SALMON AND RICE SALAD

Prep: 15 minutes   Cook: 15 to 18 minutes   Serves: 6 to 8

Since this salad can remain dressed and refrigerated for a day before serving, it's ideal for no-fuss entertaining.

4 cups reduced-sodium chicken broth	¾ teaspoon freshly ground pepper
2 cups long-grain white rice	2 cups chopped smoked salmon (10 to 12 ounces)
1 cup nonfat plain yogurt	1 (10-ounce) package frozen peas, thawed
⅓ cup chopped fresh dill	½ cup chopped chives
2 tablespoons olive oil	
2 tablespoons lemon juice	

1. In a large saucepan, bring broth to a boil over medium-high heat. Add rice and stir briefly. Reduce heat to low, cover, and cook until liquid is absorbed and rice is just tender, 15 to 18 minutes. Transfer to a large bowl and fluff with a fork to separate grains.

2. In a small bowl, whisk together yogurt, dill, oil, lemon juice, and pepper. Drizzle over rice and toss until well blended. Add salmon, peas, and chives and toss again. Serve at room temperature or chilled.

174   CRAB, CORN AND WILD RICE SALAD
Prep: 25 minutes   Cook: 35 to 40 minutes   Serves: 5 to 6

Corn, crab, and red bell pepper, all subtly sweet, complement each other beautifully in this delicious one-dish meal. Since all of the ingredients are similar in size but range wildly in color, the salad looks like edible confetti.

½ cup wild rice, rinsed
½ cup brown rice
1 (10-ounce) package frozen
    corn, thawed
8 ounces cooked or canned
    crabmeat, drained and
    picked over
4 plum tomatoes, cut into
    ½-inch dice
4 scallions, thinly sliced

1 medium red bell pepper,
    cut into ½-inch dice
1 small jalapeño pepper,
    seeded and minced
1 cup chopped parsley
½ cup olive oil
¼ cup lemon juice
    Salt and freshly ground
    pepper

1. In a medium pot, bring 4 cups of lightly salted water to a boil. Add wild rice and brown rice and stir briefly. Reduce heat to low, cover, and cook until both types of rice are just tender, about 35 to 40 minutes. Drain well and place in a large bowl. Let cool at least 10 minutes.

2. Add corn, crab, tomatoes, scallions, red bell pepper, jalapeño pepper, and parsley. Drizzle on oil and lemon juice and toss until well blended. Season with salt and pepper to taste. Serve at room temperature.

175   SHREDDED POTATO AND WILD RICE SALAD
Prep: 25 minutes   Cook: 35 to 40 minutes   Serves: 4 to 5

Based on a party salad of cookbook author Bert Greene, this lovely dish combines shiitake mushrooms, red bell pepper, and creamy fontina cheese with shredded potatoes and wild rice. Be sure to drain the rice and potatoes well, so that the dressing doesn't become diluted.

½ cup wild rice, rinsed
1 tablespoon lemon juice
1 pound russet potatoes,
    peeled
⅓ cup mayonnaise
⅓ cup nonfat plain yogurt
4 medium fresh shiitake
    mushrooms, stemmed,
    caps thinly sliced

1 cup shredded fontina
    cheese
4 paper-thin slices of
    prosciutto, shredded
1 medium red bell pepper,
    cut into slivers
1 cup chopped parsley
    Salt and freshly ground
    pepper

1. In a medium saucepan, bring 2 cups lightly salted water to a boil. Add wild rice and stir briefly. Reduce heat to low, cover, and cook until rice is just tender, 35 to 40 minutes.

2. Meanwhile, in a large bowl, combine lemon juice with 4 cups water. Shred potatoes and plunge them immediately into acidulated water. Bring a large pot of lightly salted water to a boil. Drain potatoes and add to boiling water. Cook until just tender, about 3 minutes. Drain, run under cold water, and drain again.

3. In a large bowl, blend together mayonnaise and yogurt. When cooked, drain rice, run under cold water, and drain again. With your hands, squeeze moisture from potatoes. Add rice, potatoes, mushrooms, cheese, prosciutto, bell pepper, and parsley to dressing. Toss until well blended. Season with salt and pepper to taste. Serve at room temperature.

---

176 ·MUSSEL AND LENTIL SALAD ADRIATICA
Prep: 20 minutes   Cook: 18 to 20 minutes   Serves: 3 to 4

If you're not a fan of mussels, don't forgo this stunning, satisfying salad; substitute clams or cooked shrimp. The salad is brilliantly colored with black olives, brown lentils, bright red tomatoes, clear white chunks of feta cheese, and flecks of green parsley throughout.

1 cup lentils, rinsed and picked over	½ cup crumbled feta cheese
24 mussels, preferably cultivated, in the shell	2 garlic cloves, minced
	¼ cup lemon juice
4 medium plum tomatoes, cut into ½-inch dice	¼ cup extra-virgin olive oil
	Salt and freshly ground pepper
½ cup chopped parsley	Lemon wedges
½ cup pitted kalamata olives	

1. In a medium saucepan, bring 3 cups lightly salted water to a boil. Stir in lentils. Cover and simmer until tender but not mushy, 18 to 20 minutes. Drain well.

2. Meanwhile, scrub mussels thoroughly; discard any with open shells that do not close. With a small sharp knife, cut off hairy brown "beards." Bring a large pot with 2 inches of water to a boil. Add mussels, cover, and return to a boil over high heat. Reduce heat to medium and steam for 3 to 5 minutes, or until shells open. With a slotted spoon, transfer mussels to a platter. Discard any mussels that do not open.

3. In a medium bowl, combine lentils, tomatoes, parsley, olives, cheese, and garlic. Drizzle on lemon juice and oil. Toss until well blended. Season with salt and pepper to taste.

4. To serve, mound lentil mixture in center of a platter or 3 or 4 individual plates. Arrange mussels around perimeter of salad, garnish with lemon wedges, and serve.

177 WILD RICE, SHRIMP, AND SPINACH TOSS
Prep: 25 minutes   Cook: 35 to 40 minutes   Serves: 4 to 5

Brilliantly colored and variously textured, this interesting salad is special enough for party fare. For full visual effect, serve it on a bed of large spinach leaves.

1 cup wild rice, rinsed
⅓ cup olive oil
2 tablespoons mayonnaise
2 tablespoons lemon juice
1 teaspoon Dijon mustard
1 teaspoon dried tarragon
12 ounces cooked shelled and deveined bay (tiny) shrimp
4 cups lightly packed fresh spinach, chopped

1 large red bell pepper, cut into ½-inch dice
1 (7-ounce) can sliced water chestnuts, drained
4 scallions, thinly sliced
2 celery ribs, thinly sliced
Salt and freshly ground pepper

1. In a large saucepan, bring 4 cups lightly salted water to a boil. Add wild rice and stir briefly. Reduce heat, cover, and cook until just tender, 35 to 40 minutes. Drain well and transfer to a large bowl. Let cool at least 10 minutes.

2. In a small bowl, whisk together oil, mayonnaise, lemon juice, mustard, and tarragon until smooth. Drizzle over wild rice and toss until well blended.

3. Add shrimp, chopped spinach, bell pepper, water chestnuts, scallions, and celery. Toss to mix well. Season with salt and pepper to taste and serve.

178 CONFETTI LENTIL SALAD
Prep: 25 minutes   Cook: 18 to 20 minutes   Serves: 4 to 6

1 cup lentils, rinsed and picked over
¼ cup olive oil
1 medium onion, finely chopped
1 medium carrot, peeled and finely chopped
2 celery ribs, finely chopped
1 large red bell pepper, finely chopped

1 cup shredded mozzarella cheese
½ cup chopped fresh basil
2 scallions, finely chopped
2 tablespoons red wine vinegar
1 teaspoon salt
Green leaf lettuce leaves
Freshly ground pepper

1. In a medium saucepan of lightly salted boiling water, cook lentils until just tender but not mushy, 18 to 20 minutes. Drain, run under cold water, and drain well.

2. Meanwhile, in a large skillet, heat 2 tablespoons oil over medium heat. Add onion and carrot and cook, stirring occasionally, until slightly softened, about 3 minutes. Add celery and bell pepper and cook, stirring occasionally, 5 minutes.

3. In a large bowl, combine lentils, sautéed vegetables, cheese, basil, and scallions. Drizzle with remaining 2 tablespoons oil and vinegar and sprinkle with salt. Toss until well blended. Divide among 4 to 6 lettuce-lined plates and serve warm or at room temperature with freshly ground pepper.

---

179 ANDOUILLE SAUSAGE, RICE, AND LENTIL JUMBLE
Prep: 15 minutes   Cook: 15 to 18 minutes   Serves: 4 to 6

Rice and lentils provide a nutritious backdrop in this colorful salad so that spicy Cajun andouille sausage can enjoy center stage. Mellow, poached garlic provides the basis for the creamy, lightly herbed dressing. Cooking the rice, lentils, and garlic together is a bit unorthodox, but efficient.

1 cup long-grain white rice
1 cup lentils, rinsed and
    picked over
8 garlic cloves, unpeeled
1 pound andouille or hot
    Italian sausage
¼ cup red wine vinegar
1 tablespoon Dijon mustard

1 teaspoon dried thyme
¼ cup olive oil
4 cups torn romaine lettuce
4 plum tomatoes, cut into
    ½-inch dice
Salt and freshly ground
    pepper

1. Preheat broiler. Bring a medium pan of lightly salted water to a boil. Stir in rice, lentils, and garlic. Reduce heat, cover, and cook until rice and lentils are just tender but not mushy, 15 to 18 minutes. Drain, run under cold water, and drain again well.

2. Meanwhile, prick sausage evenly with a fork and broil 4 inches from heat, turning occasionally, until evenly browned, about 10 minutes. Remove to a cutting board and slice into ¼-inch rounds.

3. Remove peel from garlic cloves and place garlic in a large bowl. Mash garlic with back of a spoon or a fork. Blend in vinegar, mustard, and thyme. Slowly whisk in oil.

4. Add rice and lentil mixture, sausage, lettuce, and tomatoes. Toss until well blended. Season with salt and pepper to taste. Serve at room temperature.

180   BLACK BEAN AND CACTUS SALAD
Prep: 20 minutes   Cook: 5 to 6 minutes   Serves: 2 to 3

Nopales, the fleshy, oval leaves, or paddles, of the prickly pear cactus are edible and gaining in popularity in the United States, particularly in areas where Mexican-Americans have settled. Chopped nopales, called *nopalitos,* can be bought prepared in jars in Mexican markets and in some supermarkets.

4 medium cactus leaves
   (about 10 ounces), or 1
   (16-ounce) jar *nopalitos,*
   drained
¼ cup vegetable oil
1 tablespoon red wine
   vinegar
1 jalapeño pepper, seeded
   and minced

1 garlic clove, minced
½ teaspoon dried oregano
1 (15-ounce) can black beans,
   rinsed and well drained
2 plum tomatoes, chopped
   Salt and freshly ground
   pepper
½ cup grated Cheddar cheese

1. If using fresh cactus, with a sharp knife, remove eyes from cactus leaves. Cut cactus into ¾-inch dice. In a medium pot of lightly salted boiling water, cook cactus until crisp-tender, about 5 to 6 minutes. Drain, run under cold water, and drain again.

2. In a large bowl, combine oil, vinegar, jalapeño pepper, garlic, and oregano. Add cactus or *nopalitos,* beans, and tomatoes. Toss until well blended. Season with salt and pepper to taste. Sprinkle cheese on top. Serve at room temperature.

181   BLACK-EYED PEA AND BACON SALAD
Prep: 10 minutes   Cook: 20 to 26 minutes   Serves: 4 to 6

2 (10-ounce) packages frozen
   black-eyed peas
6 slices of bacon
1 large onion, cut into
   ¾-inch dice
½ teaspoon sugar

¼ cup red wine vinegar
4 teaspoons lemon juice
1 tablespoon olive oil
1 teaspoon salt
   Freshly ground pepper
6 cups torn red leaf lettuce

1. In a medium saucepan of lightly salted boiling water, cook black-eyed peas until barely tender, 8 to 10 minutes. Drain, run under cold water, and drain again.

2. In a large skillet, cook bacon over medium heat until crisp, 7 to 9 minutes. Drain on paper towels. Remove all but 2 tablespoons bacon fat from skillet.

3. Add onion to drippings in skillet. Sprinkle on sugar. Cook, stirring occasionally, until softened and golden brown, 5 to 7 minutes. Remove from heat.

4. In a large bowl, combine black-eyed peas, browned onion, vinegar, lemon juice, olive oil, and salt. Crumble bacon and add to peas. Toss until well mixed. Season with pepper to taste. Divide lettuce among 4 to 6 plates and mound black-eyed peas on top. Serve at room temperature.

182 TRIPLE BEAN AND CHEESE SALAD SOUTHWESTERN STYLE
Prep: 30 minutes   Cook: none   Marinate: 2 hours   Serves: 6

Cilantro gives this slightly sweet, mildly hot three-bean salad a fragrant twist. For a complete meal, serve this colorful, meatless main course with crisp tortilla chips.

1 (15-ounce) can black beans, rinsed and drained
1 (15-ounce) can kidney beans, rinsed and drained
1 (15-ounce) can cannellini or white kidney beans, rinsed and drained
1 (10-ounce) package frozen corn, thawed
1 small red onion—½ thinly sliced, ½ chopped
1 cup fresh lime juice
1 cup cilantro sprigs
1 tablespoon sugar

1 tablespoon vegetable oil
1 jalapeño pepper, seeded
1 teaspoon salt
8 cups shredded iceberg lettuce
½ cup shredded Cheddar cheese
½ cup shredded pepper Monterey Jack cheese
½ cup shredded mozzarella cheese
1 large ripe avocado, thinly sliced
Lime wedges

1. In a large bowl, combine black beans, kidney beans, cannellini beans, corn, and sliced red onion. In a food processor or blender, combine chopped onion, lime juice, cilantro, sugar, oil, jalapeño pepper, and salt. Process until finely minced. Pour over bean mixture and toss until well blended. Cover and marinate in refrigerator at least 2 hours, stirring occasionally.

2. Just before serving, arrange lettuce on 6 plates. Stir bean mixture again and divide among lettuce-lined plates. Sprinkle Cheddar, Monterey Jack, and mozzarella cheese on top. Arrange slightly overlapping slices of avocado on top of cheese. Garnish with lime wedges and serve at once.

183   FAVA AND CANNELLINI BEAN SALAD WITH MEDITERRANEAN ACCENTS

Prep: 20 minutes   Cook: none   Serves: 8 to 10

Thanks to the availability of canned fava and cannellini beans, this one-bowl salad, bursting with robust flavors and brilliant colors, is made with ease. If you don't have caper berries on hand, substitute ¼ cup drained capers. Serve with a loaf of crusty bread.

⅔ cup extra-virgin olive oil
¼ cup red wine vinegar
4 anchovy fillets, minced
1 teaspoon salt
2 (15-ounce) cans cannellini or white kidney beans, rinsed and drained
1 (19-ounce) can fava beans, rinsed and drained
12 cups torn romaine lettuce

8 plum tomatoes, cut into ¾-inch dice
1 small red onion, thinly sliced and separated into rings
1½ cups crumbled feta cheese (6 ounces)
1 cup pitted kalamata black olives
½ cup caper berries, drained

In a large bowl, whisk together oil, vinegar, anchovy fillets, and salt until well blended. Add cannellini beans, fava beans, lettuce, tomatoes, red onion, cheese, olives, and caper berries. Toss to mix well and serve.

184   MIDDLE EASTERN CHICKPEA AND ROASTED VEGETABLE SALAD

Prep: 25 minutes   Cook: 28 to 30 minutes   Serves: 6 to 8

Served with a loaf of crusty bread, this colorful salad makes a satisfying meal. It can be made completely ahead of time, covered and refrigerated for up to 24 hours, and returned to room temperature before serving.

2 large green bell peppers
2 large red bell peppers
4 narrow Asian eggplants, stemmed
½ cup olive oil
¼ cup lemon juice
¼ cup minced parsley
4 garlic cloves, minced
1½ teaspoons honey
1 teaspoon ground coriander

½ teaspoon ground cumin
½ teaspoon paprika
¼ teaspoon cayenne
6 large plum tomatoes, cut into ¾-inch dice
2 (15-ounce) cans chickpeas, rinsed and drained
1 cup crumbled feta cheese
½ cup chopped fresh basil

1. Preheat broiler. Cut green and red bell peppers in half lengthwise. Scoop out seeds and cut out stems. Place peppers, skin side up, on a baking sheet and broil as close to heat as possible until skin is charred all over, about 10 minutes. Place peppers in a paper bag and let steam 10 to 15 minutes.

2. Preheat oven to 375°F. Place eggplants on a lightly greased baking sheet and roast until just tender when pierced with a sharp knife, 18 to 20 minutes. When cooked, cut eggplants crosswise into thin slices. Peel off blackened skin of peppers and slice into thin strips.

3. In a large bowl, blend together oil, lemon juice, parsley, garlic, honey, coriander, cumin, paprika, and cayenne. Add roasted bell peppers, eggplants, tomatoes, and chickpeas. Toss until well blended. Sprinkle cheese and basil on top. Serve at room temperature.

---

185   JEKYLL AND HYDE BLACK BEAN SALAD
Prep: 25 minutes   Stand: 8 hours   Cook: 1 hour   Serves: 8

Vibrant with contrasts, this nutritious salad plays spicy black beans against cooling fresh lime and crunchy jicama.

2½ **cups dried black beans (about 1 pound), rinsed and picked over**
3 **smoked ham hocks**
2 **(3-inch) cinnamon sticks**
2 **bay leaves**
2 **teaspoons ground cumin**
2 **teaspoons crushed hot red pepper**
¾ **cup fresh lime juice**
¼ **cup olive oil**

8 **cups torn spinach**
4 **large tomatoes, cut into ½-inch dice**
1 **medium jicama (about 1 pound), peeled and cut into ½-inch dice (about 4 cups)**
⅔ **cup coarsely chopped cilantro or parsley**
Salt and freshly ground pepper

1. In a large pot, soak beans in cold water to cover by at least 2 inches 8 hours or overnight. Drain; rinse out pot.

2. In a large pot, combine black beans, ham hocks, cinnamon sticks, bay leaves, cumin, hot pepper, and enough water to cover by 1 inch. Bring to a boil over high heat. Reduce heat to low, cover, and cook until tender but not falling apart, about 1 hour. Remove from heat and let cool. Drain mixture. Pull meat from ham hocks and chop. Discard bones, cinnamon sticks, and bay leaves.

3. In a large bowl, blend lime juice and olive oil. Add black beans, chopped meat, spinach, tomatoes, jicama, and cilantro. Toss until well blended. Season with salt and pepper to taste. Serve at room temperature.

Chapter 7

Beyond the Picnic:
Potato and Bread Salads

From humble beginnings, potato and bread salads transform the most basic, inexpensive ingredients into fabulous food. Just as most regions in Italy make clever use of day-old bread, Americans make use of a staple of their own, the potato.

America's summer comfort food, potato salads, are quintessential picnic fare and staples of home kitchens. Year-round they are big sellers at delicatessens and provide popular accompaniments to sandwiches and burgers. This much-loved side dish became popular in the second half of the nineteenth century and, even after more than a hundred years, its popularity hasn't lost any steam.

Bread salads in Italy have a far longer history; references to them go back as far as the sixteenth century. The well-known painter Bronzino wrote about bread salads, singing their praises even before the tomato—a common ingredient in bread salads today—was introduced to Italy. Today, bread salad in Italy commonly goes by the name *panzanella*.

It's easy to see why bread and potato salads enjoy immense popularity. Both foods are nutritious, filling, inexpensive, and readily available year-round. Just as chicken and pasta provide a neutral slate for creative cooks to embellish with their favorite flavors, potatoes and bread provide a bland backdrop for a variety of additions. They also provide a food that is best served at room temperature, making them easy for buffets and picnics. Although side-dish potato salads have traditionally been served cold, they deliver more flavor, as bread salads do, at room temperature.

Some tips on choosing and preparing bread and potatoes for salads follow.

Practically without exception, choosing bread for a salad is simple. It should be day-old, crusty, rustic bread—a boon for making good use of stale, leftover bread. Methods for preparing bread vary with the salad. They include soaking, baking, and grilling.

When choosing potatoes for salad, keep in mind that red-skinned potatoes have a firm, waxy texture and will not fall apart while cooking or crumble when cut. Choosing potatoes of the same size to cook at once makes judging doneness simple. The best potatoes for salads are relatively small boiling ones, since their centers will become tender before their perimeters overcook.

When cooking potatoes of various sizes, pierce each one with a sharp knife, starting with the smallest. Remove them from the heat as they become tender. To retain taste and nutrients, cook them by simmering or steaming them with their skins on. After cooking, potatoes can be easily peeled, but many salads are more appealing and nutritious with the skins left on the potatoes.

Cook potatoes until just tender. If overcooked, they will fall apart when tossed. Plunging cooked potatoes into a bowl of ice water or running them under cold water until cool will help maintain a firm, saladlike texture.

With the exception of mayonnaise-based dressings, when possible, toss freshly cooked potatoes with their dressing while still warm or at room temperature. That way they will absorb flavors and seasoning more readily.

186   RED, WHITE, AND GREEN BEAN AND POTATO SALAD

Prep: 25 minutes   Cook: 10 to 15 minutes   Serves: 4 to 6

Delightful for party or picnic pickings, this salad is brimming with colorful green beans, pearly white feta cheese, red bell pepper, and radishes.

1½ pounds new potatoes
¾ pound green beans, trimmed
6 slices of bacon
¼ cup sour cream
3 tablespoons olive oil
2 tablespoons cider vinegar
1 small bunch of radishes, trimmed and thinly sliced

1 small red bell pepper, cut into ¾-inch dice
1 cup crumbled feta cheese
Salt and freshly ground pepper

1. In a large pot of boiling water, cook potatoes until just tender when pierced with a sharp knife, 10 to 15 minutes. Meanwhile, in a large pot of lightly salted boiling water, cook green beans until crisp-tender, 2 to 4 minutes. Drain, run under cold water, and drain again. Slice into 1-inch pieces. When potatoes are cooked, drain, run under cold water, and drain again. Cut into bite-size pieces.

2. In a large skillet, cook bacon over medium heat until crisp, 7 to 9 minutes. Drain on paper towels. When cool enough to handle, crumble bacon.

3. In a large bowl, whisk together sour cream, oil, and vinegar. Add potatoes, green beans, bacon, radishes, bell pepper, and cheese. Toss to mix well. Season with salt and pepper to taste. Serve at room temperature or chilled.

187 SARDINE, APPLE, AND POTATO SALAD WITH GHERKIN-DILL DRESSING

Prep: 15 minutes   Cook: 10 to 15 minutes   Serves: 4

Apples, potatoes, and fish are enrobed in a creamy herbed dressing in this nicely balanced main course. If you're not a fan of sardines, substitute other cooked fish, shrimp, or chicken.

1½ pounds new potatoes
3 (3¾-ounce) cans sardines packed in water, drained and cut into bite-size chunks
4 hard-cooked eggs, chopped
2 tart medium apples, cut into ¾-inch dice

1 (8¼-ounce) can julienne-cut beets, drained
1 cup Gherkin-Dill Dressing (recipe follows)
4 large radicchio or red cabbage leaves

1. In a large pot of boiling water, cook potatoes until tender when pierced with a sharp knife, 10 to 15 minutes. Drain, run under cold water, and drain again. When cool enough to handle, quarter potatoes.

2. In a large bowl, combine potatoes, sardines, eggs, apples, and beets. Add dressing and toss gently to mix well. Place a leaf of radicchio on each of 4 plates. Mound salad on radicchio and serve.

188 GHERKIN-DILL DRESSING

Prep: 5 minutes   Cook: none   Makes: about 1 cup

Gherkins are small, pickled cucumbers usually packed in jars. Their addition to this creamy dressing makes it similar to tartar sauce, which also combines minced pickles and mayonnaise.

½ cup mayonnaise
¼ cup sour cream
2 tablespoons cider vinegar
4 gherkins, minced

1 tablespoon chopped fresh dill or 1 teaspoon dried
Salt and freshly ground pepper

In a small bowl, whisk together mayonnaise, sour cream, vinegar, gherkins, and dill. Season with salt and pepper to taste. If not using immediately, cover and refrigerate.

189　HEARTLAND KIELBASA POTATO SALAD

Prep: 20 minutes　Cook: 20 to 25 minutes　Serves: 6

In this hearty entree, smoked Polish sausage and potatoes are dressed while warm with a mustard and tarragon-flavored vinaigrette.

3　pounds medium red
　　potatoes
¾　pound smoked kielbasa
　　sausage
¼　cup white wine vinegar
3　garlic cloves, minced
1　tablespoon Dijon mustard
1　teaspoon dried tarragon

¾　cup olive oil
6　scallions, thinly sliced
4　celery ribs, thinly sliced
1　large red bell pepper, cut
　　into ¾-inch dice
½　cup chopped dill pickles
　　Salt and freshly ground
　　pepper

1. Preheat broiler. In a large pot of boiling water, cook potatoes until just tender when pierced with a sharp knife, 20 to 25 minutes. Drain, run under cold water, and drain again. Peel and cut into ¾-inch cubes.

2. Meanwhile, prick sausage evenly with a fork and broil 4 to 5 inches from heat, turning occasionally, until evenly browned, about 10 minutes. Transfer to a cutting board and slice into ¼-inch rounds.

3. In a large bowl, combine vinegar, garlic, mustard, and tarragon. Gradually whisk in oil. Add potatoes, sausage, scallions, celery, bell pepper, and pickles to dressing. Toss until well mixed. Season with salt and pepper to taste and serve.

190　PICK-A-PEPPER POTATO SALAD

Prep: 25 minutes　Cook: 20 to 25 minutes　Serves: 6

Three different kinds of roasted peppers, black beans, Cheddar cheese, and cilantro give this unusual potato salad Southwestern flare. If Anaheim or poblano peppers are not available, substitute 4 large green bell peppers.

2　pounds medium red
　　potatoes
6　large Anaheim or 8 large
　　poblano peppers, halved
　　lengthwise and seeded
3　or 4 jalapeño peppers,
　　halved lengthwise and
　　seeded
2　medium red bell peppers,
　　halved lengthwise
½　cup mayonnaise

½　cup nonfat plain yogurt
½　cup chopped cilantro or
　　parsley
2　garlic cloves, minced
1　(15-ounce) can black beans,
　　rinsed and drained
4　scallions, thinly sliced
　　Salt and freshly ground
　　pepper
1½　cups shredded Cheddar
　　cheese (6 ounces)

1. Preheat broiler. In a large pot of boiling water, cook potatoes until just tender when pierced with a sharp knife, 20 to 25 minutes. Drain, run under cold water, and drain again. When cool enough to handle, peel and cut into ¾-inch cubes.

2. Meanwhile, place Anaheim, jalapeño, and bell peppers skin side up on a baking sheet and broil as close to heat as possible until skin is charred all over, about 10 minutes. Place peppers in a paper bag and let steam 10 to 15 minutes. Peel off blackened skin and cut into thin strips.

3. In a large bowl, combine mayonnaise, yogurt, cilantro, and garlic. Mix well. Add potatoes, peppers, beans, and scallions. Toss until well blended and season with salt and pepper to taste. Serve at room temperature or chilled. Sprinkle with cheese just before serving.

---

191 ROASTED GARLIC AND ITALIAN SAUSAGE POTATO SALAD
Prep: 20 minutes   Cook: 1 hour   Serves: 4 to 5

Mildly flavored roasted garlic gives this salad creaminess without fat. The salad is slightly spicy and can remain dressed overnight with no loss of flavor or texture.

2 large heads of garlic, papery tips removed
2 pounds medium red potatoes
¾ pound mild or hot Italian sausages
½ cup mayonnaise
½ cup nonfat plain yogurt
2 tablespoons Dijon mustard
2 tablespoons red wine vinegar
4 celery ribs, thinly sliced
4 scallions, thinly sliced
¼ cup minced Italian flat-leaf parsley
1 (4-ounce) jar sliced pimientos
1 (2.2-ounce) can sliced ripe olives, drained
Salt and freshly ground pepper

1. Preheat oven to 350°F. Place heads of garlic in a baking dish just large enough to hold them, sprinkle with 1 tablespoon water, and cover tightly. Bake until pulp is very tender when mashed with a fork, about 1 hour.

2. Meanwhile, preheat broiler. In a large pot of boiling water, cook potatoes until just tender when pierced with a sharp knife, 20 to 25 minutes. Drain, run under cold water, and drain again. Peel and cut into ¾-inch cubes.

3. Prick sausages evenly with a fork and broil 4 to 5 inches from heat, turning occasionally, until evenly browned, about 10 minutes. Chop finely.

4. Squeeze garlic pulp into a food processor or blender. Add mayonnaise, yogurt, mustard, and vinegar. Blend until smooth. Transfer dressing to a large bowl. Add potatoes, sausage, celery, scallions, parsley, pimientos, and olives. Toss until well mixed. Season with salt and pepper to taste and serve.

192   TRUE BLUE POTATO SALAD
Prep: 15 minutes   Cook: 25 to 30 minutes   Serves: 4 to 5

Blue potatoes make this slightly sweet potato salad an eye-catching conversation piece, and red-skinned, white-fleshed apples are particularly dramatic alongside the colorful potatoes. The salad is equally tasty and slightly sweeter made with sweet potatoes.

1½ pounds medium blue
    potatoes
½ cup mayonnaise
1 tablespoon lemon juice
1 cup diced (¾-inch) cooked
    ham
2 celery ribs, thinly sliced
2 medium red-skinned
    apples, cut into ¾-inch
    dice

½ cup chopped pecans
½ cup raisins or pitted
    chopped dates
½ cup crumbled blue cheese
    Salt and freshly ground
    pepper

1. In a large pot with 1 inch of boiling water, steam potatoes, covered, until tender when pierced with a knife, 25 to 30 minutes. Run under cold water and drain. When cool enough to handle, peel and slice into ¾-inch cubes.

2. In a large bowl, blend together mayonnaise, lemon juice, and 1 tablespoon water until smooth. Add potatoes, ham, celery, apples, pecans, raisins, and cheese. Toss until well mixed. Season with salt and pepper to taste and serve.

193   SPANISH GOLD POTATO SALAD
Prep: 30 minutes   Cook: 5 minutes   Serves: 4

This exotic-looking salad appears to be painted with gold. In truth, it glistens with a saffron-spiked vinaigrette. Steamed potatoes make the perfect backdrop for the many piquant Mediterranean flavors included here. For dramatic effect, I like to serve this salad on red lettuce leaves.

2 pounds red potatoes, peeled
    and cut into ½-inch cubes
4 ounces thinly sliced
    prosciutto, shredded
12 sun-dried tomato halves
    packed in oil, drained
    and chopped
1 (8½-ounce) can quartered
    artichoke hearts, drained
½ cup pitted kalamata olives

¼ cup capers, drained
1 garlic clove
3 tablespoons red wine
    vinegar
1 tablespoon Dijon mustard
¼ teaspoon powdered saffron
½ cup extra-virgin olive oil
    Salt and freshly ground
    pepper
¼ cup minced Italian parsley

1. In a large pot of lightly salted boiling water, cook potatoes until just tender, about 5 minutes. Drain, run under cold water, and drain again.

2. In a large bowl, combine potatoes, prosciutto, tomatoes, artichoke hearts, olives, and capers.

3. Mince garlic in a food processor or blender. Add vinegar, mustard, and saffron. With machine on, drizzle in oil. Add dressing to potatoes and toss until well mixed. Season with salt and pepper to taste. Serve, with parsley sprinkled on top.

---

194   STEAK AND POTATO SALAD WITH FRESH SALSA
Prep: 25 minutes   Cook: 20 to 25 minutes   Serves: 8 to 10

Dressing traditionally mayonnaise-laden potato salad with freshly made salsa not only makes for an unusual, flavorful salad, it also makes it low in fat and unwanted calories.

3 pounds medium red potatoes
2 pounds flank steak
4 medium tomatoes, chopped
6 scallions, minced
1 medium green bell pepper, cut into small dice
3 jalapeño peppers, seeded and minced

1 cup chopped cilantro or parsley
2 garlic cloves, minced
⅓ cup red wine vinegar
2 tablespoons olive oil
Salt and freshly ground pepper

1. Light a hot fire in a barbecue grill or preheat broiler. In a large pot of boiling water, cook potatoes until tender when pierced with a sharp knife, 20 to 25 minutes. Drain, run under cold water, and drain again. Peel and cut into ¾-inch cubes.

2. Meanwhile, place steak on a lightly oiled grill rack or broil 4 to 6 inches from heat. Cook, turning once, until browned outside and still pink and juicy inside, 4 to 6 minutes per side. Transfer steak to a cutting board and let rest at least 5 minutes. Cut steak lengthwise along grain into 2-inch-wide strips; turn and slice thinly against grain.

3. In a large bowl, combine tomatoes, scallions, bell pepper, jalapeño peppers, cilantro, garlic, vinegar, and oil. Toss to mix. Add potatoes and steak and toss again. Season with salt and pepper to taste.

195   PESTO POTATO SALAD
Prep: 10 minutes   Cook: 20 to 25 minutes   Serves: 4

2   **pounds medium red
        potatoes**
¾   **cup prepared or homemade
        pesto**
½   **cup sun-dried tomatoes,
        drained and thinly sliced**
½   **cup pitted kalamata olives**

4   **thin slices of prosciutto,
        chopped**
    Red leaf lettuce leaves
1   **(3-ounce) chunk of
        Parmesan cheese,
        preferably imported**

1. In a large pot of boiling water, cook potatoes until just tender when pierced with a sharp knife, 20 to 25 minutes. Drain, run under cold water, and drain again. Peel and cut into ¼-inch slices.

2. In a large bowl, combine potatoes, pesto, tomatoes, olives, and prosciutto. Toss gently until well blended. Divide among 4 lettuce-lined plates. Using a swivel-bladed vegetable peeler, shave Parmesan cheese into slices and scatter over each salad. Serve at room temperature.

196   SWEET POTATO, HAM, AND HAZELNUT SALAD
Prep: 30 minutes   Cook: 3 to 5 minutes   Chill: 2 hours   Serves: 6

2½   **pounds sweet potatoes,
        peeled and cut into
        ¾-inch cubes**
½   **cup mayonnaise**
¼   **cup olive oil**
2   **tablespoons cider vinegar**
1   **teaspoon cinnamon**
½   **teaspoon grated nutmeg**
12   **ounces cooked ham, cut into
        ¾-inch cubes (about
        3 cups)**

2   **large tart-sweet apples,
        cored and cut into ¾-inch
        dice**
3   **scallions, thinly sliced**
    **Salt and freshly ground
        pepper**
⅔   **cup hazelnuts, lightly
        toasted**

1. In a large pot of lightly salted boiling water, cook sweet potatoes until barely tender, 3 to 5 minutes. Drain, run under cold water, and drain again. Cover and refrigerate until cool, about 2 hours.

2. In a large bowl, blend together mayonnaise, oil, vinegar, cinnamon, and nutmeg. Add sweet potatoes, ham, apples, and scallions. Toss until well mixed. Season with salt and pepper to taste. Sprinkle hazelnuts on top and serve.

197   SMOKED OYSTER AND POTATO SALAD
Prep: 10 minutes   Cook: 10 to 15 minutes   Serves: 2

This hearty salad is made practically instantly with smoked shellfish packed in oil. The oil, when paired with just lemon juice, provides all of the dressing ingredients.

8 ounces new potatoes
1 (3¾-ounce) can smoked
   oysters, undrained
2 scallions, thinly sliced
1 celery rib, thinly sliced

2 tablespoons lemon juice
   Salt and freshly ground
     pepper
   Boston lettuce leaves

1. In a medium pot of boiling water, cook potatoes until tender when pierced with a sharp knife, 10 to 15 minutes. Drain, run under cold water, and drain again. When cool enough to handle, quarter potatoes.

2. In a large bowl, combine potatoes, smoked oysters and their liquid, scallions, celery, and lemon juice. Toss gently to mix well. Season with salt and pepper to taste. Divide between 2 lettuce-lined plates and serve.

198   COBB POTATO SALAD
Prep: 25 minutes   Cook: 20 to 25 minutes   Serves: 4 to 5

Here potatoes are flavored with the classic components of a Cobb salad. Unlike the original composed presentation, this salad is casually tossed. Garlic, shallots, blue cheese, and bacon provide so much taste that little dressing is needed in this filling, colorful main course.

2 pounds medium red
   potatoes
8 slices of bacon
¼ cup olive oil
¼ cup minced parsley
4 teaspoons cider vinegar
2 small shallots, minced
2 garlic cloves, minced

1 teaspoon Dijon mustard
2 small ripe avocados, cut into
   ¾-inch dice
2 large tomatoes, cut into
   ¾-inch dice
¾ cup crumbled blue cheese
   Salt and freshly ground
     pepper

1. In a large pot of boiling water, cook potatoes until just tender when pierced with a sharp knife, 20 to 25 minutes. Drain, run under cold water, and drain again. Peel and cut into ¾-inch cubes.

2. Meanwhile, in a large skillet, cook bacon over medium heat until crisp, about 7 to 9 minutes. Drain on paper towels. When cool enough to handle, crumble bacon.

3. In a large bowl, whisk together oil, parsley, vinegar, shallots, garlic, and mustard. Add potatoes, bacon, avocados, tomatoes, and cheese. Toss until well mixed. Season with salt and pepper to taste and serve.

199   POTATO SALAD PROVENÇAL

Prep: 25 minutes   Cook: 20 to 25 minutes   Serves: 5 to 6

This robust potato salad is actually better after a day in the refrigerator, which gives its flavors a chance to meld. It's great for a picnic or buffet and can be served cold or at room temperature. To make it more substantial, add freshly cooked or canned tuna or crumbled feta cheese.

2 pounds medium red
   potatoes
½ cup extra-virgin olive oil
¼ cup balsamic vinegar
¼ cup capers, drained
1 tablespoon minced fresh
   tarragon or 1 teaspoon
   dried
1½ cups cherry tomatoes,
   halved

½ cup pitted kalamata olives
4 hard-cooked eggs, chopped
3 scallions, thinly sliced
2 celery ribs, thinly sliced
1 medium green bell pepper,
   cut into ¾-inch dice
   Salt and freshly ground
   pepper

1. In a large pot of boiling water, cook potatoes until just tender when pierced with a sharp knife, 20 to 25 minutes. Drain, run under cold water, and drain again. Slice into ¾-inch cubes.

2. In a large bowl, blend together oil, vinegar, capers, and tarragon. Add potatoes, tomatoes, olives, eggs, scallions, celery, and bell pepper. Toss gently to mix well. Season with salt and pepper to taste. Serve chilled or at room temperature.

200   SALMON-POTATO SALAD MIMOSA

Prep: 30 minutes   Cook: 12 to 13 minutes   Serves: 4

This lightly dilled salad is luxurious with silky, barely cooked fresh salmon. In a pinch, substitute drained and flaked canned salmon. Mimosa refers to a garnish of minced hard-cooked egg yolk that resembles the yellow mimosa flower.

1 pound red potatoes, peeled
   and cut into ½-inch dice
2 (6-ounce) salmon steaks,
   about ¾ inch thick
⅓ cup mayonnaise
⅓ cup nonfat plain yogurt
1 tablespoon minced fresh
   dill or 1 teaspoon dried
¾ teaspoon salt

½ teaspoon black pepper
1 small cucumber, quartered
   lengthwise and thinly
   sliced crosswise
4 scallions, thinly sliced
4 hard-cooked eggs—whites
   chopped, yolks minced
   Green leaf lettuce leaves

1. In a large pot of lightly salted boiling water, cook potatoes until just tender, about 5 minutes. Drain, run under cold water, and drain again.

2. In a medium skillet, bring 2 cups lightly salted water to a boil over high heat. Reduce heat to low and place salmon in water. Simmer, uncovered, 4 minutes. With a slotted spatula, carefully turn salmon over and cook 3 to 4 minutes, or until opaque throughout. Remove fish with slotted spatula and place on a platter. Blot excess water with a paper towel. When cool enough to handle, remove skin and bones. Break salmon into large flakes.

3. In a large bowl, blend together mayonnaise, yogurt, dill, salt, and pepper until smooth. Add potatoes, salmon, cucumber, scallions, and chopped egg whites. Toss gently to mix. Divide among 4 lettuce-lined plates, garnish with minced egg yolks, and serve.

---

201   HOT POTATO AND SPINACH SALAD WITH BACON

Prep: 15 minutes   Cook: 1 hour   Serves: 4

Baking potatoes at a high temperature gives their skin a wonderful crispness and saladlike texture. This simple main course includes bacon, scallions, and Parmesan cheese for toppings, but it's very adaptable. If you prefer, substitute a variety of cheeses for the Parmesan and sprinkle with condiments, such as sun-dried tomatoes, olives, or capers.

4 **medium baking potatoes, pierced with a sharp knife**	3 **tablespoons red wine vinegar**
8 **slices of bacon, cut into ¾-inch dice**	6 **cups torn spinach**
1 **to 2 tablespoons vegetable oil (optional)**	4 **scallions, thinly sliced**
	½ **cup grated Parmesan cheese**

1. Preheat oven to 475°F. Bake potatoes 1 hour.

2. Meanwhile, in a large skillet over medium heat, cook bacon, stirring frequently, until crisp, 7 to 9 minutes. Transfer bacon to paper towels and drain off all but 5 tablespoons fat from skillet. If there is less, add oil to up amount. Stir in vinegar and keep warm over low heat.

3. Divide spinach among 4 plates. Quarter potatoes lengthwise and arrange 4 quarters on each plate of spinach. Drizzle pan drippings and vinegar mixture over salads. Sprinkle bacon, scallions, and cheese over potatoes. Serve warm or at room temperature.

202 ROASTED VEGETABLE AND TOASTED BREAD SALAD

Prep: 25 minutes   Cook: 21 to 28 minutes   Serves: 4

Rustic and colorful, this salad features pleasantly charred vegetables and crisply toasted rustic bread. The piquant vinaigrette, complete with extra-virgin olive oil and fresh herbs, provides the perfect finish.

4 cups (1-inch) cubes crusty Italian bread
¼ cup olive oil
½ cup grated Parmesan cheese
1 medium red bell pepper, cut into 1-inch cubes
1 Japanese eggplant, cut crosswise into ½-inch slices
1 small yellow summer squash, cut crosswise into ½-inch slices

1 small zucchini, cut crosswise into ½-inch slices
1 small red onion, cut into ½-inch slices and separated into rings
¾ cup Vinaigrette Provençal (recipe follows)

1. Preheat oven to 500°F. In a large bowl, drizzle bread cubes with 2 tablespoons olive oil and toss until well blended. Spread on a baking sheet in a single layer and bake until golden brown, about 6 to 8 minutes. Return to same bowl, sprinkle with ¼ cup cheese, and let cool.

2. In another large bowl, combine bell pepper, eggplant, summer squash, zucchini, and red onion. Drizzle on remaining 2 tablespoons olive oil and toss until well blended. Spread on baking sheet in a single layer and bake, stirring occasionally, until golden brown, about 15 to 20 minutes. Return to same bowl, sprinkle with remaining ¼ cup cheese, and let cool.

3. Just before serving, combine vegetables and bread. Drizzle on vinaigrette and toss until mixed. Divide among 4 plates and serve at room temperature.

203 VINAIGRETTE PROVENÇAL
Prep: 8 minutes   Cook: none   Makes: about ³/₄ cup

⅓ cup extra-virgin olive oil
2 tablespoons balsamic
  vinegar
2 tablespoons chopped
  parsley
2 tablespoons chopped fresh
  basil

1 teaspoon Dijon mustard
2 garlic cloves, minced
1 tablespoon capers, drained
  Salt and freshly ground
  pepper

In a small bowl, whisk together olive oil, vinegar, parsley, basil, mustard, and garlic. Blend in capers. Season with salt and pepper to taste. If not using within 1 hour, cover and refrigerate. Let return to room temperature before using.

204 CROUTON SALAD WITH ROASTED PEPPERS, OREGANO, AND FETA CHEESE
Prep: 25 minutes   Cook: 20 to 22 minutes   Serves: 8

Crisp and chewy rustic bread, curly endive, roasted peppers, kalamata olives, and fragrant oregano make this blend of Mediterranean colors, textures, and flavors irresistible. The salad is lightly dressed, so that the primary ingredients can shine through.

16 cups (¾-inch) cubes French
  or Italian bread
3 large red bell peppers
8 cups torn curly endive
1 to 1½ cups crumbled feta
  cheese (4 to 6 ounces)
6 scallions, thinly sliced
¼ cup chopped fresh oregano
  or 1 tablespoon dried

½ cup extra-virgin olive oil
¼ cup red wine vinegar
1 teaspoon salt
½ teaspoon black pepper
1 cup kalamata or other
  oil-cured black olives

1. Preheat oven to 375°F. Place bread cubes in a single layer on 2 baking sheets. Bake until lightly golden, about 10 to 12 minutes.

2. Preheat broiler. Cut bell peppers in half lengthwise. Scoop out seeds and cut out stems. Place peppers, skin side up, on a baking sheet and broil as close to heat as possible until skin is charred all over, about 10 minutes. Place peppers in a paper bag and let steam 10 to 15 minutes. Peel off blackened skin and chop.

3. In a large bowl, combine bread, peppers, endive, cheese, scallions, and oregano. Drizzle with oil and vinegar and sprinkle with salt and pepper. Toss until well blended, divide among 8 plates, and sprinkle olives on top. Serve at room temperature.

205 SUMMER HARVEST BREAD SALAD

Prep: 25 minutes   Cook: 18 to 20 minutes   Serves: 4 to 5

Three classic pairings, including fresh basil and tomatoes, bread and cheese, and olive oil with balsamic vinegar, highlight this beautiful salad with its pleasing blend of textures. If you prefer, substitute provolone, Muenster, or morbier in place of the fontina cheese.

4 cups (¾-inch) cubes day-old
    French or Italian bread
2 medium red bell peppers
2 large vine-ripened
    tomatoes, cut into ¾-inch
    dice
2 cups shredded fontina
    cheese (8 ounces)
1 large cucumber, peeled,
    halved lengthwise,
    seeded, and thinly sliced
    crosswise

¼ cup minced fresh basil
3 garlic cloves, minced
⅓ cup extra-virgin olive oil
¼ cup balsamic vinegar
    Salt and freshly ground
    pepper

1. Preheat oven to 475°F. Arrange bread on a baking sheet in a single layer. Bake until lightly browned, 8 to 10 minutes.

2. Preheat broiler. Cut bell peppers in half lengthwise. Scoop out seeds and cut out stems. Place peppers, skin side up, on a baking sheet and broil as close to heat as possible until skin is charred all over, about 10 minutes. Place peppers in a paper bag and let steam 10 to 15 minutes. Peel off blackened skin and cut into ¾-inch dice.

3. In a large bowl, combine roasted bell peppers, tomatoes, cheese, cucumber, basil, and garlic. Top with toasted bread and drizzle on oil and vinegar. Toss until well mixed. Season with salt and pepper to taste and serve.

206 BREAD SALAD PROVENÇAL WITH ANCHOVY-CAPER VINAIGRETTE

Prep: 15 minutes   Cook: none   Serves: 4

Save your best vine-ripened tomatoes and most tender basil for this robustly flavored Mediterranean salad. It makes clever use of very stale, crusty bread.

10 cups (¾-inch) cubes day-old French or Italian bread	⅔ cup Anchovy-Caper Vinaigrette (recipe follows)
4 large plum tomatoes, cut into ½-inch dice	1 (2-ounce) chunk of Parmesan cheese, preferably imported
½ cup chopped fresh basil	
½ cup pitted kalamata or other oil-cured black olives	

1. Immerse bread in a large bowl of water and remove it quickly. Squeeze excess water from bread and place in a large dry bowl. Add tomatoes, basil, and olives. Drizzle on vinaigrette and toss until well mixed.

2. Divide among 4 plates. Using a swivel-bladed vegetable peeler, shave Parmesan cheese into slices and scatter over each salad. Serve within 1 hour at room temperature.

207 ANCHOVY-CAPER VINAIGRETTE

Prep: 5 minutes   Cook: none   Makes: about ⅔ cup

The strong flavors in this dressing make it ideal to pair with bland ingredients, such as bread. It's also delicious over cooked pasta or potatoes.

8 anchovy fillets, drained	¼ cup balsamic vinegar
2 tablespoons capers, drained	⅓ cup extra-virgin olive oil
3 garlic cloves	

Combine anchovy fillets, capers, and garlic in a food processor or blender. Mince together. Add vinegar and blend well. With machine on, gradually drizzle in oil. If not using within 2 hours, cover and refrigerate. Let return to room temperature before serving.

208   WHITE BREAD AND SHELLFISH SALAD

Prep: 25 minutes   Cook: none   Chill: 8 hours   Serves: 12

The idea for this recipe came from a neighbor, who raved about the salad. My aversion to sliced white sandwich bread made me curious about how a salad made with it could possibly be appealing. Wonders never cease. The recipe makes a convenient party dish, since it can be dressed and refrigerated up to 4 hours before serving.

1   (1- to 1½-pound) loaf sliced
    soft white sandwich
    bread
6   hard-cooked eggs, chopped
1   medium onion, cut into
    ½-inch dice
1   pound cooked shelled and
    deveined bay (tiny)
    shrimp

½   pound cooked or canned
    crabmeat, drained and
    picked over
6   celery ribs, thinly sliced
½   cup minced fresh parsley
¼   cup minced fresh basil
3   cups Creamy Tomato
    Dressing (recipe follows)
    Green leaf lettuce leaves

1. Remove crusts from bread and cut slices into ¾-inch cubes. In a large bowl, combine bread, eggs, and onion. Cover and refrigerate 8 hours or overnight.

2. Add shrimp, crab, celery, parsley, basil, and dressing. Toss until well blended. Divide lettuce among 12 plates. Mound salad on top. Serve at once or cover and refrigerate up to 4 hours.

209   CREAMY TOMATO DRESSING

Prep: 3 minutes   Cook: none   Makes: about 3 cups

1   cup fresh basil leaves
4   garlic cloves
1   cup tomato paste
1   cup buttermilk

1   cup mayonnaise
2   tablespoons Dijon mustard
    Salt and freshly ground
    pepper

Combine basil and garlic in a food processor or blender. Mince together. Add tomato paste, buttermilk, mayonnaise, and mustard. Blend well. Season with salt and pepper to taste. If not using immediately, cover and refrigerate.

210   GAZPACHO BREAD SALAD

Prep: 30 minutes   Cook: 10 to 12 minutes   Serves: 4 to 6

This fresh-tasting salad duplicates the ingredients of gazpacho, the well-known cold Andalusian soup, which combines raw vegetables with a garnish of croutons and hard-cooked eggs. In the salad, the croutons become an integral part of the main dish, providing pleasant crunchiness and contrast to the vegetables.

6   cups (¾-inch) cubes French
    or Italian bread
2   garlic cloves
6   large plum tomatoes—
    3 quartered, 3 cut into
    ½-inch dice
1   small red onion—½
    chopped, ½ thinly sliced
    and separated into rings
⅓   cup extra-virgin olive oil
¼   cup red wine vinegar

1   small green bell pepper, cut
    into ½-inch dice
1   small red bell pepper, cut
    into ½-inch dice
1   medium cucumber, halved
    lengthwise, seeded, and
    thinly sliced crosswise
1   cup chopped parsley
    Salt and freshly ground
    pepper
4   hard-cooked eggs, chopped

1. Preheat oven to 375°F. Arrange bread in a single layer on a baking sheet. Bake until lightly golden and crisp, 10 to 12 minutes.

2. Mince garlic in a food processor or blender. Add quartered tomatoes and chopped red onion. Mince together. Add oil and vinegar. Blend until almost smooth with just a few tiny chunks.

3. In a large bowl, combine toasted bread, diced tomatoes, sliced onion, green bell pepper, red bell pepper, cucumber, and parsley. Drizzle on dressing and toss until well mixed. Season with salt and pepper to taste. Divide among 4 to 6 plates, sprinkle eggs on top, and serve.

211 PITA BREAD SALAD
Prep: 25 minutes   Cook: 10 to 12 minutes   Serves: 5

Oven-crisped strips of pita bread blend with other Middle Eastern flavors in this unusual entree. Cucumbers, feta cheese, parsley, mint, and olives make it colorful and flavor-packed. Serve it immediately after tossing so that the pita strips stay crisp.

½ cup plus 2 tablespoons
    extra-virgin olive oil
2 garlic cloves, minced
4 (6-inch) pita breads, stacked
    and sliced into 1 x ½-inch
    strips
⅓ cup lemon juice
⅓ cup minced fresh parsley
⅓ cup minced fresh mint
4 plum tomatoes, cut into
    ½-inch dice

4 scallions, thinly sliced
1 small cucumber, quartered
    lengthwise and thinly
    sliced crosswise
1 medium green bell pepper,
    cut into ½-inch dice
1 cup crumbled feta cheese
1 (2.2-ounce) can sliced ripe
    olives, drained
Salt and freshly ground
    pepper

1. Preheat oven to 375°F. In a large bowl, combine 2 tablespoons oil and garlic. Add pita strips and toss until evenly coated. Arrange on a baking sheet in a single layer. Bake, turning occasionally, until crisp and golden, 10 to 12 minutes.

2. In same bowl, whisk together remaining ½ cup olive oil, lemon juice, parsley, and mint until well blended. Add tomatoes, scallions, cucumber, bell pepper, cheese, olives, and pita strips. Toss to mix well. Season with salt and pepper to taste and serve at once.

212 DANDELION, SUN-DRIED TOMATO, AND POTATO SALAD
Prep: 20 minutes   Cook: 20 to 25 minutes   Serves: 4

Dandelion greens are best picked when they are very young in the spring. When they are out of season, substitute arugula, watercress, or shredded spinach.

1¼ pounds medium red
    potatoes
1 tablespoon tomato paste
1 tablespoon red wine
    vinegar
1 teaspoon salt
¼ cup extra-virgin olive oil

4 slices of bacon
8 cups torn dandelion greens
4 hard-cooked eggs, chopped
½ cup sun-dried tomatoes,
    drained and chopped
½ cup pitted kalamata olives

1. In a large pot of boiling water, cook potatoes until just tender when pierced with a sharp knife, 20 to 25 minutes. Drain, run under cold water, and drain again. As soon as potatoes are cool enough to handle, peel and cut into ¼-inch slices.

2. In a large bowl, whisk together tomato paste, vinegar, salt, and 1 tablespoon water. Gradually whisk in oil. Add warm sliced potatoes to dressing and toss gently until well blended. Let cool to room temperature.

3. Meanwhile, in a large skillet, cook bacon over medium heat until crisp, 7 to 9 minutes. Drain on paper towels. When cool enough to handle, crumble bacon.

4. Add dandelion greens, eggs, tomatoes, and olives to potatoes. Toss gently to mix well. Divide among 4 plates, sprinkle bacon on top, and serve.

213 GRILLED GARLIC BREAD, FONTINA, AND TOMATO SALAD

Prep: 20 minutes   Cook: 5 minutes   Serves: 4 to 5

Crisply cooked bread provides delicious contrast in flavor and texture to creamy fontina cheese in this simple, lightly herbed salad.

½ cup extra-virgin olive oil
3 garlic cloves, minced
6 large slices of French or Italian bread, cut 1 inch thick
4 large plum tomatoes, cut into ¾-inch dice
2 cups diced (¾-inch) fontina cheese (about 8 ounces)
1 (14-ounce) can quartered artichoke hearts, drained

4 scallions, thinly sliced
2 tablespoons minced fresh oregano or 2 teaspoons dried
3 tablespoons red wine vinegar
Salt and freshly ground pepper
Red leaf lettuce leaves

1. Prepare a hot fire in a barbecue grill or preheat broiler. In a large bowl, blend oil and garlic. Brush half of mixture on both sides of bread. Place bread on a lightly oiled grill or oven rack set 4 to 6 inches from heat and cook, turning frequently, until golden on both sides, about 5 minutes total. Slice bread into 1-inch cubes.

2. Add tomatoes, cheese, artichoke hearts, scallions, oregano, and bread to remaining oil and garlic in large bowl. Drizzle on vinegar and toss until well mixed. Season with salt and pepper to taste. Divide among 4 or 5 lettuce-lined plates and serve at once.

Chapter 8

Instant Entrees: Salads on the Spot

Now more than ever, there is hope for those of us in a hurry—and who isn't—to produce healthy, delicious, and interesting meals without spending all day shopping and cooking. Main-dish salads offer a great way to serve up terrific one-dish meals in a snap. A quick glance at a typical supermarket will show you how.

Today's produce sections boast cleaned lettuce, cabbage, and spinach and freshly cut vegetables like carrots, broccoli, and cauliflower, both loose and packaged. Salad bars provide precut vegetables, cleaned and torn greens, and trimmings of all sorts. These "prepped" vegetables in no way compromise the creativity of the cook or the results on the dinner table. They just eliminate many of the chores that must be performed at some time between shopping and dining.

In their effort to make one-stop shopping possible, many supermarkets now run in-store delis where you can buy roasted chickens, cooked and sliced meats, and sliced and shredded cheeses. Many of the prepared side salads they offer, such as potato, 3-bean, and macaroni, can be transformed into main-dish salads by pairing them with prepared meats from the deli and prewashed, ready-to-eat greens.

Some markets have taken this convenience a step further and offer ethnic delis where customers can pick up Chinese barbecued pork, smoked duck, fresh salsas, guacamole, and freshly made dressings. Marinated and ready-to-cook meats, poultry, and fish are available in many markets. Packed with flavor, they need only grilling or broiling and slicing to highlight a main-course salad.

Frozen and canned fruits and vegetables also make ideal choices for salad ingredients. Many frozen vegetables, such as corn, green peas, green beans, and black-eyed peas, require only defrosting to be ready for a salad. You can place them in a colander and run cool water over them while preparing other parts of the meal.

Canned beets, corn, roasted chiles, water chestnuts, artichoke hearts, and hearts of palm make delicious, simple-to-prepare salad fare. Instead of soaking and slowly cooking beans, choose canned ones, which need only rinsing and draining. A rainbow of beans that were once considered exotic are available canned now, including cannellini, fava, and black beans.

Jars of roasted and pickled peppers, capers, and olives of all sorts are flavor-packed salad ingredients needing no more effort than the twist of a jar lid. Bottled and jarred salad dressings, once only available in French, Italian, Thousand Island, and blue cheese, are now produced in dozens of styles and flavors, including reduced-fat, oil-free, and no-fat versions.

Augment these easy salad pickings at the market by using leftovers and by planning leftovers. It's easy to cook more meat, fish, grains, or pasta than you need at the moment. Store them carefully and they become precooked, easy-to-use ingredients. This way you can stretch the time and attention spent cooking for more than one meal. More than any other type of food we eat, salads invite the use of leftovers and provide a way of transforming them into an entirely different form.

In this chapter, you'll find many of the products that markets offer for quick cooking put to good-tasting use. Most of these salads take all of 10 minutes to prepare, one bowl to toss in, and no cooking at all. It's an international array of the fastest full-meal salads possible.

---

214   ARTICHOKE AND ANGEL HAIR SALAD
Prep: 10 minutes   Cook: 45 to 60 seconds   Serves: 3

This salad takes advantage of many of the flavor-packed ingredients, including sun-dried tomatoes, marinated artichoke hearts, and quick-cooking fresh pasta that are available in supermarkets today. To save extra time, buy preshredded mozzarella cheese.

1 (9-ounce) package fresh angel hair pasta (capellini)
1 (6-ounce) jar marinated artichoke hearts, liquid reserved
½ cup sun-dried tomatoes packed in oil, drained

½ cup fresh basil leaves
  Salt and freshly ground pepper
1½ cups shredded mozzarella cheese (about 6 ounces)
⅓ cup kalamata or other oil-cured black olives

1. In a large pot of lightly salted boiling water, cook pasta until just tender, 45 to 60 seconds. Drain and transfer to a large bowl.

2. Immediately drain artichoke marinade over pasta and toss until coated. Place artichoke hearts, sun-dried tomatoes, and basil on a cutting board. Chop together and add to pasta. Toss until well mixed. Season with salt and pepper to taste. Mound on a platter or divide among 3 plates. Sprinkle cheese and olives on top and serve.

215   STUFFED GRAPE LEAVES WITH TOMATOES AND FETA CHEESE

Prep: 10 minutes   Cook: none   Serves: 4

Stuffed grape leaves, or *dolmas,* are sold freshly made in many specialty stores and delis and in cans on supermarket shelves. The very small ones in cans are particularly attractive in this dish. For entertaining, the salad can be completely set up a day ahead and refrigerated. Let it return to room temperature and drizzle it with olive oil just before serving.

Red leaf lettuce leaves
4 large plum tomatoes, thinly sliced
20 ounces grape leaves stuffed with rice (about 20 small), drained
½ small red onion, thinly sliced and separated into rings

½ cup crumbled feta cheese
⅓ cup extra-virgin olive oil
Lemon wedges
Salt and freshly ground pepper

Line 4 plates with lettuce. Arrange tomatoes in slightly overlapping slices in center of plates. Arrange grape leaves around tomatoes. Sprinkle with onion and cheese. Drizzle with olive oil and serve at once with lemon wedges and salt and pepper to taste.

216   HEARTS OF PALM AND BOURSIN SALAD

Prep: 10 minutes   Cook: none   Serves: 3

¼ cup extra-virgin olive oil
2 tablespoons balsamic vinegar
6 cups assorted baby lettuces
Salt and freshly ground pepper
1 (7.75-ounce) can hearts of palm, drained

1 (5.2-ounce) container Boursin cheese, sliced into 3 equal wedges
1 to 1½ cups seedless red grapes

In a large bowl, whisk together oil and vinegar. Add lettuces and toss until evenly coated. Season with salt and pepper to taste. Divide among 3 plates. Arrange hearts of palm and Boursin on top of lettuces. Sprinkle with grapes and serve.

217   PEAR, BLUE CHEESE, AND ARUGULA SALAD

Prep: 10 minutes   Cook: none   Serves: 6

This light, easy salad is made festive with brightly colored Red Bartlett pears, which provide stunning contrast to the pungent, deep green arugula. Accompany the salad with crusty French baguettes.

9 cups torn arugula
4 medium Red Bartlett pears, cored and cut into ¾-inch dice

⅓ cup extra-virgin olive oil
3 tablespoons balsamic vinegar
¾ cup crumbled blue cheese

In a large bowl, combine arugula and pears. Drizzle on oil and vinegar and toss gently to coat. Divide among 6 plates. Sprinkle blue cheese on top and serve at once.

218   SPINACH SALAD WITH ASIAN ACCENTS

Prep: 10 minutes   Cook: none   Serves: 8 to 10

This colorful salad comes mostly from the pantry, so if you want it cold, place the canned foods in the refrigerator a few hours before serving. Packaged spinach tends to be large-leafed. If you don't have time to stem and tear it, let your diners do the work with a knife and fork. If you can find baby spinach that's sold loose, use it; it requires no stemming or washing.

1 (10-ounce) package fresh spinach
2 (11-ounce) cans mandarin oranges, drained
2 (5-ounce) cans sliced water chestnuts, drained
1 (8-ounce) can sliced bamboo shoots, drained
1 (5.5-ounce) can baby corn, drained

1 cup bacon bits
½ to ¾ cup bottled honey-mustard dressing
Salt and freshly ground pepper
1 (6-ounce) package chow mein noodles

In a large bowl, combine spinach, oranges, water chestnuts, bamboo shoots, corn, and bacon bits. Drizzle with dressing and toss until well mixed. Season with salt and pepper to taste. Sprinkle noodles on top and serve.

219   FRESH FRUIT MÉLANGE
Prep: 15 minutes   Cook: none   Serves: 8

This healthy salad resembles a beautiful wagon wheel of vivid color. If caught without time even to cut fresh fruit into chunks, buy prepared fruit at a salad bar. If you prefer, cottage cheese can be substituted for the yogurt.

Green leaf lettuce leaves
6 cups cubed honeydew
     melon
6 cups fresh or canned
     pineapple chunks,
     drained

6 cups strawberries, trimmed
     and quartered, if large
6 cups seedless grapes
4 cups vanilla yogurt
1 cup shelled pistachios or
     pecans

Line 8 plates with lettuce. Arrange melon, pineapple, strawberries, and grapes in a spoke pattern on top of lettuce. Pour yogurt in center and sprinkle nuts on top. Serve at once or cover and refrigerate at least 2 hours to serve cold.

220   PINEAPPLE, PEPPER, AND BLACK-EYED PEA PANTRY SALAD
Prep: 15 minutes   Cook: none   Serves: 8

This very colorful salad is splendid with most fully cooked sausages or ham, since the sweetness of the pineapple and the dressing complements their saltiness. Although the lettuce and the heavier ingredients need to be tossed separately, it's all done quickly in only one bowl.

1 (16-ounce) bag prepared
     iceberg lettuce blend
     (about 14 cups)
1 cup bottled honey-mustard
     dressing
1 (15-ounce) can black-eyed
     peas, rinsed and drained
1 (20-ounce) can unsweetened
     pineapple chunks,
     drained

1 (7-ounce) jar roasted red bell
     peppers, drained and
     thinly sliced
1 pound sliced cooked ham,
     stacked and cut into
     slivers

1. In a large bowl, combine lettuce and dressing. Toss until well blended and divide among 8 plates.

2. In same bowl, combine black-eyed peas, pineapple, bell peppers, and ham. Toss until well blended, place on top of lettuce, and serve.

221   MEXICAN BEAN, CORN, AND SMOKED CHICKEN SALAD

Prep: 15 minutes   Cook: none   Serves: 5 to 7

Mildly spicy and smoky, this colorful salad is hearty and filling—a perfect winter party salad, perhaps for Superbowl Sunday. It can also be served cold if covered and refrigerated about 2 hours; just stir it well to mix again just before dividing among plates. Serve it with crisp tortilla chips and guacamole for an extra fillip.

1 (15-ounce) can black beans, rinsed and drained
1 (15-ounce) can kidney beans, rinsed and drained
1 (15¼-ounce) can whole kernel corn, drained
1 (7-ounce) can diced green chiles

6 ounces smoked chicken, shredded
1½ cups shredded Cheddar cheese (6 ounces)
2 cups bottled mild salsa
⅔ cup cilantro leaves

In a large bowl, combine black beans, kidney beans, corn, chiles, chicken, and cheese. Add salsa and toss until well blended. Serve at room temperature, sprinkled generously with cilantro.

222   ONE-BOWL, TWO-BEAN ITALIAN SALAD

Prep: 10 minutes   Cook: none   Serves: 8

If time doesn't permit, instead of making your own dressing here, use bottled Italian or Caesar dressing.

⅓ cup red wine vinegar
1 garlic clove, crushed through a press
1 teaspoon sugar
1 teaspoon salt
1 cup extra-virgin olive oil
2 (8¼-ounce) cans quartered artichoke hearts, drained
1 (15-ounce) can cannellini or white kidney beans, rinsed and drained
1 (15-ounce) can chickpeas, rinsed and drained

1 small red onion, thinly sliced and separated into rings
16 to 20 cherry tomatoes
¼ cup coarsely chopped fresh basil
16 cups assorted salad greens
1 cup kalamata or other oil-cured black olives
½ cup grated Parmesan cheese

1. In a large bowl, combine vinegar, garlic, sugar, and salt. Gradually whisk in oil. Add artichoke hearts, cannellini beans, chickpeas, red onion, tomatoes, and basil. Toss until well blended. Add salad greens and toss again.

2. Divide salad among 8 plates. Sprinkle olives and cheese on top and serve.

223 MIXED BEAN AND SMOKED TURKEY MEDLEY
Prep: 10 minutes   Cook: none   Serves: 8

Sweet and tart, this salad is also delicious with other ready-to-eat meats, such as summer sausage, ham, or Canadian bacon. If you don't have time to blend your own dressing, use 1 cup bottled honey-mustard dressing and toss it with the beans, turkey, and lettuce.

½ cup olive oil
¼ cup raspberry vinegar
4 teaspoons Dijon mustard
4 teaspoons honey
2 (16-ounce) jars marinated mixed bean salad, drained

1 pound thinly sliced smoked turkey, stacked and chopped
1 (1-pound) bag prepared iceberg lettuce blend (about 14 cups)

In a large bowl, blend together oil, vinegar, mustard, and honey until smooth. Add bean salad, smoked turkey, and lettuce. Toss until well blended. Divide among 8 plates and serve at once.

224 VEGETABLE-BEAN BEDLAM
Prep: 10 minutes   Cook: none   Serves: 4 to 5

Vivid in color and flavor, this two-bean, two-vegetable salad makes use of canned and frozen beans and vegetables, jarred garlic, and already shredded cheese. Shredded or grated Cheddar, Swiss, Parmesan, and mozzarella cheeses are available in most supermarkets. If you prefer, the salad can be prepared hours ahead of time to serve cold. Sprinkle with the onions just before serving.

½ cup mayonnaise
2 tablespoons lemon juice
1 teaspoon jarred minced garlic
1 (15-ounce) can black beans, rinsed and drained
1 (15-ounce) can chickpeas, rinsed and drained
1 (10-ounce) package frozen peas, thawed

1 (10-ounce) package frozen corn, thawed
Salt and freshly ground pepper
Green leaf lettuce leaves
1 cup shredded Cheddar cheese (about 4 ounces)
1 (2.8-ounce) can french fried real onions

1. In a large bowl, blend together mayonnaise, lemon juice, and garlic until smooth. Add black beans, chickpeas, peas, and corn. Toss until well blended. Season with salt and pepper to taste.

2. Divide salad among 4 or 5 lettuce-lined plates. Sprinkle cheese and onions on top and serve.

225   BLAZING BLACK BEAN AND CHILE SALAD WITH CREAMY SALSA DRESSING

Prep: 10 minutes   Cook: none   Serves: 3 to 4

Nobody will suspect how effortlessly this flavorful salad is put together. Be sure all the ingredients, including the salsa if it is at all watery, are well drained, so the dressing doesn't become diluted. For speed, shred the lettuce in a food processor, or use large leaves and leave whole.

⅔ cup bottled chunky salsa
¼ cup sour cream
2 tablespoons lime juice
2 (14½-ounce) cans Mexican-style stewed tomatoes, well drained
1 (15¼-ounce) can whole kernel corn, drained

1 (15-ounce) can black beans, rinsed and well drained
1 (7-ounce) can diced green chiles, drained
4 to 6 cups shredded iceberg lettuce
1 cup shredded Cheddar cheese

1. In a large bowl, whisk together salsa, sour cream, and lime juice until well blended. Add tomatoes, corn, beans, and chiles. Toss until well blended.

2. Arrange lettuce on a platter or 3 or 4 plates. Mound salad on lettuce. Sprinkle cheese on top. Serve at room temperature or chilled.

226   MEDITERRANEAN CHICKPEA SALAD WITH CAPERS AND FETA CHEESE

Prep: 10 minutes   Cook: none   Serves: 4

Piquant from capers and lemon juice, this garlic-laced salad makes a great buffet or picnic dish. Hothouse cucumbers need no peeling—just rinse well and slice in a food processor or on a hand grater.

½ seedless hothouse cucumber, thinly sliced
2 (15-ounce) cans chickpeas, rinsed and drained
2 (4-ounce) jars sliced pimientos, drained
¾ cup crumbled feta cheese

¼ cup capers, drained
3 garlic cloves, minced
¼ cup extra-virgin olive oil
2 tablespoons lemon juice
   Salt and freshly ground pepper
12 large Boston lettuce leaves

1. In a large bowl, combine cucumber, chickpeas, pimientos, feta cheese, capers, and garlic. Drizzle on oil and lemon juice and toss until well mixed. Season with salt and pepper to taste.

2. On each of 4 plates, arrange 3 lettuce leaves with stem end in center, forming a large cup. Divide salad among plates and serve at room temperature.

227 INSTANT AIOLI SALAD
Prep: 15 minutes   Cook: none   Serves: 4

Aioli is a strong, garlicky mayonnaise so popular in the south of France that it's called the "butter of Provence." It's typically served with vegetables, meats, fish, and bread. It can be ferociously pungent or mild, as it is in this recipe. Add as much garlic to the mayonnaise as you like, and you may want to make extra dressing to pass on the side.

Green leaf lettuce leaves
1 (8½-ounce) can quartered
   artichoke hearts, drained
1 (7½-ounce) jar roasted red
   peppers, drained
1 (7-ounce) can escargots,
   drained (about 24 large)

1 (4-ounce) can whole button
   mushrooms, drained
1 pint cherry tomatoes
2 cups packaged croutons
½ cup mayonnaise
2 garlic cloves, crushed
   through a press

1. Line 4 plates with lettuce. Divide artichoke hearts, roasted peppers, escargots, mushrooms, tomatoes, and croutons among plates, arranging ingredients in a spoke or linear pattern on each plate.

2. In a small bowl, stir together mayonnaise and garlic. Divide among 4 ramekins or tiny serving bowls. Place a ramekin alongside each plate for dipping and serve at room temperature.

228 TOMATO ASPIC WITH CRAB
Prep: 5 minutes   Cook: none   Serves: 2

To serve this colorful, simply composed salad cold, place the canned aspic and crab in the refrigerator when you buy it. That way the ingredients will be ready to use at a moment's notice.

Green leaf lettuce leaves
1 (13½-ounce) can tomato
   aspic, chilled
1 to 1½ cups cooked or
   canned crabmeat, drained
   and picked over

¼ cup mayonnaise
Lemon wedges

1. Line 2 plates with lettuce. Cut aspic crosswise into 6 even slices and divide among plates, overlapping slices slightly.

2. Place crab alongside aspic. Garnish each plate with 2 tablespoons mayonnaise and lemon wedges. Serve cold.

229 INSTANT CURRIED CHICKEN SALAD

Prep: 10 minutes   Cook: none   Serves: 2

¼ cup mayonnaise or nonfat
    plain yogurt
2 tablespoons chutney
2 teaspoons curry powder
2 cups bite-size pieces
    leftover cooked chicken,
    turkey, lamb, or shrimp
    (about 8 ounces)

1 cup seedless grapes,
    preferably red
¼ cup raisins or currants
¼ cup slivered almonds

In a medium bowl, stir mayonnaise, chutney, curry powder, and 1 table-spoon water until blended. Add chicken, grapes, raisins, and almonds. Toss until well mixed. Serve at room temperature or cover and refrigerate at least 2 hours to serve cold.

230 DELI CHEF'S SALAD

Prep: 10 minutes   Cook: none   Serves: 4

Choosing cooked, thin-sliced meats and cheeses from the deli makes this salad quick to fix. To cut these into slivers, stack the slices and cut through the layers into very thin strips.

8 cups assorted baby lettuces
½ cup best-quality bottled
    Italian salad dressing
2 tablespoons capers, drained
4 ounces thinly sliced cooked
    ham, cut into slivers
    (about 1 cup)
4 ounces thinly sliced cooked
    turkey, cut into slivers
    (about 1 cup)

4 ounces thinly sliced Swiss
    cheese, cut into slivers
    (about 1 cup)
1 (4-ounce) jar sliced
    pimientos, drained
1 (2.2-ounce) can sliced ripe
    olives, drained

1. In a large bowl, combine lettuces, dressing, and capers. Toss until well blended and divide among 4 plates.

2. Arrange ham, turkey, and cheese in a spoke pattern over greens. Divide pimientos among salads, arranging in a mound in center of each. Sprinkle olives on top and serve.

231 CHINESE BARBECUE PORK AND BROCCOLI SLAW WITH LYCHEES

Prep: 10 minutes   Cook: none   Serves: 4

Oven-roasted, ready-to-serve Chinese barbecued pork, available in Chinese markets and in many large supermarkets, is mildly flavored and slightly sweet. It pairs perfectly here with a hoisin-flavored broccoli slaw, sold in packages. If broccoli is unavailable, use cabbage-based packaged slaw.

¼ cup bottled Italian dressing
1 (11-ounce) can whole lychees in heavy syrup, 4 teaspoons syrup reserved
2 teaspoons hoisin sauce
1 (16-ounce) package broccoli coleslaw or cabbage coleslaw blend

12 ounces Chinese-style cured barbecue pork, thinly sliced
1 (5.5-ounce) can whole baby sweet corn, drained

1. In a large bowl, blend together dressing, reserved lychee syrup, and hoisin sauce. Add coleslaw and toss until well blended. Divide among 4 plates.

2. Arrange pork in slightly overlapping slices on one side of salad. Arrange corn alongside. Drain lychees and place on top of pork. Serve at once.

232 REUBEN SALAD

Prep: 15 minutes   Cook: none   Serves: 10 to 12

Reportedly named for Arthur Reuben, the owner of a former New York City delicatessen, the popular Reuben sandwich is made of layers of corned beef, sauerkraut, and Swiss cheese topped with creamy Thousand Island dressing. All the flavors of the classic Reuben sandwich make an appearance in this substantial salad. Serve it with chewy rye bread.

1¾ cups bottled Thousand Island dressing
3 tablespoons lemon juice
1 tablespoon caraway seed
16 cups torn romaine lettuce
4 pounds sauerkraut, rinsed and squeezed dry

8 to 10 ounces thinly sliced corned beef, cut into shreds
2 to 2½ cups shredded Swiss cheese (8 to 10 ounces)

In a large bowl, combine dressing, lemon juice, and caraway seed. Blend well. Add lettuce, sauerkraut, corned beef, and cheese. Toss until well mixed. Serve at once.

233 RED CABBAGE AND GERMAN SAUSAGE SALAD

Prep: 10 minutes   Cook: none   Serves: 4

1 tablespoon cider vinegar
1 tablespoon coarse-grained
  German-style mustard
2 teaspoons caraway seed
¼ cup olive oil
1 (16-ounce) jar
  sweet-and-sour red
  cabbage, drained

8 ounces fully cooked
  German-style sausage,
  such as knockwurst,
  thinly sliced
4 cups assorted baby greens

1. In a large bowl, combine vinegar, mustard, and caraway seed. Whisk until well blended. Slowly whisk in olive oil.

2. Add cabbage, sausage, and greens. Toss until well mixed. Serve at once.

234 KALEIDOSCOPE SUMMER SAUSAGE SALAD

Prep: 15 minutes   Cook: none   Serves: 8

Three different types of beans, crumbled feta cheese, diced tomatoes, and shredded lettuce give this salad its multicolored aspect. If you don't have time to dice tomatoes, substitute 1 (14½-ounce) can stewed tomatoes, well drained.

½ cup olive oil
2 tablespoons lemon juice
1 tablespoon chili powder
12 cups shredded iceberg
  lettuce
1 (19-ounce) can fava beans,
  rinsed and drained
1 (15-ounce) can black-eyed
  peas, rinsed and drained
1 (15-ounce) can black beans,
  rinsed and drained

4 medium plum tomatoes, cut
  into ¾-inch dice
1 cup crumbled feta cheese
  Salt and freshly ground
  pepper
1 pound fully cooked
  summer sausage, thinly
  sliced

1. In a large bowl, whisk together oil, lemon juice, and chili powder until well blended. Add lettuce, fava beans, black-eyed peas, black beans, tomatoes, and feta cheese. Toss until well mixed. Season with salt and pepper to taste.

2. Divide sausage among plates, arranging slices overlapping slightly around edges. Mound salad in center of plates and serve at room temperature.

235 SUN-DRIED TOMATO AND CRAB SALAD
Prep: 15 minutes   Cook: none   Serves: 4 to 5

Sun-dried tomatoes and lemon juice enliven commercially made mayonnaise to flavor rich crabmeat in this easy main course. If you happen to have leftover cooked salmon, tuna, or shrimp, it can be used in place of the crab.

½ cup sun-dried tomatoes
   packed in oil, drained
   and minced
½ cup mayonnaise
2 tablespoons lemon juice
1 pound fresh cooked or
   canned crabmeat, drained
   and picked over

1 (10-ounce) package frozen
   peas, thawed
1 cucumber, quartered
   lengthwise and thinly
   sliced crosswise
Green leaf lettuce leaves

In a medium bowl, blend together sun-dried tomatoes, mayonnaise, and lemon juice. Add crab, peas, and cucumber. Toss gently until well mixed. Line 4 or 5 plates with lettuce leaves. Mound crab salad in center and serve at once.

236 BASIL, SPINACH, AND SHRIMP SALAD
Prep: 10 minutes   Cook: none   Serves: 4

Flecks of black olives, small pink shrimp, dark green spinach, and shredded white mozzarella cheese give this 10-minute entree a dramatic look. Buying shredded cheese and prewashed and trimmed spinach will speed preparations considerably. A loaf of crusty bread will complete the meal.

½ cup best-quality bottled
   Italian salad dressing
1 tablespoon balsamic
   vinegar
1 garlic clove, crushed
   through a press
8 cups baby spinach leaves or
   torn spinach

1½ cups shredded mozzarella
   cheese (6 ounces)
2 cups cooked shelled and
   deveined bay (tiny)
   shrimp
3 tablespoons coarsely
   chopped fresh basil
½ cup pitted kalamata olives

In a large bowl, blend dressing, vinegar, and garlic. Add spinach, cheese, shrimp, basil, and olives. Toss until well blended. Divide among 4 plates and serve.

237   GREEN PEA AND SHRIMP SALAD WITH CURRY AND MINT

Prep: 15 minutes   Cook: none   Serves: 4

½ cup mayonnaise
½ cup nonfat plain yogurt
2 teaspoons curry powder
1 teaspoon sugar
2 (10-ounce) packages frozen peas, thawed
4 cups cooked shelled and deveined bay (tiny) shrimp (about 1 pound)

1 (7-ounce) can sliced water chestnuts, drained
Salt and freshly ground pepper
½ cup roasted cashews
3 tablespoons chopped fresh mint

1. In a large bowl, combine mayonnaise, yogurt, curry powder, and sugar. Blend well. Add peas, shrimp, and water chestnuts. Toss gently until evenly mixed. Season with salt and pepper to taste.

2. Mound salad on a platter or divide among 4 plates. Sprinkle cashews and mint on top. Serve chilled or at room temperature.

238   ORANGE AND SHRIMP-STUFFED AVOCADOS

Prep: 15 minutes   Cook: none   Serves: 8

Choose ripe, preferably Hass, avocados for this rich salad. For larger portions, serve 2 avocado halves per serving and double the filling. If you have time, peel the avocados. An avocado knife, with its slightly curved blade, makes peeling them short work by scooping the entire avocado half out of its skin.

½ cup mayonnaise
2 tablespoons orange juice concentrate
1 pound cooked shelled and deveined bay (tiny) shrimp
2 (11-ounce) cans mandarin oranges, drained
1 (14½-ounce) can boiled whole onions, drained

Salt and freshly ground pepper
12 cups shredded iceberg lettuce
4 large ripe avocados, halved lengthwise and pitted
½ cup alfalfa sprouts

1. In a large bowl, combine mayonnaise, orange juice concentrate, and ¼ cup water. Whisk until smooth. Add shrimp, mandarin oranges, and onions. Toss until well blended. Season with salt and pepper to taste.

2. Divide lettuce among 8 plates and top each with 1 avocado half. Mound shrimp salad onto avocado, allowing some to spill over onto lettuce. Sprinkle with sprouts and serve at room temperature.

239   TUSCAN TUNA AND WHITE BEAN SALAD
Prep: 15 minutes   Cook: none   Serves: 4

⅓ cup extra-virgin olive oil
¼ cup lemon juice
¼ cup chopped parsley
1 tablespoon minced fresh
   oregano or ¾ teaspoon
   dried
2 garlic cloves, minced
2 (15-ounce) cans cannellini or
   white kidney beans,
   rinsed and drained

2 (6½-ounce) cans solid white
   tuna, drained
4 plum tomatoes, cut into
   ½-inch dice
½ cup pitted kalamata or other
   black olives
Salt and freshly ground
   pepper
4 cups torn assorted salad
   greens

1. In a large bowl, combine olive oil and lemon juice. Stir in parsley, oregano, garlic, cannellini beans, tuna, tomatoes, and olives. Toss to mix well.

2. Season with salt and pepper to taste. Divide greens among 4 plates and top with tuna-bean salad. Serve at room temperature.

240   MANDARIN SMOKED SHELLFISH SALAD
Prep: 10 minutes   Cook: none   Serves: 4 to 6

Oranges and lemon juice offer a tart-sweet counterpoint to smoky, savory shellfish in this rich and satisfying salad.

4 (3½-ounce) cans smoked
   clams or mussels, liquid
   reserved
2 (11-ounce) cans mandarin
   oranges, drained
2 (8-ounce) cans sliced water
   chestnuts, drained

¼ cup lemon juice
Salt and freshly ground
   pepper
8 cups assorted baby lettuces

In a large bowl, combine clams and their liquid, mandarin oranges, water chestnuts, and lemon juice. Toss until well mixed. Season with salt and pepper to taste. Divide lettuce among 4 to 6 plates. Mound salad on top and serve.

241   COUSCOUS, SPINACH, AND SMOKED SHELLFISH SALAD

Prep: 15 minutes   Cook: none   Serves: 4

The couscous we buy in packages today is tiny pasta that's precooked, so it only needs to stand for 5 minutes in hot water.

1½ cups reduced-sodium
      chicken broth or water
1½ cups couscous
1   (14½-ounce) can stewed
      tomatoes, drained and
      coarsely chopped
1   (10-ounce) package frozen
      chopped spinach, thawed

2   (3¾-ounce) cans smoked
      clams, oysters, or
      mussels, liquid reserved
3   tablespoons lemon juice
      Salt and freshly ground
      pepper

1. In a medium saucepan, bring broth to a boil. Add couscous and stir briefly. Cover and remove from heat. Let stand 5 minutes.

2. Meanwhile, in a large bowl, combine tomatoes, spinach, smoked clams and their liquid, and lemon juice. Fluff couscous with a fork to separate grains. Add to salad and toss until well blended. Season with salt and pepper to taste. Divide among 4 plates and serve warm or at room temperature.

242   BROCCOLI AND SHELLFISH COLESLAW

Prep: 5 minutes   Cook: none   Serves: 4 to 6

If you prefer, use all shrimp or crab in this salad and regular cabbage-based coleslaw mix instead of broccoli. It's especially pretty served on green leaf lettuce, spinach, or large cabbage leaves.

½ cup mayonnaise
⅓ cup bottled chili sauce
1 teaspoon prepared white
     horseradish sauce
1 (1-pound) package broccoli
     coleslaw

6 ounces cooked or canned
     crabmeat, drained and
     picked over
6 ounces cooked shelled
     deveined bay (tiny)
     shrimp

In a large bowl, blend together mayonnaise, chili sauce, and horseradish. Add coleslaw, crab, and shrimp. Toss until mixed and divide among 4 to 6 plates. Serve at once.

Chapter 9

Party Salads

Parties make unique demands on a host or hostess, depending upon the type of occasion being planned and the food being served. It's always easier when the food can be prepared at least a day ahead of time. Buffets and picnics require dishes that can stand at room temperature without fussing over for a few hours. Festive occasions beg for out-of-the-ordinary presentations, and parties intended to impress call for extraordinary ingredients. The one common requirement of party dishes is that they taste delicious. And, of course, a party suggests quantity—enough to serve eight or more.

These are many of the reasons why particular salads were distinguished by being chosen for this special chapter. Paella Salad, Technicolor Tortilla Toss, Broccoli and Bacon Bash, and Bouillabaisse Salad with Rouille offer such festive presentations and wonderful flavors that they make ideal party fare.

Some, such as Cranberry and Turkey Strata, Smoked Trout-Stuffed Iceberg Lettuce, and Seven-Layer Potluck Salad, allow the cook the luxury of preparing the main course a day or more ahead of time, thereby providing relaxed entertaining when the guests arrive. Others, such as Vegetables à la Grecque and Tossed Antipasto Salad, can be served at varying temperatures, which makes them perfect for a buffet or picnic. And since entertaining sometimes calls for indulgence, a few luxurious salads, such as Smoked Salmon Salad with Caviar and Crème Fraîche, Shellfish Salad, and Asparagus Under Wraps, call for more expensive ingredients reserved for special occasions.

243 ASPARAGUS UNDER WRAPS
Prep: 15 minutes   Cook: 2 to 5 minutes   Serves: 8

Elegant and simple, this salad provides appealing contrasts in flavor, texture, and color. When time allows, peel the stems of the asparagus for extra tenderness and a beautiful pale green color. Serve with a loaf of crusty bread.

3 **pounds fresh asparagus, woody stems removed**	¾ **cup olive oil, preferably extra-virgin**
16 **paper-thin slices prosciutto**	⅓ **cup balsamic vinegar**
Green leaf lettuce leaves	1 **(3-ounce) chunk of**
8 **hard-cooked eggs, quartered lengthwise**	**Parmesan cheese, preferably imported**
8 **plum tomatoes, quartered lengthwise**	**Freshly ground pepper**

1. In a large pot of lightly salted boiling water, cook asparagus until barely tender, 2 to 5 minutes, depending on thickness of stalks. Drain, run under cold water, and drain again. Divide asparagus into 8 even bundles. Wrap 2 slices of prosciutto around each, leaving asparagus tips exposed.

2. Line 8 plates with lettuce and top with asparagus bundles. Alternate egg and tomato wedges around them. In a small bowl, combine oil and vinegar. Drizzle over salads. Using a swivel-bladed vegetable peeler, shave Parmesan cheese into slices and scatter over each salad. Serve at once with pepper.

244 BROCCOLI AND BACON BASH
Prep: 15 minutes   Cook: 11 to 13 minutes   Serves: 12

This broccoli-based salad is slighty sweet with chewy dried cherries, pecans, and the fruity fragrance of raspberry vinegar. Shredded baked ham can be substituted for the bacon. For pleasing color contrast, I like to serve this salad on large red cabbage leaves.

2 **pounds thickly sliced bacon, cut into ¾-inch dice**	1 **large sweet onion, such as Vidalia, cut into ½-inch dice**
24 **cups broccoli florets (about 2 pounds)**	2 **cups dried cherries, dried cranberries, or raisins**
1½ **cups mayonnaise**	1 **cup broken pecans**
¼ **cup sugar**	**Salt and freshly ground pepper**
¼ **cup raspberry vinegar**	

1. In 2 large skillets, cook bacon over medium heat until crisp, 8 to 10 minutes. Transfer to paper towels to drain.

2. In a large stockpot of lightly salted boiling water, cook broccoli until crisp-tender, about 3 minutes. Drain, run under cold water, and drain well.

3. In a large bowl, whisk together mayonnaise, sugar, and vinegar until well blended. Add bacon, broccoli, onion, dried cherries, and pecans. Toss until well mixed. Season with salt and pepper to taste. Serve at room temperature.

---

245   FIESTA FAJITA CHICKEN SALAD
Prep: 30 minutes   Marinate: 8 hours   Cook: 8 to 10 minutes
Serves: 8 to 12

A popular party staple in the Southwest, fajitas make entertaining easy. The chicken can be marinated the night before and grilled after guests arrive. All the help-yourself ingredients (except the avocado) can be arranged in bowls, covered, and refrigerated the day before. Warm the tortillas in a closed grill, if you like, after the chicken is cooked. Let guests assemble their own salads while you enjoy the party.

⅔ cup vegetable oil
⅔ cup red wine vinegar
4 teaspoons cayenne, or less to taste
2 teaspoons ground cumin
4 scallions, thinly sliced
¼ cup chopped cilantro or parsley
8 skinless, boneless chicken breast halves
16 cups chopped romaine lettuce

2 (15-ounce) cans kidney beans, rinsed and drained
8 plum tomatoes, cut into ¾-inch dice
4 cups grated Monterey Jack cheese (1 pound)
3 to 4 ripe avocados, cut into ¾-inch dice
2 tablespoons lemon juice
1 cup bottled salsa
16 flour tortillas

1. In a small bowl, blend together oil, vinegar, cayenne, cumin, scallions, and cilantro. Transfer ⅓ cup of mixture to a shallow glass dish. Add chicken and turn to coat all over. Cover and refrigerate 8 hours or overnight. Cover and refrigerate remaining marinade.

2. Light a hot fire in a barbecue grill or preheat broiler. Lift chicken breasts from marinade and place on a lightly oiled rack set 4 to 6 inches from heat. Grill or broil, turning once, until white in center but still moist, about 4 to 5 minutes per side. Remove chicken to a cutting board and let stand 5 to 10 minutes. Cut into ¾-inch dice.

3. Place chicken, lettuce, beans, tomatoes, and cheese in separate serving bowls or in separate mounds on a large platter. Gently toss avocados with lemon juice to coat and place in a serving bowl. Combine reserved marinade with salsa and pour into a medium pitcher. Place tortillas in a bread basket. Let guests assemble their own salads.

246 FALAFEL AND CUCUMBER SALAD ON A PITA PLATTER

Prep: 20 minutes   Chill: 1 hour   Cook: 16 to 19 minutes   Serves: 8

Falafel, a Middle Eastern specialty, is a dish of small deep-fried croquettes made of seasoned ground chickpeas. It's often served as an appetizer tucked inside pita bread with cucumbers and yogurt. This main-course salad pairs them with oven-crisped pita bread, a yogurt-glazed, crunchy cucumber salad, and cherry tomatoes.

2 medium cucumbers, peeled, halved lengthwise, seeded, and thinly sliced crosswise
1 teaspoon salt
8 (6-inch) pita breads
1 cup nonfat plain yogurt
¼ cup minced parsley
2 tablespoons minced fresh mint

1 tablespoon olive oil
2 teaspoons white wine vinegar
1 (10-ounce) box falafel mix
  Vegetable oil for frying
8 cups shredded iceberg lettuce
1 pint cherry tomatoes

1. In a medium bowl, toss cucumbers with salt until well blended. Cover and refrigerate 1 hour.

2. Meanwhile, preheat oven to 375°F. Split each pita bread into 2 thin rounds. Arrange in a single layer, rounded sides down, on 2 large baking sheets and bake until crisp, about 10 minutes.

3. Rinse cucumbers under cold running water, drain, and pat dry with paper towels. In a medium bowl, blend together yogurt, parsley, mint, oil, and vinegar. Add cucumbers and toss until well blended.

4. In a large bowl, combine falafel mix with 1½ cups water. Let stand 10 minutes. In a large skillet, heat at least 1 inch of vegetable oil over medium-high heat until hot, about 375°. Using a teaspoon or melon baller, dip into mix to form small balls. Drop into oil and fry in batches until golden brown, about 2 to 3 minutes per batch. Transfer to paper towels to drain.

5. Place 2 pita bread halves, rounded side down and slightly overlapping, on 8 plates, forming a platter. Divide lettuce among them. Top with cucumbers and tomatoes. Sprinkle with falafel balls (about 6 per salad). Serve at once while warm.

247   JAMBALAYA SALAD
Prep: 30 minutes   Cook: 20 to 23 minutes   Serves: 10 to 12

Jambalaya, a hallmark of Creole cooking, is a versatile dish including rice, onions, bell peppers, and a variety of meats. It's a great way to transform leftovers into a stunning, tasty main course.

2 tablespoons olive oil	1 bunch of scallions, thinly sliced
2 medium onions, chopped	
4 cups chicken stock or reduced-sodium canned chicken broth	1½ pounds cooked medium shrimp, shelled and deveined
3 bay leaves	2 cups diced (¾-inch) cooked chicken (about 8 ounces)
2 teaspoons dried thyme	
¼ teaspoon crushed hot red pepper	2 cups diced (¾-inch) cooked ham (about 8 ounces)
2 cups long-grain white rice	1 cup Jambalaya Dressing (recipe follows)
4 medium red bell peppers— 2 cut into ¾-inch dice, 2 sliced into rings	15 to 16 cups shredded iceberg lettuce
2 medium green bell peppers, cut into ¾-inch dice	

1. In a large skillet, heat oil over medium heat until hot. Add onions and cook, stirring occasionally, until softened, about 5 minutes. Add broth, bay leaves, thyme, and hot pepper. Bring to a boil over medium-high heat. Add rice and stir briefly. Reduce heat to low, cover, and cook until liquid is absorbed and rice is just tender, 15 to 18 minutes. Discard bay leaves. Transfer rice to a large bowl and let cool.

2. When rice is room temperature, add diced red and green bell peppers, scallions, shrimp, chicken, ham, and dressing. Toss until well mixed. Arrange lettuce on a large serving platter. Top with jambalaya rice and garnish with red pepper rings.

248   JAMBALAYA DRESSING
Prep: 3 minutes   Cook: none   Makes: about 1 cup

This creamy, spicy dressing is also delicious on hamburgers and in sandwiches.

3 tablespoons white wine vinegar	1 teaspoon black pepper
	⅛ teaspoon cayenne
2 tablespoons Dijon mustard	⅛ teaspoon salt
1 egg (see Note, page 6)	¾ cup mild olive oil

Combine vinegar, mustard, egg, pepper, cayenne, and salt in a food processor or blender. Blend well. With machine on, gradually drizzle in oil. If not using immediately, cover and refrigerate.

249 DILLED AND GRILLED CHICKEN-POTATO PARTY SALAD

Prep: 25 minutes   Cook: 50 to 60 minutes   Chill: 2 hours
Serves: 12 to 16

This substantial salad contains most of the same ingredients as a classic Cobb salad, including bacon, poultry, avocados, and tomatoes. It can be served cold or at room temperature, which makes it ideal for picnics and buffets.

2 (3½-pound) chickens, halved
2 tablespoons vegetable oil
4 pounds medium red potatoes
12 slices of bacon
8 large plum tomatoes, cut into ¾-inch dice
8 scallions, thinly sliced

4 celery ribs, thinly sliced
2 large ripe avocados, cut into ¾-inch dice
4 cups Tofu Ranch Dressing (recipe follows)
Salt and freshly ground pepper
Green leaf lettuce leaves

1. Prepare a medium-hot fire in a barbecue grill. Brush chicken with half of oil and place meaty side down on an oiled rack. Grill until lightly browned on bottom, about 15 minutes. Turn, brush with remaining oil, and continue cooking, turning, until golden brown and cooked through, about 15 to 20 minutes longer. When chickens are cool enough to handle, shred meat and discard skin and bones.

2. In a large pot of boiling water, cook potatoes until tender when pierced with a sharp knife, 20 to 25 minutes. Drain, run under cold water, and drain again. Peel and slice into ¾-inch cubes.

3. Meanwhile, in a large skillet, cook bacon in 2 batches over medium heat, turning until crisp, 7 to 9 minutes per batch. Drain on paper towels. Crumble bacon and reserve.

4. In a large bowl, combine chicken, potatoes, tomatoes, scallions, and celery. Cover and refrigerate at least 2 hours. Just before serving, add bacon, avocados, and dressing and toss until well blended. Season with salt and pepper to taste. Serve chilled or at room temperature.

250   TOFU RANCH DRESSING
Prep: 5 minutes   Cook: none   Chill: 1 hour   Makes: about 4 cups

All the flavor of traditional ranch dressing is here, but with much less fat and with added protein from soybean-based tofu.

3 garlic cloves	½ cup mayonnaise
7 ounces firm tofu	½ cup sour cream
1 cup buttermilk	1 tablespoon dried dill
1 cup nonfat plain yogurt	1½ teaspoons salt

Drop garlic into a food processor or blender to mince. Add remaining ingredients and blend until smooth. Cover and refrigerate at least 1 hour before using.

251   TOSSED ANTIPASTO SALAD
Prep: 30 minutes   Marinate: 8 hours   Cook: none   Serves: 8

Ideal for a buffet or picnic, this colorful, well-balanced salad has almost universal appeal. It mimics the classic Italian hors d'oeuvre antipasto ("before the pasta"), including meats and cheeses, marinated vegetables, and olives. When fresh basil is plentiful, add 1 cup minced basil leaves for added flavor. Savoy cabbage leaves form a stunning bowl for the salad.

¾ cup extra-virgin olive oil	6 cups cauliflower florets
¼ cup red wine vinegar	¾ pound mushrooms, quartered
½ cup parsley, minced	1 medium red onion, thinly sliced and separated into rings
2 garlic cloves, minced	
½ teaspoon salt	
¼ teaspoon black pepper	1 (8¼-ounce) can quartered artichoke hearts, drained
½ pound thinly sliced salami, stacked and cut into ¼-inch slices (about 2 cups)	1 large red bell pepper, cut into thin strips
	1 (8-ounce) jar pepperoncini, drained
½ pound thinly sliced provolone or fontina cheese, stacked and cut into ¼-inch slices (about 2 cups)	½ cup pitted ripe black olives
	½ cup pitted green olives

In a large bowl, whisk together oil, vinegar, parsley, garlic, salt, and pepper. Add salami, cheese, cauliflower, mushrooms, onion, artichoke hearts, bell pepper, pepperoncini, and black and green olives. Toss until well mixed. Cover and marinate in refrigerator at least 8 hours or up to 2 days before serving.

252   CORN AND PEPPER SUMMER SALAD
Prep: 25 minutes   Cook: 7 to 9 minutes   Serves: 8 to 10

1 pound sliced bacon
8 fresh ears of corn, husked
2 pints cherry tomatoes, halved
6 scallions, thinly sliced
2 large red bell peppers, cut into thin strips about 1½ inches long

1 large green bell pepper, cut into thin strips about 1½ inches long
1 cup chopped fresh basil
½ cup extra-virgin olive oil
⅓ cup balsamic vinegar
Salt and freshly ground pepper

1. In 2 large skillets or in 2 batches, cook bacon over medium heat until crisp, 7 to 9 minutes. Drain on paper towels. When cool enough to handle, crumble bacon.

2. Meanwhile, in a large pot of boiling water, cook corn until just barely tender, 2 to 4 minutes. Remove ears and run under cold water to cool. With a large sharp knife, cut kernels off cobs.

3. Place corn kernels in a large bowl. Add tomatoes, scallions, red bell peppers, green bell pepper, basil, and bacon. Drizzle on oil and vinegar and toss until well blended. Season with salt and pepper to taste and serve.

253   PEARS AND PROSCIUTTO ON BITTER GREENS WITH CASHEWS
Prep: 15 minutes   Cook: none   Serves: 8

For a formal version of this casually tossed salad, toss the greens and radicchio with the dressing and divide among plates. Instead of dicing the pears, cut them into thin wedges and arrange in slightly overlapping slices on one side of greens. Leave the prosciutto slices whole and drape them alongside. Sprinkle with onion and nuts. Red Bartlett pears are especially stunning in this salad due to their bright red skin. If you prefer, substitute shredded spinach for the greens and radicchio.

16 cups assorted baby bitter greens
16 paper-thin slices of prosciutto, cut into slivers
4 large ripe pears, cored and cut into ½-inch dice
1 small red onion, thinly sliced and separated into rings

1 cup roasted cashews or macadamia nuts
1½ cups Pear Vinaigrette (recipe follows)

In a large bowl, combine all ingredients. Toss until well blended. Divide among 8 plates and serve at once.

254 PEAR VINAIGRETTE
Prep: 3 minutes   Cook: none   Makes: about 1½ cups

Sweet and highly fragrant, this pear-based dressing complements most salads that contain some amount of fruit. It keeps up to a week refrigerated.

1 small ripe pear, peeled, quartered, and cored
2 tablespoons honey
2 tablespoons Dijon mustard
⅓ cup berry vinegar
1 cup extra-virgin olive oil
Salt and freshly ground pepper

Combine pear, honey, and mustard in a food processor or blender. Blend together. Add vinegar. With machine on, gradually drizzle in oil. Season with salt and pepper to taste. If not using within 2 hours, cover and refrigerate. Let return to room temperature before serving.

255 SEVEN-LAYER POTLUCK SALAD
Prep: 25 minutes   Cook: 7 to 9 minutes   Serves: 12

Easy to make, transport, and serve, this sturdy salad is distinguished by seven brightly colored layers. It's simple, basic, and delicious food. The salad is best made a day ahead, so there's no last-minute fussing.

16 cups shredded iceberg lettuce
3 large red bell peppers, chopped
2 (10-ounce) packages frozen green peas, thawed
2 (3.8-ounce) cans sliced ripe olives, drained
1 large bunch of scallions, thinly sliced
1 cup mayonnaise
1 cup nonfat plain yogurt
1½ tablespoons sugar
5 cups shredded Cheddar cheese (10 ounces)
1 pound sliced bacon

1. In two 9 x 13-inch baking pans, layer lettuce, bell peppers, peas, olives, and scallions. In a small bowl, blend together mayonnaise, yogurt, and sugar. Spread evenly over salad. Sprinkle with cheese. Cover and refrigerate overnight.

2. In 2 large skillets or in 2 batches, cook bacon over medium heat until crisp, 7 to 9 minutes. Drain on paper towels. When cool enough to handle, crumble bacon.

3. To serve, sprinkle bacon on top of salad. Cut into squares, so everyone gets some of each layer.

256 SPINACH SALAD WITH ROSEMARY RANCH DRESSING AND PEPPERY GARLIC CROUTONS

Prep: 25 minutes   Chill: 1 hour   Cook: 7 to 9 minutes
Serves: 9 to 10

Cooling ranch dressing provides pleasant contrast to spicy croutons in this colorful, lightly herbed spinach salad. To keep the dressing lean, you can use low-fat or nonfat mayonnaise.

1 cup mayonnaise
1 cup buttermilk
2 tablespoons fresh rosemary, minced, or 1 tablespoon dried
2 garlic cloves, minced
¼ teaspoon salt
12 slices of bacon
2 bunches of radishes, trimmed and thinly sliced

16 medium mushrooms, thinly sliced (about 12 ounces)
8 cups torn spinach
8 cups torn romaine lettuce
8 hard-cooked eggs, chopped
1 small red onion, thinly sliced and separated into rings
4 cups Peppery Garlic Croutons (recipe follows)
Freshly ground pepper

1. In a medium bowl, whisk together mayonnaise, buttermilk, rosemary, garlic, and salt until well blended. Cover and refrigerate at least 1 hour before serving.

2. Meanwhile, in a large skillet, cook bacon over medium heat until crisp, 7 to 9 minutes. Drain on paper towels. When cool enough to handle, crumble bacon.

3. In a large bowl, combine radishes, mushrooms, spinach, lettuce, eggs, onion, croutons, and bacon. Drizzle on dressing and toss until well mixed. Season with pepper to taste and serve.

257 PEPPERY GARLIC CROUTONS

Prep: 10 minutes   Cook: about 20 minutes   Makes: 4 cups

Cayenne, black pepper, and ground cumin pack a lot of heat into these crunchy, garlicky croutons. If you prefer to bake the croutons, rather than fry them, arrange the bread cubes in a single layer on a baking pan and bake in a preheated 325°F oven until crisp and golden, about 25 minutes.

4 tablespoons butter or ¼ cup olive oil
2 tablespoons minced garlic
¼ teaspoon black pepper
¼ teaspoon cayenne

¼ teaspoon ground cumin
¼ teaspoon dry mustard
4 cups (½-inch) cubes French or Italian bread

In a large skillet, melt butter over medium-low heat. Blend in garlic, pepper, cayenne, cumin, and mustard. Add bread and toss quickly until well blended. Cook, stirring frequently, over low heat until cubes are crisp and golden, about 20 minutes. Transfer to paper towels and let cool. Store in an airtight container up to 3 days.

258 VEGETABLES À LA GRECQUE
Prep: 30 minutes   Cook: 55 minutes   Marinate: 8 hours
Serves: 8 to 10

This marinated vegetable dish can be made a full 3 days ahead and can be served at various temperatures, so it makes an easy salad for a buffet or picnic. To easily peel boiling onions, trim their tips and stem end and blanch them briefly in boiling water. Place them under cold running water and their skins will slip off easily when pinched.

3 cups reduced-sodium chicken broth
1 cup dry white wine
1 cup olive oil
½ cup lemon juice
2 garlic cloves, minced
1 teaspoon salt
½ teaspoon dried thyme
24 small boiling onions, peeled
2 medium zucchini, sliced ½ inch thick (about 1 pound total)
2 medium yellow squash, sliced ½ inch thick (about 1 pound total)

2 cans quartered artichoke hearts, drained
3 medium red bell peppers, cut into 1-inch cubes
24 medium mushrooms (about 18 ounces), stemmed
Salt and freshly ground pepper
Leaf lettuce leaves
2 cups crumbled feta cheese (8 ounces)

1. In a large nonreactive saucepan, combine broth, wine, oil, lemon juice, garlic, salt, and thyme. Bring to a boil over high heat. Reduce heat, cover partially, and simmer 15 minutes.

2. Add onions to saucepan, cover, and cook 20 minutes. With a slotted spoon, remove onions to a large bowl. Add zucchini, yellow squash, and artichokes to liquid and simmer 12 minutes. Remove vegetables to bowl with onions. Add bell peppers and mushrooms to liquid and simmer 8 minutes. Transfer vegetables and cooking liquid to bowl. All vegetables should be at least partly covered with liquid. Cover and marinate refrigerated 8 hours or overnight.

3. Drain vegetables and discard marinade. Season with salt and pepper to taste. Mound on a lettuce-lined platter and sprinkle with cheese. Serve chilled or at room temperature.

259   TOMATO SALAD WITH ARUGULA AND POACHED GARLIC

Prep: 20 minutes   Cook: 15 to 20 minutes   Marinate: 30 minutes
Serves: 8

Perfect for a casual summer party when vine-ripened tomatoes and sun-loving fresh basil are plentiful, this salad makes a special meal with a crusty loaf of bread and a bottle of dry red wine. It's slightly sweet and light, and assertive arugula provides welcome contrast.

1 cup dry vermouth
¾ cup unpeeled garlic cloves
¾ cup extra-virgin olive oil
⅓ cup balsamic vinegar
¼ cup chopped fresh basil
Salt and freshly ground pepper
8 medium vine-ripened tomatoes, thinly sliced
1 small red onion, thinly sliced and separated into rings

2 small heads of Boston lettuce, separated into leaves
8 cups torn arugula
1 (4-ounce) chunk of Parmesan cheese, preferably imported

1. In a small nonreactive saucepan, combine vermouth and garlic. Bring to a boil over medium-high heat. Reduce heat, cover, and simmer until garlic is tender when pierced with a sharp knife, 12 to 15 minutes. Remove garlic and reserve. Bring liquid to a boil and cook until reduced to 2 or 3 tablespoons, 3 to 5 minutes. Transfer to a large dish and let liquid cool at least 5 minutes.

2. Add oil, vinegar, and basil and whisk until well blended. Season with salt and pepper to taste. Add tomatoes and red onion. Toss until well blended and marinate at room temperature 30 to 45 minutes.

3. When cool enough to handle, peel garlic. Arrange lettuce around a large platter or 8 individual plates. Top with arugula and place tomatoes and onion in center. Sprinkle garlic cloves on top. Using a swivel-bladed vegetable peeler, shave Parmesan cheese into thin slices and scatter over each salad. Serve at room temperature.

260   BOW TIES WITH BLUE CHEESE, MIXED GREENS, AND CAPER VINAIGRETTE

Prep: 20 minutes   Cook: 10 minutes   Serves: 8

This tasty pasta salad is a favorite of mine for buffets. It can be made and dressed ahead of time and served casually at room temperature. The fanciful shape of the pasta as well as the bright red, green, and white colors of the ingredients make it look as special as it tastes. If watercress is unavailable, use all shredded spinach.

12 ounces bow-tie pasta (farfalle)	1½ cups crumbled blue cheese (about 6 ounces)
4 large ripe tomatoes, cut into ½-inch dice	1¼ cups Caper Vinaigrette (recipe follows)
2 cups watercress, tough stems removed	¼ cup pine nuts (pignoli), lightly toasted
2 cups shredded spinach	

1. In a large pot of lightly salted boiling water, cook pasta until just tender, about 10 minutes. Drain, run under cold water, and drain again well.

2. In a large bowl, combine pasta, tomatoes, watercress, spinach, blue cheese, vinaigrette, and pine nuts. Toss until well blended. Divide among 8 plates and serve at room temperature or cover and refrigerate up to 24 hours. Let return to room temperature before serving.

261   CAPER VINAIGRETTE

Prep: 5 minutes   Cook: none   Makes: about 1¼ cups

This creamy vinaigrette is a favorite of mine. The piquancy of capers and lemon juice coupled with fragrant extra-virgin olive oil makes it a natural with fish, chicken, pasta, tomatoes, or on a simple mixed green salad.

1 garlic clove	2 tablespoons lemon juice
½ teaspoon salt	1 teaspoon Dijon mustard
¼ teaspoon pepper	¾ cup extra-virgin olive oil
3 tablespoons balsamic vinegar	¼ cup capers, drained

1. Combine garlic, salt, and pepper in a food processor or blender. Mince together. Add vinegar, lemon juice, and mustard. Blend together until smooth.

2. With machine on, gradually drizzle in oil. Stir in capers. If not using immediately, cover and refrigerate. Let return to room temperature before serving.

262   CRANBERRY AND TURKEY STRATA
Prep: 20 minutes   Cook: 3 minutes   Chill: 3 hours   Serves: 8 to 10

Perfect for transforming leftover holiday turkey into a special dish, this double-layer salad is refreshing enough to serve on the hottest summer day. It's composed of two distinct layers: a bright red layer of cranberry sauce and mandarin oranges and a white, crunchy bottom layer of mayonnaise-glazed turkey.

2 (11-ounce) cans mandarin
    oranges, juices reserved
4 (¼-ounce) envelopes
    unflavored gelatin
2 (1-pound) cans whole berry
    cranberry sauce
1 cup chopped pecans

1 cup mayonnaise
1 teaspoon salt
6 cups leftover cooked turkey
    (about 1½ pounds), finely
    chopped
4 celery ribs, finely chopped
⅔ cup minced parsley

1. In a small nonreactive saucepan, combine mandarin orange juice and 2 envelopes gelatin. Let soften 5 minutes. Place over low heat and stir occasionally until dissolved, about 3 minutes. Place orange segments in a medium bowl. Add dissolved gelatin, cranberry sauce, and pecans. Stir, breaking up cranberry sauce gently with a spoon, until well blended. Divide between 2 (2-quart) molds or individual molds and refrigerate until firm, at least 1 hour.

2. In a medium bowl, combine remaining 2 envelopes gelatin and ½ cup cold water. Let soften 5 minutes. Add 1 cup hot water and stir until dissolved. Add mayonnaise and salt and whisk until well blended. Add turkey, celery, and parsley and stir until well blended. Pour carefully over cranberry layer and smooth with back of a spoon until level and solid. Cover and place in coldest part of refrigerator until firm, at least 2 hours, preferably overnight.

3. To unmold, run a knife around inside edge of molds. Dip into a large container of hot water up to rim of molds. After 30 seconds, invert onto a cutting board or 2 plates. With a sharp knife, cut into even slices. Serve cold.

263 SILKEN NOODLE AND GRILLED CHICKEN SALAD

Prep: 25 minutes   Marinate: 30 minutes   Cook: 11 to 14 minutes
Serves: 8 to 10

Crisp raw vegetables and a bed of silky, smooth noodles provide appealing contrasts in texture in this well-balanced salad. Fresh ginger and a generous dose of cayenne leave a warm glow in the mouth. Since it's best served at room temperature, this salad is a delight for parties.

1 cup peanut oil
½ cup dark molasses
½ cup cider vinegar
½ cup lemon juice
¼ cup Dijon mustard
4 garlic cloves, minced
2 tablespoons minced fresh
ginger
¾ teaspoon cayenne
8 skinless, boneless chicken
breast halves (about
5 ounces each)

1 pound angel hair pasta
6 tablespoons Asian sesame
oil
½ pound snow peas, trimmed
and thinly sliced
2 (8-ounce) cans sliced
bamboo shoots, drained
2 medium carrots, peeled and
shredded

1. In a small bowl, whisk together peanut oil, molasses, vinegar, lemon juice, mustard, garlic, ginger, and cayenne. Pour 1 cup of dressing into a shallow glass dish. Add chicken breasts and turn to coat all sides. Cover and marinate for 30 minutes at room temperature or refrigerate overnight. Cover and refrigerate remaining dressing.

2. Light a medium-hot fire in a barbecue grill. In a large pot of lightly salted boiling water, cook pasta until just tender, about 3 to 4 minutes. Drain, run under cold water, and drain again. Transfer to a large bowl and toss with sesame oil. Arrange noodles on a platter.

3. Lift chicken from marinade and place on a lightly oiled grill rack set 4 to 6 inches from coals. Cook, turning once, until white in center but still moist, 4 to 5 minutes on each side. Transfer to a cutting board and let rest 5 to 10 minutes. Cut crosswise into ¼-inch slices.

4. In a large bowl, combine chicken, snow peas, bamboo shoots, and carrots. Drizzle with reserved dressing and toss until well blended. Place on top of noodles and serve warm or at room temperature.

264   TECHNICOLOR TORTILLA TOSS

Prep: 25 minutes   Cook: 10 minutes   Serves: 8 to 12

Brilliant with contrasting colors, this crunchy mélange of beans, vegetables, and tortillas is a feast for the eyes. The dressing is sprightly with lime and hot with serrano peppers. Be sure to serve the salad immediately after tossing it, so that the tortilla strips stay crisp.

Vegetable oil for frying
16 corn tortillas, stacked and
     sliced into 2 x ½-inch
     strips
 1 (15-ounce) can black beans,
     rinsed and drained
 1 (10-ounce) package frozen
     corn, thawed
 1 small jicama, peeled and cut
     into ½-inch dice

 1 medium red bell pepper,
     cut into ½-inch dice
 1 medium green bell pepper,
     cut into ½-inch dice
 2 cups Serrano-Cilantro
     Dressing (recipe follows)
Green leaf lettuce leaves

1. In a large skillet, heat at least 1 inch vegetable oil to 375°F. Separate tortillas strips. Fry in batches until golden and crisp, about 2 minutes per batch. Drain on paper towels.

2. In a large bowl, combine beans, corn, jicama, red bell pepper, green bell pepper, and tortilla strips. Drizzle on dressing and toss until well blended. Divide among 8 to 12 lettuce-lined plates and serve at once.

265   SERRANO-CILANTRO DRESSING

Prep: 15 minutes   Cook: none   Makes: about 2 cups

 1 cup vegetable oil
 ¾ cup fresh lime juice
 ¼ cup minced cilantro
 8 serrano peppers, stemmed
     and minced

 4 garlic cloves, minced
 1 teaspoon salt

In a small bowl, whisk together all ingredients until well blended. If not using within 1 hour, cover and refrigerate. Let return to room temperature before serving.

266 SHELLFISH SALAD
Prep: 25 minutes   Cook: 15 to 18 minutes   Serves: 8

This beautiful salad is a simple, straightforward treatment of five types of shellfish. It can be served as soon as the shellfish is cooked, or the components can be cooked ahead and refrigerated to serve cold. The piquant, creamy dressing is especially attractive placed in the top shell of an oyster, which would otherwise be discarded. If lobster is too pricey, double up on the shrimp or mussels.

1 (1¼-pound) lobster
2 dozen small mussels, preferably cultivated, in the shell
1 pound medium shrimp
Large Boston lettuce leaves
1 pound cooked or canned crabmeat, drained and picked over
8 fresh oysters, shucked
4 hard-cooked eggs, sliced

3 tablespoons caviar (optional)
Lemon wedges
1 cup mayonnaise
¼ cup minced parsley
1 medium shallot, minced
1 tablespoon Dijon mustard
1 tablespoon capers, drained
1 tablespoon chopped dill pickle

1. Bring a large pot of water to a boil over high heat. Add lobster and cover. Reduce heat to medium and boil until bright red in color, about 10 minutes. Lift lobster from pot with tongs and run under cold water. Set in a colander. When lobster is cool enough to handle, remove meat from shells and cut into 1-inch chunks.

2. Meanwhile, prepare mussels. Scrub mussels thoroughly; discard any with open shells that do not close. With a small sharp knife, cut off hairy brown "beards." In a large saucepan or flameproof casserole, bring about 2 inches of water to a boil over medium-high heat. Add mussels, cover, reduce heat to medium, and steam until shells open, 3 to 5 minutes. With a slotted spoon, transfer mussels to a platter. Discard any mussels that do not open.

3. In a large saucepan of boiling water, cook shrimp until pink and loosely curled, 2 to 3 minutes. Drain and run under cold water to cool. Shell and devein shrimp.

4. Divide lettuce among 8 plates. Arrange lobster, mussels, shrimp, crab, and oysters in small bunches on each plate. Garnish with slightly overlapping slices of egg, a spoonful of caviar, and lemon wedges. In a small bowl, blend together mayonnaise, parsley, shallot, mustard, capers, and pickle. Divide among small ramekins or upper shell of shucked oysters. Place alongside salads and serve at once.

267   BOUILLABAISSE SALAD WITH ROUILLE

Prep: 35 minutes   Cook: 20 to 24 minutes   Serves: 8

Bouillabaisse, the famous fish stew from Marseilles, requires a lengthy list of locally caught fish and shellfish, much of it unavailable outside the Mediterranean. For that reason, chefs improvise and make their own signature versions with fish available in their region. For this salad version of the dish, choose the freshest fish available in your area that suits your palate. Serve with plenty of French bread, toasted if you like.

3 **cups dry white wine**
3 **medium shallots, chopped**
3 **garlic cloves, minced**
2 **teaspoons black peppercorns**
1½ **teaspoons dried oregano**
1 **pound small mussels, preferably cultivated, in the shell**
1½ **pounds small sea scallops**
2 **pounds firm-textured white fish, such as halibut, cod, or rockfish, cut into 1-inch cubes**

4 **celery ribs, thinly sliced**
4 **scallions, thinly sliced**
1½ **cups Rouille (recipe follows)**
12 **to 16 cups assorted baby lettuces**
8 **plum tomatoes, cut into wedges**

1. In a large pot, combine wine, shallots, garlic, peppercorns, oregano, and 2 cups water. Bring to a boil, reduce heat to low, and simmer 10 minutes.

2. Meanwhile, scrub mussels thoroughly; discard any with open shells that do not close. With a small sharp knife, cut off hairy brown "beards." Add mussels to wine mixture, cover, and cook just until shells open, about 3 to 5 minutes. With a slotted spoon or skimmer, transfer to a plate. Discard any mussels that do not open.

3. Return broth to a simmer and add scallops. Cover and cook 2 to 4 minutes, or until just opaque throughout but still moist. Transfer scallops to a medium bowl. Return broth to a simmer and add fish. Cover and cook until opaque throughout but still moist, about 5 minutes. Transfer to bowl with scallops. Reserve 6 tablespoons cooking liquid to make Rouille.

4. Drain off any accumulated juices from scallops and fish and blot dry with paper towels. Add celery, scallions, and Rouille and toss until well blended.

5. Scatter lettuces on a platter or 8 individual plates and top with fish. Arrange mussels and tomato wedges around rim of salad and serve at once.

268   ROUILLE
Prep: 5 minutes   Cook: 10 minutes   Makes: 1½ to 2 cups

Traditional rouille, used to stir into bouillabaisse, is a thick sauce made from roasted sweet red peppers and hot peppers. It's garlicky and mildly spicy. This version is thinner, so that it lightly coats the salad ingredients.

6 tablespoons poaching liquid from Bouillabaisse Salad (page 190) or fish broth	2 tablespoons lemon juice
	2 eggs (see Note, page 6)
	1 teaspoon salt
	½ teaspoon black pepper
¼ teaspoon powdered saffron	¼ teaspoon cayenne
1 small red bell pepper	1 cup extra-virgin olive oil

1. Preheat a broiler. Strain poaching liquid through cheesecloth and into a small bowl. While warm, stir in saffron. Set aside and let cool.

2. Cut bell pepper in half lengthwise. Scoop out seeds and cut out stem. Place pepper, skin side up, on a baking sheet and broil as close to heat as possible until skin is charred all over, about 10 minutes. Place pepper in a paper bag and let steam 10 to 15 minutes. Peel off blackened skin.

3. Place bell pepper in a food processor and mince. Add cooled broth, lemon juice, eggs, salt, pepper, and cayenne. With machine on, slowly drizzle in oil. If not using immediately, cover and refrigerate.

269   NEW ORLEANS SHRIMP RÉMOULADE
Prep: 15 minutes   Cook: 2 to 3 minutes   Serves: 8

2 pounds large shrimp, shelled and deveined	8 hard-cooked eggs, chopped
	4 celery ribs, thinly sliced
16 cups assorted baby lettuces	6 scallions, thinly sliced
1½ cups Rémoulade Dressing (recipe follows)	

1. In a large saucepan of simmering water, cook shrimp until pink and loosely curled, 2 to 3 minutes. Drain, run under cold water to cool, and drain again.

2. In a large bowl, combine lettuces and half of dressing. Toss until well blended and divide among 8 plates. In same bowl, combine shrimp, eggs, celery, and scallions. Toss with remaining dressing, divide among lettuce-lined plates, and serve.

270   RÉMOULADE DRESSING
Prep: 5 minutes   Cook: none   Makes: 1½ cups

Spicy, garlicky, and lemony, this colorful dressing is a natural with shrimp. It also goes well with chicken and other fish and shellfish.

8 sprigs of parsley, tough
     stems removed
3 or 4 garlic cloves
6 tablespoons lemon juice
¼ cup Dijon mustard
2 tablespoons prepared white
     horseradish

2 teaspoons Worcestershire
     sauce
2 teaspoons paprika
½ teaspoon cayenne
1 cup olive oil
   Salt and freshly ground
     pepper

1. Place parsley and garlic in a food processor or blender. Mince together. Add lemon juice, mustard, horseradish, Worcestershire, paprika, and cayenne. Blend together.

2. With machine on, slowly drizzle in oil. Season with salt and pepper to taste. If not using immediately, cover and refrigerate.

271   SMOKED SALMON SALAD WITH CAVIAR AND CRÈME FRAÎCHE
Prep: 15 minutes   Cook: none   Serves: 8

This luxurious salad depends upon the quality of its ingredients and how they are handled. Be sure to chop the salmon into tiny chunks with a sharp knife; if it's mashed it becomes pasty, a texture unbecoming to salad. Serve with toast points or a French baguette.

1 pound smoked salmon,
     chopped
1 small red onion, minced
¼ cup capers, drained
1½ tablespoons fresh thyme or
     ¾ teaspoon dried
1 teaspoon freshly ground
     pepper
½ cup rice vinegar

½ cup extra-virgin olive oil
   Salt
12 cups assorted baby lettuces
1 cup Crème Fraîche,
     purchased or homemade
     (recipe follows)
¼ cup caviar, preferably
     sevruga

In a medium bowl, combine salmon, onion, capers, thyme, and pepper. Drizzle on vinegar and oil and toss until well mixed. Season with salt to taste. Divide among 8 lettuce-lined plates. Dollop about 2 tablespoons Crème Fraîche on one side of each plate. Top with caviar and serve at once.

272 CRÈME FRAÎCHE
Makes about 2 cups

1 cup heavy cream
1 cup sour cream

In a 1-pint glass jar, stir together cream and sour cream until well blended. Let stand at room temperature, uncovered, until very thick, about 24 hours. Cover and refrigerate at least 6 hours or up to 10 days before using.

273 SUNBURST SHRIMP AND FRUIT PLATTER, INDONESIAN STYLE
Prep: 30 minutes   Cook: 2 to 3 minutes   Serves: 8 to 10

This dazzling salad will grab the attention of any party. The beautiful arrangement of fruit and plump shrimp coupled with its unusual dressing make a stunning main course. If you like, save the top of pineapple to include in a dramatic presentation. Platters or plates of the salad can be arranged hours ahead of time and refrigerated, but drizzle the dressing over them just before serving.

2 pounds medium shrimp
3 large pink grapefruit
   Green leaf lettuce leaves
3 medium papayas, peeled, seeded, and thinly sliced
2 large Granny Smith apples, thinly sliced
1 small pineapple (about 3½ pounds), peeled, quartered lengthwise, cored, and thinly sliced

1 cup cilantro sprigs—½ cup whole, ½ cup chopped
½ cup fresh lime juice
½ cup firmly packed brown sugar
¼ cup Asian fish sauce
2 tablespoons Asian sesame oil
1 teaspoon crushed hot red pepper

1. In a medium pot of boiling water, cook shrimp until pink and loosely curled, 2 to 3 minutes. Drain, run under cold water, and drain again. When cool enough to handle, shell and devein shrimp.

2. Cut ends off grapefruit and cut away skin and white pith. Cut into segments. Line a large platter with lettuce. Arrange shrimp in center. Arrange grapefruit, papayas, apples, and pineapple around shrimp. Sprinkle whole cilantro sprigs over fruit.

3. In a small bowl, blend together chopped cilantro, lime juice, sugar, fish sauce, sesame oil, and hot pepper. If not using within 1 hour, cover and refrigerate dressing and salad separately. Just before serving, drizzle dressing over shrimp and fruit.

274   PAELLA SALAD

Prep: 30 minutes   Cook: about 19 to 24 minutes   Serves: 8 to 12

This sumptuous feast of saffron-glazed rice studded with lobster, mussels, clams, shrimp, and more is worth every ounce of effort for a special party. It's festive, colorful, and delicious. The salad is named for and modeled after the classic Spanish rice preparation.

2 tablespoons vegetable oil
1 small onion, chopped
2 cups long-grain white rice
4 cups reduced-sodium
    chicken broth
½ teaspoon crumbled saffron
    threads
1 (1¼-pound) lobster
    (optional)
1 pound large shrimp
12 mussels, preferably
    cultivated, in the shell
12 small hard-shelled clams,
    such as cherrystones
2 cups shredded cooked ham
    (about 8 ounces)

2 cups shredded cooked
    chicken or turkey (about
    8 ounces)
1 cup frozen green peas,
    thawed
½ cup minced parsley
4 scallions, thinly sliced
1 medium red bell pepper,
    cut into ¾-inch dice
2 garlic cloves, minced
½ cup extra-virgin olive oil
¼ cup lemon juice
    Salt and freshly ground
    pepper
    Lemon wedges

1. In a large saucepan, heat vegetable oil over medium heat. Add onion and cook, stirring occasionally, until softened, 3 to 5 minutes. Add rice and cook, stirring, 1 minute. Stir in broth and saffron. Bring to a boil over medium-high heat. Reduce heat to low, cover, and cook until rice is tender and all liquid is absorbed, 15 to 18 minutes. When rice is cooked, transfer to a large bowl and let cool at least 10 minutes.

2. Meanwhile, if using lobster, in a large pot of boiling water, cook lobster until bright red in color, about 10 minutes. Drain, run under cold water, and drain again. When cool enough to handle, remove meat from shells and cut into 1-inch chunks. In a medium saucepan of boiling water, cook shrimp until pink and loosely curled, 2 to 3 minutes. Drain, run under cold water, and drain again. Shell and devein shrimp.

3. Scrub mussels and clams thoroughly; discard any with open shells that do not close. With a small sharp knife, cut off hairy brown "beards" of mussels. Bring a large pot with 2 inches of water to a boil. Add mussels and clams, cover, and return to a boil over high heat. Reduce heat to medium and steam until shells open, 4 to 6 minutes. With a slotted spoon, transfer to a bowl. Discard any mussels or clams that do not open.

4. Add lobster, shrimp, ham, chicken, peas, parsley, scallions, bell pepper, and garlic to rice. Drizzle on olive oil and lemon juice and toss until well blended. Season with salt and pepper to taste. Place on a platter or 8 to 12 individual plates and surround with mussels and clams. Serve at once with lemon wedges.

275 SMOKED TROUT-STUFFED ICEBERG LETTUCE

Prep: 15 minutes   Chill: 2 hours   Cook: none   Serves: 8

Crisp iceberg lettuce frames creamy, flavor-packed wedges of smoked trout in this striking salad. Perfect party food, it can be made 2 days ahead for frantic-free entertaining.

- 2 small heads of iceberg lettuce
- 8 ounces cream cheese, at room temperature
- ½ cup sour cream
- 2 cups finely chopped smoked trout (about 10 ounces)
- ½ cup chopped chives
- 6 tablespoons minced fresh dill or 1½ tablespoons dried
- 8 hard-cooked eggs, quartered lengthwise
- 8 small plum tomatoes, quartered lengthwise
- Lemon wedges

1. Core lettuces, then rinse with water. Drain well on paper towels. Hollow out center of lettuce (save center lettuce for use another time), making a large hole to stuff. Be sure to leave a 1- to 1½-inch lettuce shell all around. Refrigerate while making filling.

2. In a medium bowl, blend together cream cheese and sour cream until smooth. Add smoked trout, chives, and dill and mix until well blended. Stuff mixture solidly without gaps or holes into center of lettuce shells, smoothing opening. Wrap in plastic wrap and refrigerate at least 2 hours before serving.

3. Cut each stuffed lettuce into 12 thin wedges and divide among 8 plates, allowing 3 slices per serving. Surround lettuce with alternating slices of eggs and tomatoes. Serve at once with lemon wedges.

276   RIGATONI WITH PESTO AND SHRIMP
Prep: 15 minutes   Cook: 15 to 19 minutes   Serves: 10 to 12

For a lovely, fragrant flourish to this salad, buy extra fresh basil to place a sprig or two among the pasta. If hurried, use 2 cups purchased pesto and eliminate the basil, garlic, pine nuts, olive oil, and Parmesan cheese from the recipe.

1 **cup pine nuts (pignoli)**	1 **cup grated Parmesan cheese**
2 **pounds rigatoni**	8 **medium plum tomatoes, cut**
2 **pounds medium shrimp**	**into ½-inch dice**
2 **cups fresh basil leaves**	**Salt and freshly ground**
3 **garlic cloves**	**pepper**
1 **cup extra-virgin olive oil**	

1. Preheat oven to 350°F. Spread out pine nuts on a baking sheet and toast until fragrant and golden brown, 5 to 7 minutes.

2. In a large pot of lightly salted boiling water, cook rigatoni until just tender, 10 to 12 minutes. At same time, in a large pot of boiling water, cook shrimp until pink and loosely curled, 2 to 3 minutes. Drain pasta and shrimp separately, run under cold water, and drain again well. When shrimp are cool enough to handle, shell and devein them.

3. Place basil, pine nuts, and garlic in a food processor. Mince together. Add olive oil and cheese and process until pesto is well blended and evenly minced.

4. In a large bowl, combine pasta, shrimp, pesto, and tomatoes. Toss until well mixed. Season with salt and pepper to taste. Serve at room temperature or cover and refrigerate at least 2 hours to serve cold.

Chapter 10

Spa Salads

By their nature, salads provide the ideal balance and proportion of food groups in our diet. The bulk of salads are generally greens and vegetables, grains, beans, and pasta —the very foods that nutritionists tell us should compose the bulk of our diets.

The real culprit in adding calories and fat to salads is rarely the salad itself, but most often, the dressing. A fat-laden dressing can destroy the healthfulness of a salad, and overdressing a salad can ruin the inherent taste of its ingredients. Here are some tips to help you produce salads that are truly slimming and healthy.

Choose mild, mellow vinegars, such as balsamic and rice, so that the vinegar's sharpness doesn't need to be tamed by large quantities of calorie-laden oil. Use low-fat liquids, such as defatted chicken broth, fruit juices, buttermilk, evaporated skim milk, and nonfat plain yogurt, to extend and give body to dressings.

Pick low-fat foods that pack a lot of flavor. Garlic, chiles, onions, vinegars, and herbs and spices heighten the flavor of other salad ingredients with few additional calories.

Choose the leanest meats and fish available. Lean fish, including cod, pollock, halibut, and orange roughy, contain less than 5 percent fat and yield about 100 calories per 4-ounce serving. Fatty fish, including salmon, bluefish, and mackerel, contain between 5 and 10 percent fat and yield about 200 calories per 4-ounce serving. Choose canned fish packed in water instead of oil.

Trim off all visible fat from meats and poultry before cooking and remove poultry skin before or after cooking. After cooking oily fish, such as salmon, remove the brown layer of fat underneath its skin before serving.

Use nonstick or well-seasoned cookware to eliminate the need for much cooking oil. When you do cook with oil or butter, be sure it's hot before adding the food. That way the food is more likely to resist absorbing much fat.

Brown or grill foods for fat-free cooking and alluring flavor. If an outdoor grill is not available, use a simple stove-top grill pan. It can be used with a gas or electric stove. Spray baking pans and grill racks with vegetable cooking spray instead of brushing with oil.

277   LOW-FAT CAESAR SALAD

Prep: 20 minutes   Chill: 3 hours   Cook: 12 minutes   Serves: 8

Tart with lemon and pungent with raw garlic, this Caesar delivers much of the flavor of the traditional salad without all the calories and fat. Buttermilk and yogurt make the dressing creamy, and croutons made of unadorned bread crisped in an oven carry on the low-fat treatment. If you like, garnish the salad with lemon wedges and extra anchovy fillets.

4 anchovy fillets, drained
3 garlic cloves, smashed
1 small shallot, quartered
½ cup nonfat plain yogurt
½ cup buttermilk
¼ cup lemon juice
1 teaspoon Worcestershire
   sauce

6 cups cubes (¾-inch) French
   or Italian bread
16 cups torn romaine lettuce
½ cup grated Parmesan cheese
   Salt and freshly ground
   pepper

1. In a food processor or blender, combine anchovy fillets, garlic, and shallot. Mince together. Add yogurt, buttermilk, lemon juice, and Worcestershire sauce. Blend until smooth. Cover dressing and refrigerate until cold and slightly thickened, about 3 hours.

2. Preheat oven to 375°F. Arrange bread cubes in a single layer on a baking sheet. Bake until lightly golden and crisp, about 12 minutes.

3. In a large bowl, combine lettuce, cheese, croutons, and dressing. Toss until well mixed. Season with salt and pepper to taste. Divide among 8 plates and serve at once.

278   SOUTH-OF-THE-BORDER BARLEY AND SUCCOTASH SALAD

Prep: 20 minutes   Cook: 35 to 40 minutes   Serves: 4 to 5

3 cups canned
   reduced-sodium chicken
   broth
1 cup pearl barley
1 (10-ounce) package frozen
   baby lima beans
½ cup tomato juice
¼ cup fresh lime juice
2 tablespoons chopped
   cilantro
1 teaspoon ground cumin

1 teaspoon chili powder
1 (10-ounce) package frozen
   corn, thawed
1 cup diced (½-inch) 95
   percent fat-free ham
   (about 4 ounces)
4 plum tomatoes, cut into
   ½-inch dice
   Salt and freshly ground
   pepper
   Lime wedges

1. In a medium saucepan, bring broth to a boil over medium-high heat. Add barley and stir briefly. Reduce heat to low, cover, and cook until tender, 35 to 40 minutes.

2. Meanwhile, in a medium saucepan of boiling water, cook lima beans until just tender, about 5 minutes. Drain, run under cold water, and drain again. When barley is cooked, drain, run under cold water, and drain again well.

3. In a large bowl, blend together tomato juice, lime juice, cilantro, cumin, and chili powder. Add barley, lima beans, corn, ham, and tomatoes. Toss until well mixed. Season with salt and pepper to taste. Serve at room temperature with lime wedges.

---

279 RAMEN NOODLE AND VEGETABLE SALAD

Prep: 20 minutes   Cook: 5 to 7 minutes   Serves: 2

Slightly sweet and slightly hot, this nutritious salad is a delicious combination of contrasting textures and colors. Black sesame seeds, available in Asian groceries, lend an intriguing look and crunchiness.

1 (3-ounce) package ramen noodles, seasoning packet reserved for another use
1 cup snow peas, trimmed (about 2 ounces)
1 medium carrot, peeled and cut into matchstick strips
2 tablespoons soy sauce
2 tablespoons rice vinegar
4 teaspoons sugar

1 teaspoon Asian sesame oil
¼ teaspoon hot chili oil or crushed hot red pepper
2 cups shredded Chinese (Napa) cabbage
2 scallions, thinly sliced
1 cup cooked shelled deveined bay (tiny) shrimp (4 to 5 ounces)
½ teaspoon black sesame seeds (optional)

1. In a medium pot of lightly salted boiling water, cook noodles until just tender, about 2 to 3 minutes. As noodles cook, separate strands with 2 forks. Drain, run under cold water, and drain again.

2. In a small pot of boiling water, cook snow peas until crisp-tender, about 1 minute. With a slotted spatula, remove peas to a colander. Drain, run under cold water until cool, and drain again. Add carrot to same boiling water and cook until crisp-tender, 2 to 3 minutes. Drain, run under cold water until cool, and drain again.

3. In a large bowl, whisk together soy sauce, vinegar, sugar, sesame oil, and hot oil until sugar dissolves. Add noodles, snow peas, carrot, cabbage, scallions, and shrimp. Toss until well mixed and divide between 2 plates. Sprinkle sesame seeds on top and serve.

280   MIXED FRUITS AND GREENS WITH BANANA-PINEAPPLE CREAM

Prep: 25 minutes   Cook: none   Serves: 8

Colorful fruits and greens, punctuated with a strong cheese and an aromatic dressing, make a flavorful, low-fat meal. Serve with a loaf of crusty bread.

8   cups torn red leaf lettuce
6   cups torn watercress or
    arugula
½   cup crumbled blue or feta
    cheese
8   kiwi, peeled, quartered
    lengthwise, and thinly
    sliced
4   pears, preferably Red
    Bartlett, quartered, cored,
    and thinly sliced

2   bananas, thinly sliced
1   small red onion, thinly
    sliced and separated into
    rings
1¼ cups Banana-Pineapple
    Cream (recipe follows)

In a large bowl, combine all ingredients and toss until well mixed. Divide among 8 plates and serve at once.

281   BANANA-PINEAPPLE CREAM

Prep: 5 minutes   Cook: none   Makes: 1¼ cups

This tropical-tasting dressing gets its body from pureed banana—a healthy alternative to oil-laden dressings. This one is pleasantly sweet, subtly spiced, and keeps well refrigerated. It pairs nicely with ham, chicken, and most salads that contain some fruit.

1   ripe banana
⅓   cup unsweetened pineapple
    juice
1   garlic clove, crushed
2   tablespoons lemon juice

1   tablespoon sugar
½   teaspoon salt
½   teaspoon paprika
¼   teaspoon grated nutmeg
2   tablespoons vegetable oil

In a food processor or blender, combine banana, pineapple juice, garlic, lemon juice, sugar, salt, paprika, and nutmeg. Blend together. With machine on, slowly drizzle in oil. If not using within 1 hour, cover and refrigerate. Let return to room temperature before using.

282   LASAGNE ROLLS FLORENTINE
Prep: 20 minutes   Cook: 10 minutes   Chill: 1 hour   Serves: 4

Spiral circles of spinach-stuffed lasagne not only make an unusual salad that is low in calories, but also one so striking that it makes a lovely party dish. For a special occasion, each circle of lasagne can be tied with a blanched scallion.

- 4 lasagne noodles
- 1 (10-ounce) package frozen chopped spinach, thawed and squeezed dry
- ¼ cup grated Parmesan cheese
- 2 hard-cooked eggs, finely chopped
- 1 large shallot, minced

- 1 garlic clove, minced
- ½ cup Basic Spa Vinaigrette (recipe follows)
- Salt and freshly ground pepper
- 6 cups shredded fresh spinach leaves

1. In a large pot of lightly salted boiling water, cook lasagne noodles until just tender, about 10 minutes. Drain, run under cold water, and drain again. Arrange noodles on a flat surface.

2. In a medium bowl, blend together chopped spinach, cheese, eggs, shallot, garlic, and ¼ cup vinaigrette. Season with salt and pepper to taste. Spread mixture evenly over noodles, leaving a 1-inch margin at one end of each noodle. Starting with filled ends, roll up each noodle tightly. Place seam side down on a platter. Cover and refrigerate at least 1 hour.

3. Divide shredded spinach among 4 plates. With a sharp knife, slice each lasagne roll into 3 equal circles. Divide among plates and drizzle remaining vinaigrette over lasagne rolls. Serve chilled or at room temperature.

283   BASIC SPA VINAIGRETTE
Prep: 3 minutes   Cook: none   Makes: about ½ cup

- ¼ cup balsamic vinegar
- ¼ cup fat-free chicken broth
- 1 teaspoon Dijon mustard
- 1 tablespoon plus 1 teaspoon extra-virgin olive oil

- Salt and freshly ground pepper

In a medium bowl, combine vinegar, broth, and mustard. Slowly whisk in oil. Season with salt and pepper to taste. If not using within 2 hours, cover and refrigerate. Let return to room temperature before using.

284   PEAR, BLUE CHEESE, AND KUMQUAT SALAD

Prep: 25 minutes   Cook: none   Serves: 8

Kumquats, totally edible except for their seeds, are too often neglected. They deliver sweet and tart tang to salads, and they're delicious eaten out of hand.

½ cup buttermilk
½ cup nonfat plain yogurt
3 garlic cloves, crushed
    through a press
⅛ teaspoon cayenne
½ cup crumbled blue cheese
24 kumquats, thinly sliced and seeded

8 scallions, thinly sliced
4 large pears, cored and cut into ¾-inch dice
1 large cucumber, quartered lengthwise, seeded, and thinly sliced crosswise
16 cups torn red leaf lettuce

In a large bowl, whisk together buttermilk, yogurt, garlic, and cayenne until smooth. Blend in blue cheese. Add kumquats, scallions, pears, and cucumber. Toss until well mixed. Divide among 8 lettuce-lined plates and serve at once.

285   SEVICHE

Prep: 25 minutes   Cook: none   Marinate: 4 hours
Chill: 1 hour   Serves: 8

Seviche is a Latin American dish of raw fish that is "cured" by marinating in lime juice. The juice firms the fish and turns it opaque, just as it would be if it were cooked with heat. Use very fresh fish for seviche, and vary it seasonally by what is fresh and abundant.

1 pound bay scallops
1 pound firm white fish, such as halibut or red snapper, cut into ¾-inch cubes
¾ cup fresh lime juice
¾ cup rice vinegar
3 garlic cloves, minced
2 medium red bell peppers, cut into ¾-inch dice

2 medium mangoes, peeled, pitted, and cut into ¾-inch dice
1 small red onion, chopped
    Salt and freshly ground pepper
    Green leaf lettuce
⅓ cup coarsely chopped cilantro

1. In a large bowl, combine scallops, fish, lime juice, vinegar, and garlic. Toss until well blended. Cover and refrigerate 4 hours or overnight, stirring occasionally.

2. About 1 hour before serving, add bell peppers, mangoes, and onion to fish. Toss gently to mix. Cover and refrigerate again until cold.

3. When ready to serve, season with salt and pepper to taste. Divide among 8 lettuce-lined plates. Sprinkle cilantro on top and serve.

286 BASMATI RICE AND CRAB SALAD WITH SPA RUSSIAN DRESSING

Prep: 15 minutes   Cook: 10 minutes   Serves: 4 to 5

Bright, contrasting colors and delicate flavors make this salad memorable. Aromatic basmati rice and rich crab need little adornment, so that their inherent flavors shine through. Reduced-fat Russian dressing coats and complements the ingredients without overwhelming them.

1 cup basmati rice
1 (10-ounce) package frozen green peas, thawed
1½ cups cooked fresh or canned crabmeat, drained and picked over

1 large red bell pepper, cut into ½-inch dice
¾ cup Spa Russian Dressing (recipe follows)
Salt and freshly ground pepper

1. In a medium saucepan, bring 2 cups lightly salted water to a boil. Add rice and stir briefly. Reduce heat to low, cover, and cook until just tender, about 10 minutes. Drain, run under cold water, and drain again well. Transfer to a large bowl and let cool about 10 minutes.

2. Add green peas, crab, bell pepper, and dressing. Toss until well mixed. Season with salt and pepper to taste. Serve at once or chilled.

287 SPA RUSSIAN DRESSING

Prep: 5 minutes   Chill: 1 hour   Cook: none   Makes: about ¾ cup

Creamy and mild, this low-fat dressing is also delicious on coleslaw and chef's salads. With the addition of minced dill pickle, it also makes a healthy alternative to tartar sauce.

½ cup buttermilk
3 tablespoons fat-free sour cream
1 tablespoon tomato paste
1 garlic clove, minced

1 teaspoon Dijon mustard
½ teaspoon Worcestershire sauce
¼ teaspoon sugar

In a small bowl, whisk together all ingredients until well blended. Cover and refrigerate at least 1 hour before serving.

288 TUNISIAN GRILLED VEGETABLE SALAD WITH TUNA

Prep: 10 minutes   Cook: 7 to 10 minutes   Serves: 2

Tunisians are justly famous for their grilled salads, which convey a roasted flavor, even when chilled. This salad is traditionally chopped fine and spread on bread or eaten as a condiment for meats and fish. Here, the vegetables are chopped, and canned tuna is added to make a simple, flavor-packed, one-dish meal. Serve with a thinly sliced French baguette.

6 New Mexican or Anaheim peppers, halved lengthwise and seeded
1 medium red bell pepper, halved lengthwise and seeded
3 plum tomatoes, halved lengthwise

6 garlic cloves
1 (6½-ounce) can solid white tuna, drained and flaked
2 tablespoons capers, drained
1 tablespoon lemon juice
2 teaspoons olive oil
½ teaspoon ground cumin

1. Light a hot fire in a barbecue grill or preheat broiler. Place New Mexican peppers, bell pepper, and tomatoes cut sides down on a lightly oiled rack as close to heat as possible. Grill or broil until skin is charred, 7 to 10 minutes.

2. At same time, place garlic cloves in a small grilling basket or wrap in foil. Place on grill alongside peppers and cook, turning frequently. As vegetables and garlic blacken, transfer them to a paper bag and let steam 10 to 15 minutes. Peel off blackened skin from peppers, tomatoes, and garlic. Cut vegetables into bite-size pieces.

3. In a medium bowl, combine roasted vegetables with tuna, capers, lemon juice, oil, and cumin. Toss gently until well mixed. Serve at room temperature.

289 WHITE AND JADE SESAME SHRIMP SALAD

*Prep: 15 minutes   Cook: 5 minutes   Marinate: 30 minutes
Serves: 6*

3 tablespoons soy sauce
3 tablespoons rice vinegar
2½ tablespoons honey
1½ tablespoons Asian sesame oil
¼ teaspoon hot chili oil or crushed hot red pepper
8 cups broccoli florets (about 1 large head)

8 cups cauliflower florets (about 1 large head)
1 large red bell pepper, thinly sliced
1 pound cooked shelled and deveined bay (tiny) shrimp
2 teaspoons sesame seeds

1. In a large bowl, whisk together soy sauce, vinegar, honey, sesame oil, and chili oil until honey dissolves.

2. In a large pot, bring 1 inch of water to a boil over high heat. Add broccoli and cauliflower and cover. Reduce heat to medium and steam until crisp-tender, about 5 minutes. Drain, run under cold water, and drain again, pressing on broccoli to remove water. Add to dressing and toss until well mixed. Marinate at room temperature at least 30 minutes or cover and refrigerate 2 hours, stirring occasionally.

3. When ready to serve, add bell pepper and shrimp to vegetables. Toss again to mix. Divide among 6 plates and sprinkle with sesame seeds. Serve at once.

---

290 CHICKEN SALAD WITH GREEN PEPPERCORNS AND STRAWBERRY VINAIGRETTE
Prep: 15 minutes   Cook: 12 to 14 minutes   Serves: 4

Peppery with watercress and green peppercorns, this beautiful salad suffers no loss of flavor despite its lack of calories. Strawberries make up the bulk of the dressing, eliminating the need for much oil and lending the salad a pink, shiny tinge. Sliced star fruit provides a dramatic, edible garnish.

2 chicken breast halves on the bone (about 1 pound)
1 (14½-ounce) can reduced-sodium chicken broth
1 cup trimmed and quartered strawberries plus 12 whole berries for garnish
1 garlic clove, smashed
2½ tablespoons balsamic vinegar
1 tablespoon olive oil
1 teaspoon green peppercorns in brine, drained
Salt and freshly ground pepper
6 cups torn Boston lettuce
2 cups watercress, tough stems removed
1 star fruit (carambola), thinly sliced crosswise

1. In a medium saucepan, place chicken breasts skin side down with chicken broth. Bring to a simmer over medium-high heat. Reduce heat to low, cover, and cook until chicken is white in center but still moist, 12 to 14 minutes. Let cool in broth. When cool enough to handle, pull meat off bones and shred. Discard skin and bones; reserve broth for another use.

2. Combine quartered strawberries and garlic in a blender or small food processor. Mince together. Add vinegar. With machine on, slowly drizzle in oil. Stir in green peppercorns and season with salt and pepper to taste.

3. Divide lettuce and watercress among 4 plates. In a medium bowl, combine chicken and dressing and toss until well blended. Divide among lettuce-lined plates. Arrange star fruit and whole strawberries around chicken. Serve at room temperature.

291 BAYOU CRAWFISH COLESLAW
Prep: 20 minutes   Cook: 3 minutes   Serves: 2

Fresh and frozen crawfish are becoming more readily available through-out the country, but if you can't find them, use 6 to 8 ounces of cooked shelled and deveined shrimp. This colorful coleslaw is hot and sweet, with practically no fat.

6 **to 8 ounces peeled crawfish tails**	1 **cup peeled and shredded carrots**
¼ **cup seasoned rice vinegar**	1 **cup shredded green bell pepper**
¼ **cup 2 percent milk**	1 **cup shredded red bell pepper**
¼ **cup firmly packed brown sugar**	**Salt and freshly ground pepper**
¼ **to ½ teaspoon Tabasco sauce**	
4 **cups finely shredded cabbage**	

1. In a medium pot of lightly salted boiling water, cook crawfish until they are loosely curled and opaque, about 3 minutes. Do not overcook. Drain, run under cold water, and drain again. If not using at once, cover and refrigerate.

2. In a large bowl, whisk together vinegar, milk, sugar, and Tabasco sauce until sugar dissolves. Add cabbage, carrots, green bell pepper, and red bell pepper. Toss until well mixed. Season with salt and pepper to taste. If not using immediately, cover and refrigerate up to 4 hours. Serve coleslaw topped with crawfish.

292 SMOKED SALMON, GREEN BEAN, AND PICKLED ONION SALAD
Prep: 15 minutes   Marinate: 1 hour   Cook: 4 to 5 minutes
Serves: 4 or 5

1 **tablespoon sugar**	**Red leaf lettuce leaves**
1 **tablespoon salt**	6 **to 8 ounces smoked salmon, chopped**
½ **cup boiling water**	4 **teaspoons green peppercorns in brine, drained**
1 **medium sweet onion, such as Vidalia, Walla Walla, Texas, or Maui**	
1 **cup cider vinegar**	
1 **pound green beans, trimmed and cut into 1-inch lengths**	

1. In a large glass bowl, combine sugar, salt, and boiling water. Stir until sugar and salt dissolve. Thinly slice onion, separate into rings, and add to water. Stir in ½ cup cold water and distribute onion so that all rings are covered. Marinate at room temperature 30 minutes. Drain onion and return to bowl. Pour vinegar over onion, cover, and marinate 30 minutes longer. Drain, run under cold water, and drain again.

2. In a large pot of lightly salted boiling water, cook beans until crisp-tender, 4 to 5 minutes, depending upon their size and age. Drain, run under cold water, and drain again.

3. Line 4 or 5 plates with lettuce leaves. Divide beans among plates. Top with pickled onion rings and scatter salmon and peppercorns on top. Serve at once or chilled.

293 SWORDFISH ON WARM LENTIL SALAD

Prep: 15 minutes   Cook: 27 to 30 minutes   Chill: 2 hours
Serves: 2

Hearty and substantial, this salad is a gorgeous grouping of meaty white swordfish on a bed of brown lentils atop bright greens. Swordfish is so firm and dense that it's steaklike in texture, making it a satisfying alternative to red meat.

½ pound swordfish cut 1 inch
    thick, halved
½ cup lentils, rinsed and
    picked over
1 small red bell pepper, cut
    into ½-inch dice
2 scallions, thinly sliced
1 teaspoon Asian sesame oil

Salt and freshly ground
    pepper
1 small bunch of arugula or
    6 leaves green leaf lettuce
1 tablespoon balsamic
    vinegar
2 teaspoons soy sauce

1. In a medium skillet, bring 2 cups lightly salted water to a boil over medium heat. Reduce heat to low and place swordfish in water. Simmer, uncovered, 5 minutes. With a slotted spatula, carefully turn swordfish over and cook 4 to 5 minutes, or until opaque throughout. Remove fish with slotted spatula and place on a platter. Blot excess water with a paper towel. Cover and refrigerate until cold, about 2 hours.

2. Meanwhile, in a medium saucepan, bring 1½ cups lightly salted water to a boil. Stir in lentils. Cover and simmer until tender but not mushy, about 18 to 20 minutes. Drain well. While warm, place lentils in a medium bowl. Add bell pepper, scallions, and sesame oil. Toss to mix well. Season with salt and pepper to taste. Line 2 plates with arugula or lettuce. Top with lentil salad. Set swordfish on lentils. Drizzle vinegar and soy sauce over fish and serve.

294   FALL POTATO AND HAM SALAD WITH BUTTERMILK-MUSTARD DRESSING

Prep: 25 minutes   Cook: 5 to 7 minutes   Serves: 4

The tang of mustard and creaminess of buttermilk belie the slimming qualities of this filling salad. The dressing, complete with only 2 ingredients, yields about 10 calories per tablespoon, so use it freely wherever its flavor complements a dish.

1 **pound red potatoes, peeled and cut into ½-inch dice**
½ **cup buttermilk**
¼ **cup Dijon mustard**
6 **cups torn curly endive**
1 **large red-skinned apple, cored and cut into ¾-inch dice**

¼ **pound slivered 95 percent fat-free ham (about 1 cup)**
4 **scallions, thinly sliced**
   Salt and freshly ground pepper

1. In a large pot of boiling water, cook potatoes until just tender, 5 to 7 minutes. Drain, run under cold water, and drain again.

2. In a large bowl, whisk together buttermilk and mustard until smooth. Add potatoes, endive, apple, ham, and scallions. Toss until well mixed. Season with salt and pepper to taste.

295   KUMQUAT MAY CHICKEN SALAD

Prep: 25 minutes   Cook: 13 to 16 minutes   Serves: 4

Soy sauce, Asian sesame oil, fresh mint, and ginger provide plenty of flavor for this delicious salad with little fat. Tart orange kumquats and bright green snow peas make it a feast for the eyes.

2 **chicken breast halves on the bone (about 1 pound)**
1 **(14½-ounce) can reduced-sodium chicken broth**
½ **pound fresh snow peas, trimmed**
12 **kumquats, finely chopped and seeded**
2 **tablespoons finely chopped fresh mint**

1 **tablespoon soy sauce**
2 **teaspoons Asian sesame oil**
1 **(1-inch) piece of fresh ginger, peeled and minced**
2 **garlic cloves, minced**
1 **(7-ounce) can sliced water chestnuts, drained**
8 **cups shredded iceberg lettuce**

1. In a medium nonreactive saucepan, place chicken breasts skin side down with chicken broth. Bring to a boil over medium-high heat. Reduce heat to low, cover, and cook until chicken is white in center but still moist, 12 to 14 minutes. Let cool in broth. When cool enough to handle, pull meat off bones and shred. Discard skin and bones.

2. In a medium saucepan of boiling water, cook snow peas until crisp-tender, about 1 to 2 minutes. Drain, run under cold water, and drain again.

3. In a large bowl, combine kumquats, mint, soy sauce, sesame oil, ginger, and garlic. Add chicken, snow peas, and water chestnuts and toss to mix. Divide lettuce among plates. Mound chicken salad on top and serve.

---

296 PORK TENDERLOIN SALAD WITH PINEAPPLE SALSA

Prep: 25 minutes   Cook: 15 to 20 minutes   Serves: 8

Pineapple, strawberries, and kiwi combined with jalapeño peppers make a pale pink, tart-sweet salsa that's a perfect accompaniment for pork tenderloin.

1 pork tenderloin (about 12 ounces)	8 kiwi—4 peeled and quartered, 4 peeled and thinly sliced lengthwise
½ teaspoon salt	½ cup fresh mint
½ teaspoon black pepper	2 jalapeño peppers, seeded
1 medium pineapple (about 3½ pounds)	4 teaspoons Dijon mustard
2 pints strawberries	Red leaf lettuce leaves

1. Prepare a hot fire in a barbecue grill. Trim fat and silver membrane off pork and rub with salt and pepper. Cook pork on an oiled rack set 4 to 6 inches from heat, turning occasionally, until just cooked through with no trace of pink in center, about 15 to 20 minutes. Meat should register 160 to 165°F on an instant-reading thermometer. Let meat stand while making salsa.

2. Using a sharp knife, remove top and bottom of pineapple. Cut 3 crosswise slices each ¾ inch thick from center of pineapple, leaving skin intact. Cut each slice into 6 wedges and remove core from each. Remove skin and eyes from remaining pineapple. Chop enough pineapple to equal 2 cups.

3. Quarter 1 pint of strawberries; leave remainder whole. Combine chopped pineapple, quartered strawberries, quartered kiwi, mint, jalapeño peppers, and mustard in a food processor or blender. Mince finely.

4. Line 8 plates with lettuce. Slice pork thinly and divide among plates, arranging in slightly overlapping slices. Spoon salsa over pork. Arrange pineapple wedges and kiwi slices alongside pork. Garnish salads with whole strawberries. Serve at once.

297   EGGPLANT SALAD PROVENÇAL

Prep: 25 minutes   Stand: 45 minutes
Cook: 5 minutes   Serves: 2 to 3

Packed with the robust flavors of Provence, this brilliantly colored salad invites tasting. It can be served warm, at room temperature, or cold, making it convenient party fare for a buffet or picnic. For an even more substantial main course, add ¼ to ½ cup crumbled feta cheese.

1   medium eggplant (about 1 pound), peeled and cut into ¾-inch cubes
1½   teaspoons salt
1½   tablespoons vegetable oil
2   cups sliced mushrooms (about 6 medium)
3   garlic cloves, minced
4   plum tomatoes, cut into ¾-inch dice

4   scallions, thinly sliced
⅓   cup pitted kalamata or other oil-cured black olives
¼   cup minced fresh basil
2   tablespoons capers, drained
1½   tablespoons extra-virgin olive oil
2   teaspoons lemon juice
     Salt and freshly ground pepper

1. Place eggplant in a colander and sprinkle with salt. Toss until well blended. Let stand about 45 minutes to drain off any bitter liquid. Rinse eggplant under cold water, drain, and pat dry.

2. In a large nonstick skillet, heat vegetable oil over medium heat until hot. Add eggplant, mushrooms, and garlic. Cook, stirring occasionally, until vegetables soften, about 5 minutes. Remove vegetables to a large bowl and let cool briefly, about 5 minutes.

3. Add tomatoes, scallions, olives, basil, and capers. Drizzle with olive oil and lemon juice and toss until well blended. Season with salt and pepper to taste. Serve warm, at room temperature, or chilled.

298   HONEYDEW, HAM, AND JICAMA SALAD

Prep: 25 minutes   Cook: none   Serves: 8 to 12

Gently gingered, this amply dressed salad combines sweet and savory components with little fat and few calories.

1¾   cups nonfat plain yogurt
2   tablespoons Dijon mustard
1   tablespoon finely minced fresh ginger
1   large honeydew melon, cut into ¾-inch dice (about 12 cups)

4   cups diced (¾-inch) peeled jicama
4   cups seedless red grapes
3   cups shredded radicchio or red cabbage
½   pound 95 percent fat-free ham, cut into ¾-inch dice

In a large bowl, whisk together yogurt, mustard, and ginger until well blended. Add honeydew, jicama, grapes, radicchio, and ham. Toss until well mixed. Serve at room temperature.

299 RED LENTIL, PINEAPPLE, AND CHICKEN SALAD WITH RAITA DRESSING

Prep: 20 minutes   Cook: 1 to 1¼ hours   Serves: 6

Red lentils, which do not contain the seed coat of the more common brown lentil, give this well-balanced, nutritious salad an intriguing look, and are very quick-cooking.

1 (3½- to 4-pound) whole chicken
2½ cups reduced-sodium chicken broth
1 cup red lentils, rinsed and picked over
2 teaspoons lemon juice
1½ cups diced fresh pineapple or unsweetened canned chunks

4 scallions, thinly sliced
1 medium cucumber, quartered lengthwise and thinly sliced crosswise
1½ cups Raita Dressing (recipe follows)
Salt and freshly ground pepper

1. Preheat oven to 375°F. Rinse chicken inside and out and pat dry. Set in a baking dish and roast for 1 to 1¼ hours, or until thigh juices run clear when pierced with a sharp knife. When cool enough to handle, pull meat off bones and shred; discard skin and bones.

2. Meanwhile, in a medium saucepan, combine broth, lentils, and lemon juice. Bring to a boil over medium-high heat. Reduce heat to low, cover, and cook until lentils are just tender but not mushy, about 8 minutes. Drain, run under cold water, and drain again.

3. In a large bowl, combine chicken, lentils, pineapple, scallions, cucumber, and dressing. Toss until well mixed. Season with salt and pepper to taste. Serve warm or chilled.

300 RAITA DRESSING

Prep: 10 minutes   Cook: none   Makes: about 1½ cups

Raita is a refreshing Indian yogurt-based condiment used to tame hot curries. It often contains spices, vegetables, or fruit.

⅔ cup nonfat plain yogurt
⅓ cup fat-free sour cream
½ cup seeded, peeled, and shredded cucumber
1¼ teaspoons sugar

1 teaspoon salt
¼ teaspoon curry powder
¼ teaspoon turmeric
⅛ teaspoon ground cumin

In a small bowl, stir together all ingredients until well blended. If not using immediately, cover and refrigerate.

301   HAM SALAD WITH WATERCRESS AND BEETS

Prep: 15 minutes   Cook: none   Serves: 8

This fast-to-fix, one-bowl salad is packed with pepperiness from watercress and horseradish. Buying prepackaged, thin-sliced ham makes it easy to slice the stacks thinly to mimic the julienne cut of canned beets. For festive occasions, serve the ham mixture pouring out of large radicchio leaves or with spokes of Belgian endive spears around each plate. If you like, add 4 quartered hard-cooked eggs for a substantive garnish.

1½ cups nonfat plain yogurt
2 tablespoons prepared white horseradish
1 tablespoon sugar
3 (15-ounce) cans julienne-cut beets, drained

1 pound cooked 95 percent fat-free ham, cut into matchstick strips
2 scallions, thinly sliced
12 cups watercress, tough stems removed

1. In a large bowl, whisk together yogurt, horseradish, and sugar until smooth. Add beets, ham, and scallions. Toss until well mixed.

2. Make a bed of watercress on a platter or on 8 individual plates. Mound salad on watercress and serve.

302   COOL THAI CHICKEN-NOODLE SALAD

Prep: 25 minutes   Cook: 14 to 17 minutes   Serves: 6

This refreshing, nutritious salad delivers a clean, light taste. Unlike many Thai dishes, it contains no heat at all. Its lovely blend of colorful vegetables combined with a sweet-and-savory dressing makes it a favorite, especially for summertime. Even dressed, the salad can stay in the refrigerator for hours, so it's a good choice for easy entertaining.

3 chicken breast halves (about 1½ pounds)
1 (14½-ounce) can reduced-sodium chicken broth
6 ounces bean thread or cellophane noodles
½ cup rice vinegar
⅓ cup Asian fish sauce
2 tablespoons sugar

3 garlic cloves, minced
6 cups shredded Chinese (Napa) cabbage
4 scallions, thinly sliced
3 medium carrots, peeled and shredded
1 medium cucumber, peeled, seeded, and shredded
⅓ cup fresh mint leaves

1. In a medium saucepan that will just hold chicken in a single layer, place breasts skin side down with chicken broth. Bring to a simmer over medium-high heat, reduce heat to low, cover, and cook until chicken is white in center but still moist, 12 to 14 minutes. Let cool in broth. When cool enough to handle, pull meat off bones and shred. Discard skin and bones; reserve broth for another use.

2. Bring a large pot of water to a boil. Drop noodles into water and stir briefly to separate strands. Remove from heat and let stand until softened, 15 to 20 minutes. Drain well.

3. In a large bowl, blend together vinegar, fish sauce, sugar, and garlic until sugar dissolves. Add chicken, noodles, cabbage, scallions, carrots, and cucumber. Toss until well mixed. Mound on a platter or divide among 6 plates. Scatter mint on top. Serve at room temperature or slightly chilled.

---

303 DRUNKEN FRUIT WITH GRILLED PORK TENDERLOIN

Prep: 20 minutes   Cook: 25 to 30 minutes   Chill: 4 hours
Serves: 8

Port, intensely flavored dried fruits, and yogurt team up to make a creamy, palate-pleasing dressing with no fat and few calories. If you prefer, use a bit more pork tenderloin. Since the meat isn't dressed, it won't affect the balance of the salad itself.

2 cups port	1½ cups nonfat plain yogurt
¾ cup dried apricots, chopped	¼ cup cider vinegar
¾ cup prunes, chopped	2 apples, cored and cut into
1 pork tenderloin (about	½-inch dice
12 ounces)	8 scallions, thinly sliced
2½ teaspoons salt	6 celery ribs, thinly sliced
¾ teaspoon black pepper	Green leaf lettuce leaves

1. In a small saucepan, combine port, apricots, and prunes. Bring to a boil over medium-high heat. Reduce heat to medium-low and simmer 5 minutes. With a slotted spoon, remove apricots and prunes and reserve. Boil port until reduced to ½ cup, about 5 minutes. Transfer to a small bowl and refrigerate until thickened, about 4 hours.

2. Prepare a hot fire in a barbecue grill. Trim fat and silver membrane off pork and rub with 1½ teaspoons salt and ½ teaspoon pepper. Grill pork on an oiled rack set 4 to 6 inches from coals, turning occasionally, until just cooked through with no trace of pink in center, about 15 to 20 minutes. Meat should register 160° to 165°F on an instant-reading thermometer. Let meat stand while making salad.

3. In a large bowl, combine reduced port, yogurt, vinegar, and remaining 1 teaspoon salt and ¼ teaspoon pepper. Whisk until smooth. Add apricots, prunes, apples, scallions, and celery. Toss until well mixed. Divide among 8 lettuce-lined plates. Slice pork thinly and arrange alongside fruit. Serve at once.

304 PROSCIUTTO AND FRUIT WITH CREAMY LIME SAUCE

Prep: 25 minutes   Chill: 30 minutes   Cook: none   Serves: 4

Particularly on a hot day, this salad is a must-do. Its tart, sweet, and salty components give the salad a pleasant roundness of flavor, and the yogurt-based dressing defies spa cuisine with its richness. It would also make a wonderful part of a buffet, since it's eye-catching and holds up well over an hour or two out of the refrigerator.

¾ cup nonfat plain yogurt
3 tablespoons fresh lime juice
2 tablespoons firmly packed
   brown sugar
12 red leaf lettuce leaves
4 cups diced (¾-inch)
   honeydew melon

¾ cup seedless red grapes
4 paper-thin slices of
   prosciutto, trimmed of fat
4 kiwis, peeled and quartered
   lengthwise
4 fresh figs, quartered
   lengthwise

1. In a small bowl, whisk together yogurt, lime juice, and sugar until well blended. Cover and refrigerate dressing at least 30 minutes.

2. Divide lettuce among 4 plates. Mound honeydew in center of each plate and top with grapes. Drape prosciutto around honeydew. Surround with alternating quarters of kiwi and fig. Drizzle dressing over salads and serve.

305 SPINACH, SMOKED CHICKEN, AND STRAWBERRY SALAD

Prep: 15 minutes   Cook: none   Serves: 4

2 cups diced (¾-inch) smoked
   chicken or turkey (about
   8 ounces)
2 cups strawberries, trimmed
   and quartered
2 cups fresh or canned
   pineapple chunks,
   drained

1 small red onion, thinly
   sliced and separated into
   rings
⅔ cup Pineapple-Dijon
   Vinaigrette (recipe
   follows)
6 cups torn fresh spinach

In a large bowl, combine chicken, strawberries, pineapple, and red onion. Drizzle on vinaigrette and toss to mix. Serve at once on 4 spinach-lined plates.

306 PINEAPPLE-DIJON VINAIGRETTE

Prep: 3 minutes   Chill: 1 hour   Cook: none   Makes: about ²/₃ cup

Pineapple juice provides fruity aroma and garlic delivers a lot of punch in this low-fat dressing.

2 garlic cloves, smashed
½ cup unsweetened pineapple
   juice
1 tablespoon red wine
   vinegar

1 tablespoon Dijon mustard
1 tablespoon olive oil
   Salt and freshly ground
   pepper

In a blender or small food processor, mince garlic. Add pineapple juice, vinegar, and mustard. With machine on, drizzle in olive oil. If needed, season with salt and pepper to taste. Cover and refrigerate at least 1 hour before serving.

307 SOBA NOODLE SALAD WITH POACHED SWORDFISH

Prep: 20 minutes   Cook: 11 to 13 minutes   Serves: 6

This salad is packed with flavor and nutrition, and it's quick to put together. If you prefer, substitute other firm, white fish for the swordfish or substitute small cooked shrimp.

12 ounces swordfish steaks, cut
   1 inch thick
1 pound soba (Japanese
   buckwheat) noodles
2 tablespoons rice vinegar
2 tablespoons soy sauce
1 tablespoon vegetable oil
1 teaspoon Asian sesame oil
¼ teaspoon hot chili oil or
   crushed hot red pepper

1 teaspoon sugar
3 garlic cloves, minced
2 cups shredded Chinese
   (Napa) cabbage
4 scallions, thinly sliced
1 small carrot, peeled and
   shredded
¼ cup shredded drained
   pickled ginger

1. In a medium skillet, bring 2 cups lightly salted water to a boil over medium heat. Reduce heat to low and place swordfish in water. Simmer, uncovered, 5 minutes. With a slotted spatula, carefully turn swordfish over and cook 4 to 5 minutes, or until opaque throughout. Remove fish with a slotted spatula and place on a platter. Blot excess water with a paper towel. When cool enough to handle, remove skin and bones. Break swordfish into small chunks.

2. In a large pot of lightly salted boiling water, cook noodles until just tender, 2 to 3 minutes. Drain, run under cold water, and drain again.

3. In a large bowl, combine vinegar, soy sauce, vegetable oil, sesame oil, chili oil, sugar, and garlic. Add noodles, shredded cabbage, scallions, carrot, and pickled ginger. Toss until well mixed. Transfer to a platter or 6 individual plates. Top with swordfish and serve.

Chapter 11

Warm and Wilted Salads

Warm salads, newly in vogue, are more complex than a mere temperature difference between ingredients that are eaten together. When just-cooked meat is added to a salad, the natural juices in the meat are still unstable. As the meat is sliced through by a knife or crushed by chewing, its juices are released and become a vital part of the salad dressing. Even cheeses that are served warm in a salad become an integral part of the salad in texture and flavor as they melt onto fruits or greens.

Another effect of warm ingredients on raw salad greens is that the heat of the food wilts the greens, so using sturdy greens is advisable. Curly endive, spinach, and kale and other cabbages hold up well to heat. On the other hand, fragile baby greens are best left to lightly dressed cold or room-temperature salads. Unless the greens in a warm salad are tossed in a hot dressing, only those that come into contact with the warm food are affected. So, only the greens that are underneath or alongside the meat or its juices will wilt. The result is an intriguing blend of warm meat and variously crisp and wilted greens.

We are most sensitive to foods served slightly warm or at room temperature. Cold and very hot foods numb our palates to varying degrees, so we don't appreciate all the potential of the food at hand. Consequently, warm or room-temperature salads are at their peak of flavor-giving potential.

Warm salads are ideal for the last-minute cook. Foods that are best served cold require planning ahead to allow plenty of cooling time in the refrigerator. Cooking food immediately before adding it to a salad allows for immediate consumption.

A few salads in this chapter, such as Warm Chicken Liver Salad with Port Vinaigrette and Warm Seafood Salad, incorporate delightfully warm dressings as well as just-cooked ingredients. One typically French salad, Dandelion Salad with Poached Eggs, includes just-poached eggs that, when pierced, become an integral part of the dressing.

As you gear up for some of the most fascinating and flavorful salads available, remember that your sauté pan, wok, broiler, and barbecue grill can be as important to the salad as the salad bowl.

308   BRONZED CAJUN CHICKEN SALAD
Prep: 20 minutes   Cook: 8 to 10 minutes   Serves: 4

Blackening, the technique of coating fish or meat in spices and pan-frying it over intense heat, was popularized by Cajun cooking guru Paul Prud-homme. While tasty, it's a smoky technique that's not too practical for the home kitchen. Bronzing is a tamer alternative that gives a similar, safer result. This interesting salad combines warm and cold temperatures and hot and sweet flavors.

2 teaspoons paprika	2 tablespoons mild honey
1 teaspoon black pepper	⅓ cup olive oil
1 teaspoon cayenne	8 cups shredded romaine or
½ teaspoon salt	iceberg lettuce
4 skinless, boneless chicken	4 plum tomatoes, cut into
breast halves	½-inch dice
2 tablespoons vegetable oil	3 scallions, thinly sliced
3 tablespoons Dijon mustard	Salt and freshly ground
3 tablespoons red wine	pepper
vinegar	

1. In a shallow dish, blend together paprika, black pepper, cayenne, and salt until well mixed. Add chicken and turn to coat evenly. Heat vegetable oil in a large, preferably nonstick skillet over medium-high heat. Add chicken and cook, turning once, until opaque throughout but still juicy, about 4 to 5 minutes per side. Transfer to a cutting board and let rest while making salad.

2. In a large bowl, blend together mustard, vinegar, and honey until smooth. Slowly whisk in olive oil. Add lettuce, tomatoes, and scallions. Toss until well mixed. Season with salt and pepper to taste.

3. Divide among 4 plates. Slice chicken crosswise into thin slices, retaining shape of breasts. Arrange 1 breast half over each salad. Serve warm.

309 WARM CHICKEN LIVER SALAD WITH PORT VINAIGRETTE

Prep: 20 minutes   Cook: 4 to 5 minutes   Serves: 8 to 10

16 cups torn butter lettuce
2 cups torn radicchio
1 medium red onion, thinly sliced and separated into rings
1 cup crumbled blue cheese
1⅓ cups Port Vinaigrette (recipe follows)

2 tablespoons butter
1½ pounds chicken livers, trimmed
Salt and freshly ground pepper
8 to 10 fresh figs, quartered lengthwise

1. In a large bowl, combine lettuce, radicchio, red onion, and blue cheese. Drizzle on vinaigrette and toss until well blended; divide among 8 to 10 plates.

2. In a large skillet, melt butter over medium-high heat. Add livers and sauté until brown outside but still pink and juicy inside, 4 to 5 minutes. Season with salt and pepper to taste. Divide warm livers among salads and surround each with 4 pieces of fig. Serve at once.

310 PORT VINAIGRETTE

Prep: 3 minutes   Cook: 10 minutes   Makes: about 1⅓ cups

Port, a sweet fortified wine, is a favorite ingredient of mine to make a pan sauce after sautéing meat. It becomes syrupy and intensely flavored, a pleasant counterpoint to savory ingredients. In this salad dressing, reduced port teams up with mellow balsamic vinegar and extra-virgin olive oil, resulting in a memorable vinaigrette. Use it with other salads that combine meat and fruit.

¾ cup port
¾ cup extra-virgin olive oil
⅓ cup balsamic vinegar

½ teaspoon salt
¼ teaspoon pepper

1. In a small nonreactive saucepan, bring port to a boil over medium-high heat. Reduce heat and simmer until reduced to ¼ cup, about 10 minutes.

2. In a small bowl, blend together oil, vinegar, salt, and pepper. Whisk in reduced port. If not using within 2 hours, cover and refrigerate. Let return to room temperature before using.

311   CHICKEN SATAY SALAD
Prep: 20 minutes   Cook: 10 minutes   Serves: 6 to 8

Traditionally an Indonesian grilled snack food or hors d'oeuvre, satay is extended in this dish to a main course. This tantalizing combination of warm and cold, nutty and spicy, charred and crisp makes a great party salad, especially in summer when the lure of the grill beckons.

2 pounds skinless, boneless chicken breasts, cut into 1-inch cubes
3 medium red bell peppers, cut into 1-inch cubes
¼ cup vegetable oil
9 to 10 cups shredded iceberg lettuce

1 cup Satay Sauce (recipe follows)
¼ cup coarsely chopped cilantro
½ cup chopped roasted peanuts

1. If using bamboo skewers, soak them in water for 30 minutes to prevent burning. Light a medium-hot fire in a barbecue grill or preheat broiler. Thread chicken and bell peppers alternately onto skewers. Brush lightly with oil. Grill on a lightly oiled rack or broil 4 to 6 inches from heat, turning frequently, until chicken is browned outside and white in center but still moist, about 10 minutes.

2. Divide lettuce among 6 to 8 plates. Top with skewers of satays. Drizzle dressing over chicken and lettuce. Sprinkle cilantro and peanuts on top and serve warm.

312   SATAY SAUCE
Prep: 10 minutes   Cook: none   Makes: about 1 cup

Indonesian in origin, this quick peanut butter–based sauce is slightly sweet, garlicky, and nutty. It's typically served over grilled meats, but its well-rounded flavor would also be welcome over pasta.

4 garlic cloves, smashed
1 tablespoon sugar
⅓ cup fresh lime juice
¼ cup creamy peanut butter

1½ tablespoons soy sauce
½ to 1 teaspoon crushed hot red pepper
¼ cup vegetable oil

Place garlic and sugar in a blender or small food processor. Mince together. Add lime juice, peanut butter, soy sauce, and hot pepper. With machine on, drizzle in oil. If not using within 2 hours, cover and refrigerate. Let return to room temperature before serving.

313 PESTO SALAD WITH CHARRED CHICKEN AND GOAT CHEESE CROUTONS

Prep: 15 minutes   Cook: 18 to 20 minutes   Serves: 4

Basil-based pesto and grilled chicken make a feast for the nose in this delightful salad. It's truly a complete meal. Even the bread, slathered here with soft goat cheese, is included.

4 skinless, boneless chicken breast halves
⅓ cup plus 2 tablespoons extra-virgin olive oil
8 large slices of French or Italian bread, cut ½ inch thick
4 ounces mild goat cheese, such as Montrachet
¼ cup prepared or homemade pesto

2 tablespoons red wine vinegar
8 cups torn assorted salad greens
Salt and freshly ground pepper
¼ cup pine nuts (pignoli), preferably lightly toasted

1. Light a medium-hot fire in a barbecue grill or preheat broiler. Brush chicken breasts with 2 tablespoons oil. Grill on a lightly oiled rack set 4 to 6 inches from coals or broil, turning once, until just opaque throughout but still moist, about 4 to 5 minutes per side. Transfer chicken to a cutting board and let rest 5 to 10 minutes.

2. Meanwhile, preheat oven to 325°F. Arrange bread in a single layer on a wire rack and place in oven to dry, about 8 minutes. Spread goat cheese evenly over each slice. Place in oven until warmed through but not brown, about 2 minutes.

3. In a large bowl, mix remaining ⅓ cup olive oil, pesto, and vinegar. Add greens and toss until evenly coated. Season with salt and pepper to taste. Divide among 4 plates.

4. Slice chicken thinly on diagonal, retaining shape of breasts. Arrange 1 chicken breast half on each plate and sprinkle with pine nuts. Garnish each salad with 2 croutons and serve.

314   DUCK WITH CRACKLINGS, CANNELLINI, AND PORT–RED CURRANT DRESSING

Prep: 20 minutes   Cook: about 17 to 23 minutes   Serves: 4

Cracklings, the crisp pieces of duck skin that have been rendered of fat, give this salad appealing crunchiness. As you eat warm duck meat over cool spinach and white beans in this salad, the duck juices combine with the dressing ingredients to make a unique vinaigrette.

4 **small boneless duck breast halves, skin removed and reserved**
1 **large shallot, minced**
1 **cup port**
2 **tablespoons red wine vinegar**
2 **tablespoons red currant jelly**

8 **cups torn spinach**
1 **(15-ounce) can cannellini or white kidney beans, rinsed and drained**
Salt and freshly ground pepper

1. Cut duck skin into ¹/₂-inch dice. In a large heavy skillet, cook duck skin over medium heat, stirring occasionally, until crisp and brown, 7 to 10 minutes. With a slotted spoon, transfer cracklings to paper towels to drain. Pour off all but 2 tablespoons fat from skillet.

2. Increase heat to medium-high. Add duck breasts and cook, turning once, until golden brown outside but still pink and juicy inside, about 3 minutes per side. Transfer to a cutting board. Reduce heat to low. Add shallot and cook, stirring, until softened, 1 to 2 minutes. Add port and return pan to medium-high heat, scraping up any browned bits from bottom of pan. Simmer and reduce to about ¹/₃ to ¹/₂ cup, about 3 to 5 minutes. Add vinegar and jelly and whisk together until well blended. Keep warm over low heat.

3. In a large bowl, combine spinach and cannellini beans. Drizzle on warm dressing and toss to mix well. Season with salt and pepper to taste. Divide among 4 plates. Cut duck breasts crosswise on diagonal into thin slices and arrange on top of spinach. Sprinkle cracklings on top and serve at once.

315   PAN-SEARED CHICKEN SALAD WITH OYSTER MUSHROOMS AND FRESH CURRANTS

Prep: 15 minutes   Cook: about 13 to 18 minutes   Serves: 4

Shimmering with jewel-like fresh red currants, this salad combines just-cooked chicken and golden oyster mushrooms with a warm raspberry vinaigrette. When currants are unavailable, substitute fresh raspberries or blueberries.

¼ cup olive oil
4 skinless, boneless chicken
    breast halves
4 ounces oyster mushrooms
¾ cup raspberry vinegar
1½ teaspoons honey
¾ teaspoon Dijon mustard
    Salt and freshly ground
    pepper

6 cups assorted baby lettuces
4 ounces mild goat cheese,
    such as Montrachet,
    crumbled
1 cup fresh red currants,
    stemmed

1. In a large skillet, heat 2 tablespoons oil over medium-high heat until it shimmers. Add chicken and cook, turning occasionally, until golden brown on both sides and opaque throughout but still moist, 8 to 10 minutes. Transfer to a cutting board.

2. Add mushrooms to skillet in a single layer and cook, turning occasionally, until golden brown, 2 to 3 minutes. Transfer mushrooms to a plate. Pour vinegar into skillet, scraping up browned bits from bottom of pan. Boil until reduced to about ¼ cup, 3 to 5 minutes. Let cool briefly, about 5 minutes. Add remaining 2 tablespoons oil, honey, and mustard and whisk together until smooth. Season with salt and pepper to taste.

3. Divide lettuce among 4 plates. Sprinkle cheese and currants over lettuce. Cut chicken crosswise into thin slices, retaining shape of breasts. Arrange chicken and mushrooms on top. Drizzle warm dressing over salads and serve at once.

316   GLAZED DUCK SALAD WITH ORANGE-SOY VINAIGRETTE

Prep: 15 minutes   Cook: 1¼ hours   Serves: 8 to 10

Orange and duck are a classic pair. The sweetness and acidity of orange cut through some of duck's richness, so they complement each other whether served warm or cold. In this salad, curly endive contributes pleasing bitterness, and it's sturdy enough to stand up to a warm, meaty salad.

2 (4½- to 5-pound) ducks, trimmed of excess fat
⅔ cup orange juice
1½ tablespoons Thai red curry paste
1 garlic clove, minced

½ cup honey
4 medium oranges
8 cups torn Boston lettuce
8 cups torn curly endive
1¼ cups Orange-Soy Vinaigrette (recipe follows)

1. Preheat oven to 425°F. Place ducks in a lightly oiled roasting pan and prick skin all over without piercing meat. Roast 45 minutes.

2. Meanwhile, in a small saucepan, blend together orange juice, curry paste, and garlic. Bring to a boil over medium-high heat, reduce heat slightly, and boil until liquid is reduced to ⅓ cup, about 3 minutes. Remove from heat. Add honey and whisk until basting sauce is well blended.

3. After ducks have roasted 45 minutes, brush with sauce and reduce oven temperature to 350°. Roast 30 minutes, basting frequently with sauce. Remove from oven and let rest while preparing salad.

4. Cut ends off oranges and cut away skin and white pith. Slice oranges into segments. Remove duck meat from bones and slice into thin strips, leaving some crisp skin on each piece. In a large bowl, combine lettuce and endive. Drizzle on vinaigrette and toss to mix well. Divide greens among 8 to 10 plates. Arrange slightly overlapping strips of duck on salads. Arrange orange segments alongside duck and serve at once.

317   ORANGE-SOY VINAIGRETTE

Prep: 5 minutes   Cook: none   Makes: 1¼ cups

Marmalade and mustard give this sweet, peppery dressing body, and soy sauce lends it depth of flavor.

¼ cup red wine vinegar
3 tablespoons orange marmalade, melted
3 tablespoons soy sauce
2 tablespoons dry sherry

1 teaspoon freshly ground pepper
½ teaspoon Dijon mustard
½ cup olive oil

In a small bowl, whisk together vinegar, marmalade, soy sauce, sherry, pepper, and mustard until well blended. Slowly whisk in oil. If not using within 2 hours, cover and refrigerate. Let return to room temperature before using.

318 DANDELION SALAD WITH POACHED EGGS

Prep: 15 minutes   Cook: 13 to 17 minutes   Serves: 6

Topping a salad with a just-poached egg is a French tradition. Not only is the dressing warm, but the liquid egg yolk runs when pierced, contributing to the dressing. If dandelion greens are out of season, substitute arugula or spinach.

6 large slices of French or Italian bread, cut ¾ inch thick	2 teaspoons sugar
	9 slices of bacon
	1 small red onion, chopped
12 cups trimmed and torn dandelion greens	2 tablespoons lemon juice
⅓ cup extra-virgin olive oil	6 eggs
¼ cup red wine vinegar	Salt and freshly ground pepper
2 teaspoons Dijon mustard	

1. Preheat broiler. Place bread on a rack 4 to 6 inches from heat and broil, turning once, until croutons are golden on both sides, 3 to 5 minutes total. Place greens in a large bowl. In a small bowl, whisk together oil, vinegar, mustard, and sugar until dressing is smooth.

2. In a large skillet, cook bacon over medium heat until crisp, 7 to 9 minutes. Drain on paper towels. Pour off all but 2 tablespoons of fat from skillet. Add onion and cook, stirring frequently, until just beginning to soften, about 3 minutes. Remove skillet from heat and stir in dressing. Reduce heat to low and keep warm.

3. Bring a large pan of 3 inches of water to a boil. Add lemon juice and reduce to a simmer. One at a time, crack eggs and gently slip into water. Cover pan and remove from heat. Let stand until whites are set and yolks are still runny, about 3 minutes. Meanwhile, pour warm dressing over greens and toss until wilted. Season with salt and pepper to taste. Divide greens among 6 plates and top each with a crouton. Lift eggs from water with a slotted spoon, drain briefly, and place 1 on top of each crouton. Crumble bacon over salads and serve at once.

319 BABY ARTICHOKE SALAD WITH PARMESAN CHEESE
Prep: 15 minutes   Cook: 15 to 17 minutes   Serves: 4

Tender baby artichokes, most commonly available in springtime, range in size from 1 to 3 inches high. Since they're so young, a choke hasn't had time to develop, so they need very little trimming and are completely edible. This simple salad features a ring of just-cooked, halved baby artichokes, showing off all of their layers of inner leaves.

¼ cup plus 1 tablespoon extra-virgin olive oil
12 baby artichokes, stems and outer leaves removed
2 tablespoons lemon juice
8 cups torn red leaf lettuce
1½ tablespoons balsamic vinegar
Salt and freshly ground pepper
1 (2-ounce) can flat anchovy fillets, drained
½ cup grated Parmesan cheese

1. In a large skillet, heat 1 tablespoon oil over medium heat. Add artichokes and sauté, stirring occasionally, 5 minutes. Add lemon juice and 1 cup water. Cover tightly and simmer, shaking pan occasionally, until tender when pierced with a sharp knife, about 10 to 12 minutes. Meanwhile, prepare salad.

2. Place lettuce in a large bowl. Drizzle with remaining ¼ cup olive oil and vinegar. Toss until well blended and season with salt and pepper to taste. Divide among 4 plates. Drain artichokes and slice each in half. Arrange artichokes, cut side up, in a ring over lettuce. Garnish with anchovies. Sprinkle with cheese and serve warm.

320 FALL FRUIT SALAD WITH BACON
Prep: 30 minutes   Cook: 18 to 25 minutes   Serves: 8 to 10

Pomegranates, red-skinned pears, and kumquats make this a festive-looking salad for holidays. Serve it with crusty bread and cheese.

16 cups torn spinach (about 1¼ pounds)
16 kumquats, thinly sliced and seeded
8 scallions, thinly sliced
4 medium Red Bartlett pears, cut into ½-inch dice
2 cups pomegranate seeds (about 2 medium pomegranates)
1 pound sliced bacon
1 large onion, chopped
4 garlic cloves, minced
¾ cup cider vinegar
¼ cup sugar
Salt and freshly ground pepper

1. In a large bowl, toss spinach, kumquats, scallions, pears, and pomegranate seeds. Refrigerate while cooking bacon.

2. In a large skillet, cook bacon in 2 batches over medium heat until crisp, 7 to 9 minutes per batch. Drain on paper towels. Add onion and garlic to drippings in skillet and cook until softened, 3 to 5 minutes. Add vinegar and sugar and cook, stirring, until sugar dissolves and dressing is hot, 1 to 2 minutes.

3. Drizzle warm dressing with onion over salad and toss until spinach is wilted. Season with salt and pepper to taste. Divide among 8 to 10 plates. Crumble bacon over salads and serve at once.

321 WARM SEAFOOD SALAD
Prep: 30 minutes   Cook: about 7 to 9 minutes   Serves: 6

This company-worthy salad is a delicious blend of herbs, cooked and raw vegetables, and warm bay scallops, shrimp, and cod. It's dressed simply with extra-virgin olive oil, balsamic vinegar, and the pan juices left from cooking the seafood.

4 cups torn Chinese (Napa) cabbage	½ pound medium shrimp, shelled and deveined
4 cups torn romaine lettuce	½ pound fresh cod or halibut, cut into ¾-inch cubes
4 large plum tomatoes, cut into ¾-inch dice	½ pound bay scallops
⅔ cup plus 2 tablespoons extra-virgin olive oil	3 garlic cloves, minced
⅓ cup balsamic vinegar	½ cup dry vermouth or water
½ cup chopped parsley	Salt and freshly ground pepper
¼ cup chopped fresh basil	
1 medium onion, thinly sliced and separated into rings	

1. In a large bowl, combine cabbage, lettuce, and tomatoes. In a small bowl, combine ⅔ cup olive oil, vinegar, parsley, and basil.

2. In a large nonstick skillet, heat remaining 2 tablespoons oil over medium heat. Add onion and cook, stirring frequently, until softened, 3 to 5 minutes. Add shrimp and cook, stirring frequently, until shrimp starts to turn pink, about 2 minutes. Add cod, scallops, and garlic and cook, turning frequently, until just opaque throughout but still moist, about 2 minutes. With a slotted spatula, transfer seafood to a platter.

3. Add vermouth to skillet and stir to loosen any brown bits on bottom of pan. Boil until almost all liquid has evaporated and pan juices are reduced to a glaze. Remove skillet from heat and pour dressing into pan. Stir to blend well. Pour two-thirds of dressing over cabbage mixture and toss until well blended. Season with salt and pepper to taste and divide among 6 plates. In same bowl, combine seafood, accumulated juices, and remaining dressing. Toss until well blended and place on top of cabbage. Serve at once.

322 LEEK SALAD WITH TARRAGON-DIJON VINAIGRETTE
Prep: 15 minutes   Cook: 8 to 10 minutes   Serves: 4

Mildly flavored leeks are sprinkled with salty prosciutto and Parmesan cheese in this unusual salad. For a special presentation, do not chop the prosciutto but drape the slices around the stem end of the leeks. A large number of these salads look particularly dramatic on a special platter for a buffet.

12 small leeks (white and
      tender green), trimmed
      Large red or green leaf
      lettuce leaves
 4 thin slices of prosciutto or
      ham, chopped
 2 hard-cooked eggs, chopped

 1 (3-ounce) chunk of
      Parmesan cheese,
      preferably imported
¾ cup Tarragon-Dijon
      Vinaigrette (recipe
      follows)

1. Holding root end of leeks, quarter lengthwise, leaving 1 inch of root end intact. In a large bowl of water, swish leeks back and forth to clean. In a large saucepan of 2 inches of lightly salted boiling water, cook leeks until tender when pierced with a sharp knife, 8 to 10 minutes. Drain well.

2. Divide lettuce among 4 plates. Top with leeks, fanning them out slightly, and sprinkle with prosciutto and eggs. Using a swivel-bladed vegetable peeler, shave Parmesan cheese into slices and scatter over each salad. Drizzle vinaigrette over leeks and serve warm or at room temperature.

323 TARRAGON-DIJON VINAIGRETTE
Prep: 5 minutes   Cook: none   Makes: about ¾ cup

2 tablespoons red wine
      vinegar
2 tablespoons Dijon mustard
2 teaspoons lemon juice

1 teaspoon dried tarragon
1 garlic clove, crushed
      through a press
½ cup extra-virgin olive oil

In a small bowl, combine vinegar, mustard, lemon juice, tarragon, and garlic. Slowly whisk in olive oil. If not using within 2 hours, cover and refrigerate. Let return to room temperature before using.

324 SPINACH AND BLUE CHEESE SALAD WITH WARM APPLE VINAIGRETTE

Prep: 15 minutes   Cook: 14 to 20 minutes   Serves: 4

8 slices of bacon
1 medium onion, chopped
1½ cups apple juice
2 tablespoons cider vinegar
2 tablespoons olive oil
1 tablespoon Dijon mustard
8 cups torn fresh spinach

2 Granny Smith or other tart apples, cut into ¾-inch dice
Salt and freshly ground pepper
½ cup crumbled blue cheese

1. In a large skillet, cook bacon over medium heat until crisp, 7 to 9 minutes. Drain on paper towels. Pour off all but 2 tablespoons of fat from skillet.

2. Add onion to drippings in skillet and cook over medium heat, stirring occasionally, until slightly softened, 3 to 5 minutes. Add apple juice and vinegar to pan and bring to a boil over medium-high heat. Cook, stirring occasionally, until liquid is reduced to ½ cup, 4 to 6 minutes. Remove from heat and whisk in oil and mustard.

3. In a large bowl, combine spinach and apples. Drizzle on warm dressing and toss until spinach is wilted. Season with salt and pepper to taste. Divide among 4 plates. Crumble bacon over salads and sprinkle blue cheese on top. Serve at once.

325 ROASTED RATATOUILLE

Prep: 20 minutes   Cook: 30 minutes   Serves: 2 to 3

1 small eggplant, peeled and cut into 3 x ½-inch sticks
2 plum tomatoes, quartered lengthwise
1 small zucchini, quartered lengthwise and cut into 1-inch pieces
1 small yellow squash, quartered lengthwise and cut into 1-inch pieces

1 medium red bell pepper, cut into thin strips about 1½ inches long
1 small red onion, cut into ¼-inch-thick slices
½ cup Herbed Roasted Garlic Vinaigrette (recipe follows)
Red leaf lettuce leaves
¼ cup grated Parmesan cheese

1. Preheat oven to 475°F. Arrange eggplant, tomatoes, zucchini, squash, bell pepper, and onion in a single layer on 2 lightly greased large baking sheets. Roast, turning vegetables occasionally, until onion is golden and vegetables are softened, about 30 minutes.

2. Transfer vegetables to a large bowl. Top with vinaigrette and toss gently until evenly coated. Serve warm, at room temperature, or lightly chilled on lettuce-lined plates. Sprinkle Parmesan cheese on top.

326 HERBED ROASTED GARLIC VINAIGRETTE
Prep: 5 minutes   Cook: about 1 hour   Makes: about ½ cup

Slowly baked garlic gives this dressing body and mellow, nutty flavor. It's delicious over pasta as well as the ratatouille salad, and for purely roasted garlic flavor, try it without the herbs.

1 small head of garlic, papery tips removed
1 tablespoon balsamic vinegar
2 tablespoons minced fresh basil
1 teaspoon minced fresh thyme or ½ teaspoon dried

3 tablespoons extra-virgin olive oil
Salt and freshly ground pepper

1. Preheat oven to 350°F. Place garlic in a small ovenproof dish, sprinkle with a tablespoon of water, and cover tightly with foil. Bake until pulp is very tender, about 1 hour.

2. When cool enough to handle, squeeze soft garlic pulp into a small bowl (you should have about 1 heaping tablespoon). Add vinegar, basil, and thyme. Slowly whisk in olive oil. Season with salt and pepper to taste. If not using within 2 hours, cover and refrigerate. Let return to room temperature before serving.

327 GOAT CHEESE AND PEAR SALAD WITH WARM BACON–RED WINE DRESSING
Prep: 10 minutes   Cook: 8 to 10 minutes   Serves: 4

This very rich salad makes a substantial meal with just a slice or two of bread. The warm, highly aromatic dressing of red wine, Dijon mustard, and bacon makes the soft goat cheese melt in your mouth. To slice the cheese neatly, be sure to have it well chilled ahead of time and use a sharp knife.

8 slices of bacon
Olive oil
6 cups torn curly endive
2 cups torn radicchio
6 ounces Montrachet or other mild goat cheese, well chilled and sliced into 12 even rounds

2 large pears, preferably Red Bartlett, thinly sliced
⅓ cup dry red wine
3 tablespoons Dijon mustard

1. In a large skillet, cook bacon over medium heat until crisp, 7 to 9 minutes. Drain on paper towels. Pour drippings into a measuring cup and, if needed, add enough olive oil to measure ½ cup. When cool enough to handle, crumble bacon.

2. In a large bowl, combine endive and radicchio. Divide among 4 plates and sprinkle with bacon. Top each with 3 slightly overlapping slices of goat cheese. Divide pears among plates, arranging in slightly overlapping slices alongside cheese.

3. Return drippings and olive oil to pan over medium heat. Add wine and mustard and whisk until smooth, warm, and bubbling, about 1 minute. Drizzle over salads and serve at once.

---

328 WILTED RED CABBAGE SALAD WITH BACON AND BROILED GOAT CHEESE

Prep: 25 minutes   Cook: 14 to 18 minutes   Serves: 5 or 6

A soft round of goat cheese on glistening red cabbage sprinkled with crisp bits of bacon make an unusual salad of many textures. It's particularly stunning on a bed of dark green spinach leaves.

10 ounces mild goat cheese, such as Montrachet, formed into 10 or 12 equal ½-inch-thick rounds

2 tablespoons olive oil

¾ cup fresh bread crumbs

8 ounces thick-sliced bacon, cut into ½-inch dice

1 small red cabbage (about 2¼ pounds), cored and shredded

2 large shallots, minced

1 large Granny Smith apple, cut into ½-inch dice

2 tablespoons cider vinegar
    Salt and freshly ground pepper
    Large spinach leaves

1. Place goat cheese on a lightly greased baking sheet and brush tops and sides with 2 tablespoons oil. Coat tops and sides of each round with bread crumbs. Shake off excess crumbs. Refrigerate until ready to broil.

2. In a large skillet, cook bacon over medium heat, stirring frequently, until crisp, 8 to 10 minutes. With a slotted spoon, transfer to paper towels to drain.

3. Add cabbage, shallots, and apple to skillet and cook, stirring constantly, until cabbage starts to wilt, 3 to 5 minutes. Transfer to a large bowl. Remove pan from heat and add vinegar and 3 tablespoons water, scraping bottom of skillet to release any browned bits. Drizzle over cabbage and toss to coat well. Season with salt and pepper to taste.

4. Preheat broiler. Place goat cheese 4 inches from heat and broil until golden brown, about 3 minutes. Watch carefully as topping can burn easily. Divide cabbage among 5 or 6 spinach-lined plates and top with warm cheese. Sprinkle with bacon and serve at once.

329 OYSTER MUSHROOM SALAD WITH BRESAOLA AND POLENTA CROUTONS

Prep: 15 minutes   Cook: 4 minutes   Serves: 4

Delicately flavored oyster mushrooms and Italian bresaola grace this unusual salad. If bresaola is unavailable, substitute its better-known pork counterpart, prosciutto, or Westphalian ham.

6 to 8 cups torn arugula
4 cups oyster mushrooms (about 6 ounces), separated at base
¼ cup plus 1 tablespoon extra-virgin olive oil
2 small red bell peppers, cut into ¼-inch strips

2 tablespoons balsamic vinegar
Salt and freshly ground pepper
12 ounces bresaola,* thinly sliced
2 cups Parmesan Polenta Croutons (recipe follows)

1. Divide arugula among 4 plates. In a large nonstick skillet over medium heat, cook mushrooms in 1 tablespoon oil, turning at least once, until lightly golden, about 3 minutes. Arrange mushrooms with stems toward center on one side of plates. Add bell peppers to skillet and cook, stirring frequently, until just warm, about 1 minute. Divide among plates.

2. Drizzle salads with remaining ¼ cup olive oil and vinegar. Sprinkle with salt and pepper to taste. Divide bresaola among salads, draping slices to one side. Sprinkle with croutons and serve at once.

* Air-dried beef fillet that is available at Italian markets and specialty food shops.

330 PARMESAN POLENTA CROUTONS

*Prep: 5 minutes   Cook: 1 hour 15 minutes to 1 hour 25 minutes
Chill: 2 hours   Makes: about 2 cups*

Made with cornmeal, cheese, and chicken broth, these croutons are more substantial than those made of bread. They have a crispy exterior and soft center and can be served warm or at room temperature. For very crisp croutons, leave in the oven an extra 15 minutes. If you must make them ahead, store airtight for up to 2 days or freeze them. Just before serving, recrisp them in a hot oven.

1¼ cups reduced-sodium chicken broth
½ cup yellow cornmeal

⅓ cup grated Parmesan cheese
1½ tablespoons butter

1. In a medium saucepan, combine broth and 1½ cups water. Bring to a boil over high heat and slowly whisk in cornmeal to prevent lumps. Reduce heat to low and stir continually until mixture pulls from sides of pan, about 15 minutes. Remove from heat and blend in cheese and butter. Pour onto a lightly greased 7 x 7-inch baking pan and spread mixture to an even thickness. Cover and refrigerate until cold and firm, at least 2 hours.

2. Preheat oven to 375°F. Slice polenta into ¹/₂- to ³/₄-inch cubes. Arrange in a single layer on a lightly oiled large baking sheet. Bake, turning occasionally with a sharp spatula, until lightly browned and crisp, 60 to 70 minutes.

331 SPINACH AND CANNELLINI SALAD WITH WARM PANCETTA VINAIGRETTE
Prep: 15 minutes   Cook: 6 to 8 minutes   Serves: 6 to 8

This salad, a lovely jumble of nutritious beans and fresh vegetables, is highlighted by slightly salty pancetta, the cured but unsmoked Italian bacon. You can find it at Italian markets and specialty food shops and in the deli section of some supermarkets. This simple dressing is also delicious over pasta and potato salads and strong greens, such as arugula.

6 ounces pancetta, cut into
    ¹/₄-inch dice
²/₃ cup plus 1 tablespoon
    extra-virgin olive oil
¹/₄ cup red wine vinegar
12 cups torn spinach
1 (15-ounce) can cannellini or
    white kidney beans,
    rinsed and drained
2 cups sliced mushrooms
    (about 8 ounces)

1 small red onion, thinly
    sliced and separated into
    rings
Salt and freshly ground
    pepper
6 hard-cooked eggs,
    quartered lengthwise
¹/₂ cup shredded Romano
    cheese

1. In a medium skillet, combine pancetta and 1 tablespoon olive oil. Cook over medium heat, stirring frequently, until lightly browned, 6 to 8 minutes. Transfer to paper towels to drain. Add remaining ²/₃ cup olive oil to drippings in skillet. Blend in vinegar and keep warm over low heat.

2. In a large bowl, combine spinach, beans, mushrooms, and red onion. Drizzle on warm vinaigrette and toss until well blended. Season with salt and pepper to taste. Divide among 6 to 8 plates. Arrange eggs around salads. Sprinkle Romano cheese on top and serve at once.

332   GRILLED SHIITAKE AND POTATO SALAD

Prep: 20 minutes   Marinate: 1 hour   Cook: 10 minutes   Serves: 4

The meatiness of shiitake mushrooms and potatoes provides a pleasant contrast to the greens in this flavor-packed main-course salad. For an easy accompaniment, place some slices of whole grain or peasant bread on the grill while cooking the mushrooms and potatoes.

½ cup olive oil
¼ cup balsamic vinegar
1 teaspoon Dijon mustard
3 garlic cloves, crushed
   through a press
1 shallot, minced
½ teaspoon salt
½ teaspoon freshly ground
   pepper
1 pound large red potatoes,
   cut into ¼-inch-thick
   slices

4 large fresh shiitake
   mushrooms, stemmed
1 medium red bell pepper,
   cut into ¼-inch rings
8 cups shredded assorted
   salad greens
1 (2-ounce) chunk of
   Parmesan cheese,
   preferably imported

1. In a small bowl, blend together oil, vinegar, mustard, garlic, shallot, salt, and pepper. Pour half of dressing into a shallow dish. Add potatoes, mushrooms, and bell pepper and turn vegetables to coat well. Cover and marinate at room temperature 1 hour or refrigerate up to 8 hours, turning at least once. Cover remaining dressing. If not serving within 2 hours, refrigerate and let return to room temperature before using.

2. Light a medium-hot fire in a barbecue grill. Lift vegetables from marinade and place on a lightly oiled rack 4 to 6 inches from heat. Cook, turning frequently, until golden brown on both sides and tender inside, about 10 minutes total.

3. Divide greens among 4 plates and top with layers of warm potatoes, peppers, and mushrooms. Using a swivel-bladed vegetable peeler, shave Parmesan cheese into thin slices and scatter over each salad. Drizzle on reserved dressing and serve.

333 BROILED TOFU AND SPINACH SALAD WITH CREAMY SESAME-GINGER DRESSING

Prep: 15 minutes   Cook: 4 to 5 minutes   Serves: 8

Stunning with brilliantly colored spinach, red bell peppers, pale tofu, and black sesame seeds, this salad is a picture of contrasting colors and textures.

16 cups torn spinach
6 ounces medium fresh shiitake mushrooms, stemmed, caps thinly sliced
2 medium red bell peppers, quartered and thinly sliced
1 cup Sesame-Ginger Dressing (recipe follows)

2 (14-ounce) packages firm tofu, quartered horizontally
2 tablespoons Asian sesame oil
¾ cup enoki mushrooms
1 tablespoon sesame seeds, preferably black

1. Preheat broiler. In a large bowl, combine spinach, shiitake mushrooms, and bell peppers. Drizzle on dressing and toss until well mixed. Divide among 8 plates.

2. Place tofu slices on a lightly oiled baking sheet in a single layer and brush with sesame oil. Broil 4 to 5 inches from heat until light golden, 4 to 5 minutes. Top each salad with a piece of warm tofu and garnish with enoki mushrooms and sesame seeds. Serve at once.

334 SESAME-GINGER DRESSING

Prep: 5 minutes   Cook: none   Makes: about 1 cup

1½ tablespoons rice vinegar
1 (1½-inch) piece of fresh ginger, peeled and minced
1 garlic clove, minced

¾ teaspoon sugar
¾ teaspoon salt
¾ cup vegetable oil
2 to 3 teaspoons Asian sesame oil

In a small bowl, blend together vinegar, ginger, garlic, sugar, and salt until sugar dissolves. Whisk in vegetable oil and sesame oil to taste. If not using within 2 hours, cover and refrigerate. Let return to room temperature and stir before using.

Chapter 12

Cheese, Please

As an avid cook, I've always been frustrated that I could spend hours fixing a fussy pâté or a seven-layer torte, only to find that the most appreciated part of a dinner party was the cheese, whether served before or after the meal. What could possibly top this sublime food that's been described by author Clifton Fadiman as "milk's leap to immortality"? It's delectable, satisfying, and best of all, it's ready to eat with little or no preparation.

Cheese is a natural in salads. Its richness invites a pairing with light ingredients of different textures, making it the perfect companion for leafy greens, and the acidity of vinaigrettes makes an ideal foil for the smooth, creamy texture of soft and semisoft cheeses. Since the range of cheeses offers a diversity of flavors—from sharp feta and Stilton to mild goat cheese and Brie—it can be cleverly paired with a variety of fruits, vegetables, nuts, and greens.

What's more, salads featuring cheese have a special versatility. While they make satisfying main courses for either lunch or supper, in smaller portions they provide the perfect way to start a formal dinner or to end one, combining the salad and cheese courses in one.

Mild cheeses temper the sharpness of strong greens, as in the striking Arugula-Montrachet Salad with Country Mustard Vinaigrette and the simply made Winter Pear, Goat Cheese, and Hazelnuts on Watercress. Salty cheeses provide pleasing contrast to the sweetness of fruits, as in Bitter Greens with Grapes and Cheese and Grilled Pear, Pine Nut, and Gorgonzola Salad.

Some unique salads in this chapter feature unusual treatments and combinations of ingredients. Red Grapes and Belgian Endive with Blue Cheese Timbales includes a colorful array of fruits and vegetables with a velvety blue cheese-flavored custard. A Mixed Green Salad with Feta Cheese, Peppery Pecans, and Caramelized Onions combines marinated, cooked sweet onions with cayenne-spiked nuts, watercress, and a crumbly, tangy cheese. Two unusual Italian combinations are Fennel Salad with Figs, Prosciutto, and Parmesan Cheese and Fresh Pecorino and Walnut Salad.

As I've become more relaxed about cooking, I've come up with a solution to the ego-versus-cheese dilemma: instead of competing with this culinary coup, use it as a focal point to create a delicious entree. Let it star in your next main-course salad and save yourself hours in the kitchen to boot.

335   ARUGULA SALAD WITH HONEY-GLAZED PECANS AND CAMBOZOLA

Prep: 15 minutes   Cook: 4 minutes   Serves: 2

Peppery and nutty, this salad features creamy, mild blue Cambozola cheese, a staple in my house. If arugula is unavailable, substitute watercress. Serve with a crusty baguette and a special bottle of red wine.

1 tablespoon honey
1 teaspoon butter
½ cup pecans
2 tablespoons walnut or hazelnut oil
2 teaspoons sherry vinegar
¼ teaspoon salt
2 cups torn arugula

2 cups torn Boston lettuce
2 (¼- to ½-inch) wedges of Cambozola cheese (about 3 ounces total)
1 large Granny Smith apple, cored and thinly sliced
Freshly ground pepper

1. In a small skillet, melt honey and butter over medium heat, stirring occasionally, about 1 minute. Add pecans and cook, stirring constantly, until most of liquid is evaporated and nuts are coated with glaze, about 3 minutes. At first sign of smoke, remove skillet from heat. Transfer pecans to a plate and let cool.

2. In a large bowl, blend together oil, vinegar, and salt. Add arugula and lettuce and toss until evenly coated. Divide between 2 plates.

3. Place a wedge of cheese on each plate. Arrange apple slices overlapping slightly, alongside cheese. Sprinkle pecans on top and serve. Pass a peppermill at table.

336   CAMEMBERT AND RASPBERRIES ON MIXED LETTUCES

Prep: 15 minutes   Cook: none   Serves: 4

At about 6 weeks of age, Camembert is at its creamy, spreadable best. Here it's paired with raspberries and mint to create an elegant main-course salad that also works beautifully as a starter in smaller portions. Serve with a loaf of crusty bread.

¼ cup minced fresh mint
3 tablespoons rice vinegar
2 tablespoons raspberry preserves, melted
3 garlic cloves, minced
1 teaspoon Dijon mustard
¼ cup extra-virgin olive oil
4 cups torn curly endive
2 cups torn radicchio

2 cups torn Boston lettuce
Salt and freshly ground pepper
4 small wedges of Camembert cheese (about 8 ounces total), at room temperature
1 cup fresh raspberries

1. In a large bowl, blend together mint, vinegar, preserves, garlic, and mustard. Slowly whisk in oil.

2. Add endive, radicchio, and lettuce. Toss until well blended. Season with salt and pepper to taste.

3. Divide salad among 4 plates. Place a wedge of cheese on each salad, sprinkle raspberries on top, and serve.

---

337   CAESAR SALAD SANTA FE
Prep: 15 minutes   Cook: 25 minutes   Serves: 6

Anchovy paste and Dijon mustard give this salad dressing thickness without the traditional addition of a coddled egg. Smoky canned chipotle chiles add mild Southwestern heat. If you prefer not to make your own croutons, choose the best-quality packaged ones that you can find and eliminate step 1.

4 tablespoons butter, melted, or ¼ cup olive oil	1 tablespoon Dijon mustard
7 garlic cloves, minced	4 anchovy fillets, minced, or 2 teaspoons anchovy paste
3 cups cubes (¾-inch) French or Italian bread	¾ cup extra-virgin olive oil
3 tablespoons lemon juice	Salt and freshly ground pepper
1 tablespoon tamarind paste, or increase lemon juice by 1 tablespoon	14 cups torn romaine lettuce
1 tablespoon canned chipotle chiles in adobo sauce, minced, or 1 teaspoon hot pepper sauce	4 ounces Parmesan cheese, preferably imported, 1½ ounces grated, 2½ ounces in 1 piece

1. Preheat oven to 325°F. In a large bowl, combine melted butter and half of minced garlic. Add bread and toss quickly until evenly moistened. Transfer to a large baking sheet and arrange in a single layer. Bake, stirring occasionally, until crisp and golden, about 25 minutes. Transfer croutons to paper towels and let cool. If not using within 2 hours, store in an airtight container for up to 3 days. If necessary, recrisp in a 325° oven.

2. In a medium bowl, whisk together lemon juice, tamarind paste, chipotle chiles, mustard, anchovies, and remaining garlic. While whisking, gradually drizzle in olive oil. Season with salt and pepper to taste. If not using within 2 hours, cover and refrigerate. Let return to room temperature before serving.

3. In a large bowl, combine lettuce and croutons. Drizzle on dressing and grated cheese and toss until well mixed. Divide among 6 plates. Using a swivel-bladed vegetable peeler, shave remaining cheese into slices and scatter over salads. Serve at once.

338   FRESH PECORINO AND WALNUT SALAD

Prep: 15 minutes   Marinate: 30 minutes   Cook: none   Serves: 4

This simple, very rich salad comes from the restaurant Cibrèro in Florence. It combines fresh, young Pecorino cheese and lightly toasted walnuts that are marinated in wine, herbs, vinegar, and extra-virgin olive oil. It's a full meal with sliced fruit and crisp crackers or bread.

⅓ cup dry white wine
¼ cup minced parsley
2 tablespoons balsamic vinegar
1 tablespoon dried oregano
½ teaspoon crushed hot red pepper
1 garlic clove, minced
¼ cup extra-virgin olive oil

3 cups chopped fresh Pecorino cheese (about 12 ounces)
1 cup walnuts, lightly toasted
Red leaf lettuce leaves
Optional accompaniments: Slices of apples, pear, or plum; crackers or bread

In a medium bowl, blend together wine, parsley, vinegar, oregano, red pepper, and garlic. While whisking, drizzle in oil. Add cheese and walnuts and toss until well blended. Cover and marinate at room temperature 30 to 45 minutes. Divide among 4 lettuce-lined plates and serve at room temperature with slices of fruit and crackers or bread.

339   JARLSBERG AND MUSHROOM SALAD

Prep: 20 minutes   Marinate: 30 minutes   Cook: none Serves: 6 to 8

Porcini, enoki, shiitake, and oyster mushrooms are a few of the wild mushrooms that can be eaten raw. Dark cremini and light domestic mushrooms make an intriguing combination, especially when they're soaked with lemon juice as they are in this salad. The lemon juice intensifies the whiteness of light-colored mushrooms, so it heightens the contrast between their white caps and brown gills. It also shows off the difference between dark and light mushrooms.

2 pounds very fresh wild or domestic mushrooms, thinly sliced
½ cup lemon juice
2 cups finely diced Jarlsberg cheese (about 8 ounces)
½ cup extra-virgin olive oil
¼ cup minced parsley

1½ tablespoons minced fresh tarragon or 1¾ teaspoons dried
1 garlic clove, minced
½ teaspoon salt
Freshly ground pepper
Arugula leaves or other greens

1. In a large bowl, combine mushrooms and lemon juice. Toss until well blended. Marinate at room temperature 30 to 40 minutes.

2. Add cheese, oil, parsley, tarragon, garlic, and salt to mushrooms. Toss to mix well. Season generously with pepper.

3. Line a platter or individual plates with arugula. Divide mushroom and cheese mixture among 6 to 8 plates and serve at room temperature.

---

340 POACHED PEAR, WATERCRESS, AND CAMBOZOLA SALAD

Prep: 20 minutes   Cook: 6 to 8 minutes   Serves: 4

This combination of smooth poached pears, creamy blue Cambozola cheese, and crisp watercress is elegant and simple. It's actually delicious warm, cold, or at room temperature. If you're serving the pears warm and they cool too much while handling them, return them to the poaching liquid briefly to reheat. Remove them with a slotted spatula and place on salads.

½ cup sugar
   Zest and juice of 1 lemon
10 black peppercorns
 4 small firm ripe pears,
     peeled, cored, and halved
 4 cups torn Boston lettuce
 4 cups watercress, tough
     stems removed

⅓ cup extra-virgin olive oil
 2 tablespoons red wine
     vinegar
   Salt and freshly ground
     pepper
 4 (¼- to ½-inch) wedges
     Cambozola cheese (about
     6 ounces total)

1. In a medium nonreactive saucepan, combine sugar, lemon zest, lemon juice, peppercorns, and 2 inches of water. Bring to a simmer over medium-high heat, stirring until sugar dissolves. Reduce heat to low, add pears, and poach until barely tender, 6 to 8 minutes. Let pears cool in liquid until cool enough to handle, about 10 minutes.

2. With a slotted spatula, transfer pears to a cutting board cut side down. Holding stem end intact, slice each pear half lengthwise with 6 to 8 parallel cuts. Press gently on each half to spread into a fan shape.

3. In a large bowl, combine lettuce and watercress. Drizzle on oil and vinegar and toss until well mixed. Season with salt and pepper to taste. Divide among 4 plates. Arrange 2 pear halves and a wedge of cheese on each salad. Serve at once.

341 BERRIES AND BAKED BRIE ON MIXED LETTUCES

Prep: 10 minutes   Cook: none   Serves: 4

This smashing salad highlights a classic pairing of fruit and cheese. All that's needed to make it a complete meal is a loaf of crusty French bread. In smaller portions, it makes a lovely first course for an elegant meal. Or, for a very substantial meal, double the amount of Baked Brie and serve 2 wedges per salad. If fresh raspberries are unavailable, blackberries make a fine substitute.

¼ cup extra-virgin olive oil
2 tablespoons raspberry
    vinegar
1 teaspoon Dijon mustard
6 cups torn green leaf lettuce
2 cups torn radicchio

Salt and freshly ground
    pepper
4 servings Baked Brie (recipe
    follows)
1 cup fresh raspberries

In a large bowl, whisk together oil, vinegar, and mustard until well blended. Add lettuce and radicchio. Toss until well blended and season with salt and pepper to taste. Divide among 4 plates and top each salad with a warm wedge of cheese. Sprinkle with berries and serve at once.

342 BAKED BRIE

Prep: 5 minutes   Cook: 17 to 19 minutes   Serves: 4

Baked Brie, served warm or at room temperature, also makes a wonderful hors d'oeuvre surrounded with fruit or bread. Watch the cheese carefully as it cooks so that you can remove it from the oven as soon as it begins to melt.

¾ cup fresh bread crumbs
⅔ cup pecans
¼ cup flour
1 egg

1 (8-ounce) round of ripe Brie
    cheese, sliced into 4 even
    wedges

1. Preheat oven to 350°F. Spread bread crumbs on a baking sheet and bake until dry, about 10 minutes. Let cool at least 5 minutes. Place pecans in a food processor and mince. Add bread crumbs and blend together. Transfer to a small plate. Place flour in a shallow dish. In a small bowl, whisk egg until smooth.

2. Dip each wedge of cheese into flour. Turn to coat all sides and shake off excess. Dip into egg and turn to coat all sides. Dip into bread crumbs, turning to coat all surfaces. If necessary, press crumbs onto cheese to make them adhere. Transfer to a baking sheet and bake until warm, 7 to 9 minutes.

343   GRILLED PEAR, PINE NUT, AND GORGONZOLA SALAD

Prep: 15 minutes   Cook: 6 to 10 minutes   Serves: 8

Golden, buttery pears are featured in this light main course. For a crisp, easy accompaniment, grill large slices of crusty bread brushed with olive oil alongside the pears as they cook.

½ cup pine nuts (pignoli), toasted
3 tablespoons lemon juice
2 tablespoons honey
1½ tablespoons Dijon mustard
½ cup walnut or olive oil
4 large firm ripe pears, halved lengthwise and cored

12 to 16 cups torn red leaf lettuce
Salt and freshly ground pepper
1 cup crumbled Gorgonzola cheese

1. In a large dry skillet, toast nuts over medium heat, shaking pan often, until fragrant and golden brown, 3 to 5 minutes. Transfer nuts to a small dish and set aside.

2. Prepare a medium-hot fire in a barbecue grill or preheat broiler. In a large bowl, whisk together lemon juice, honey, and mustard until dressing is smooth. Slowly whisk in oil.

3. Lightly brush cut surfaces of pears with dressing. Place pears on an oiled rack 4 to 6 inches from heat. Grill or broil, turning and basting with a bit more dressing, until just warm and tender, 3 to 5 minutes. Transfer pears to a cutting board, rounded sides up, and make 6 or more equally spaced vertical cuts down length of each pear half without cutting completely through stem. Gently flatten each half so that slices fan out.

4. Add lettuce to remaining dressing and toss until evenly coated. Season with salt and pepper to taste. Divide among 8 plates. Top each salad with a pear half and sprinkle with cheese and nuts. Serve while pears are warm.

344   FENNEL SALAD WITH FIGS, PROSCIUTTO, AND PARMESAN CHEESE

Prep: 15 minutes   Cook: none   Serves: 4

Fennel is so popular in Tuscany that many people eat it with little adornment—perhaps a drizzle of extra-virgin olive oil and a sprinkling of salt. It's even served as an accompaniment to cheese and fruit for dessert. If figs are not available for this striking salad, substitute kiwi. Be sure to pass a loaf of crusty French or Italian bread.

1 large fennel bulb (about 1 pound)
4 teaspoons extra-virgin olive oil
4 teaspoons fresh lime juice
   Salt and freshly ground pepper
   Green leaf lettuce leaves

4 ripe figs, quartered lengthwise
4 paper-thin slices of prosciutto, quartered lengthwise
1 (2- to 3-ounce) chunk of Parmesan cheese, preferably imported

1. Trim enough feathery greens from tops of fennel to equal 1 tablespoon. Mince and reserve. Discard thin stems. Quarter and core bulb. Slice into thin strips. In a medium bowl, combine strips of fennel with oil and lime juice. Toss until well blended. Season with salt and pepper to taste. Divide among 4 lettuce-lined plates.

2. Wrap each quarter of fig with a length of prosciutto and arrange around fennel. Sprinkle with minced fennel tops. Using a swivel-bladed vegetable peeler, shave Parmesan cheese into thin slices and scatter over each salad. Serve at once.

345   BITTER GREENS WITH GRAPES AND CHEESE

Prep: 20 minutes   Cook: none   Serves: 6

4 cups torn Boston lettuce
4 cups torn curly endive
4 cups radicchio
3 cups red seedless grapes, halved
1 small red onion, thinly sliced and separated into rings

1 cup crumbled blue or feta cheese
1 cup hazelnuts, chopped
¾ cup Honey-Mustard Vinaigrette (recipe follows)

In a large bowl, combine lettuce, endive, radicchio, grapes, red onion, cheese, and hazelnuts. Drizzle on vinaigrette and toss until well blended. Serve at room temperature.

346 HONEY-MUSTARD VINAIGRETTE
Prep: 5 minutes   Cook: none   Makes: ³/₄ cup

1 tablespoon raspberry
   vinegar
1 tablespoon lemon juice
4 teaspoons Dijon mustard
4 teaspoons mild honey

2 garlic cloves, minced
¹/₃ cup extra-virgin olive oil
¹/₃ cup hazelnut or walnut oil
   Salt and freshly ground
   pepper

In a small bowl, combine vinegar, lemon juice, mustard, honey, and garlic. Slowly whisk in olive and hazelnut oils. Season with salt and pepper to taste. If not using within 2 hours, cover and refrigerate. Let return to room temperature before using.

347 BEETS, BROWN SUGAR–GLAZED WALNUTS, AND ROQUEFORT ON MIXED LETTUCES
Prep: 15 minutes   Cook: 1 hour   Serves: 6

Beautiful enough for special company, this salad combines beets and radicchio, whose shades of purple against creamy Boston lettuce create a lovely picture. Serve with crusty French baguettes.

3 medium beets, trimmed
1 cup walnuts
¹/₄ cup firmly packed brown
   sugar
¹/₃ cup extra-virgin olive oil
¹/₄ cup balsamic vinegar
2 tablespoons chopped fresh
   mint

1 large shallot, minced
9 cups torn Boston lettuce
3 cups torn radicchio
   Salt and freshly ground
   pepper
³/₄ cup crumbled Roquefort
   cheese

1. Preheat oven to 350°F. Wrap beets in foil and bake until tender when pierced with a sharp knife, about 1 hour. When cool enough to handle, peel beets and slice thinly.

2. Meanwhile, in a medium skillet, combine walnuts, brown sugar, and ¹/₄ cup water. Cook over medium heat, stirring occasionally, until sugar dissolves and becomes syrupy, 2 to 3 minutes. Continue to cook, stirring constantly, until syrup coats nuts and all liquid is absorbed, 6 to 8 minutes. Transfer to a plate. When cool enough to handle, separate nuts.

3. In a large bowl, blend together oil, vinegar, mint, and shallot. Add lettuce and radicchio. Toss well. Season with salt and pepper to taste. Divide among 6 plates. Top with beets, arranging in slightly overlapping slices. Sprinkle cheese and glazed walnuts on top and serve.

348   RED GRAPES AND BELGIAN ENDIVE WITH BLUE CHEESE TIMBALES

Prep: 20 minutes   Cook: 20 minutes   Serves: 6

A timbale is a mold used to cook various foods; in this case, a simple custard of blue cheese, eggs, and cream. For an elegant evening when a light meal is in order, serve this salad with crusty bread and a glass of wine or port. The timbales can be served at room temperature, warm, or cold.

½ cup crumbled blue cheese
2 eggs
1 cup heavy cream
12 cups torn assorted salad greens
3 cups seedless red grapes, halved

6 scallions, thinly sliced
3 Belgian endive, cored and sliced crosswise
1 cup Berry Vinaigrette (recipe follows)

1. Preheat oven to 325°F. Lightly butter 6 (½- to ¾-cup) timbales or ovenproof dishes and place in a large baking dish. Combine cheese and eggs in a small food processor or blender and puree. Add cream and blend just until smooth. Divide among timbales, filling no more than three-quarters full. Pour boiling water around dishes to reach to level of filling. Cover baking dish with foil and bake until a knife inserted in timbales comes out clean, about 20 minutes.

2. Remove timbales from water and place on a wire rack. Let cool at least 10 minutes. If serving cold, cover and refrigerate at least 2 hours and up to 2 days before unmolding. To unmold, run a knife around inside edge of each dish, cover each with an individual salad plate, and invert onto plate.

3. In a large bowl, combine salad greens, grapes, scallions, and endive. Drizzle with vinaigrette and toss until well blended. Surround each timbale with greens and serve.

349   BERRY VINAIGRETTE

Prep: 5 minutes   Cook: none   Makes: about 1 cup

This slightly sweet and garlicky dressing complements most salads that contain fruit. The raspberry (you may substitute blueberry) vinegar delivers a pleasant fruity aroma. For a very creamy dressing, make the vinaigrette in a food processor or blender. If you don't keep nut oils on hand, use all olive oil.

3 tablespoons raspberry or blueberry vinegar
2 teaspoons Dijon mustard
2 teaspoons honey
1 garlic clove, minced

½ teaspoon salt
¼ teaspoon pepper
½ cup extra-virgin olive oil
¼ cup walnut oil

In a small bowl, whisk together vinegar, mustard, honey, garlic, salt, and pepper until well blended. While whisking, slowly drizzle in olive and walnut oils. If not using within 2 hours, cover and refrigerate. Let return to room temperature before serving.

---

350   OVEN-DRIED FALL FRUIT WITH BLUE CHEESE AND CARAMELIZED HAZELNUTS

Prep: 40 minutes   Cook: 3 hours   Serves: 8

Glistening hazelnuts and intensely flavored oven-dried pears and apples make this fall salad memorable. Slowly drying fruits in the oven concentrates the fruits' sweetness and gives them a chewy texture. The fruits and nuts can be prepared a day ahead of serving.

4 firm ripe pears, peeled, cored, and cut into ¼-inch slices
4 apples, peeled, cored, and cut into ¼-inch slices
1 cup hazelnuts
¼ cup sugar
6 cups torn Boston lettuce

4 cups torn arugula
4 cups torn radicchio
1 cup crumbled blue cheese
½ cup extra-virgin olive oil
3 tablespoons cider vinegar
Salt and freshly ground pepper

1. Preheat oven to 250°F. Arrange pear and apple slices in a single layer on a lightly greased baking sheet. Bake, turning once, until almost dry but still pliable, about 3 hours. Check fruit frequently during last half hour of drying, to be sure none dries out completely. When cooled, chop fruit into bite-size pieces.

2. Meanwhile, in a medium skillet, preferably nonstick, combine hazelnuts, sugar, and ¼ cup water. Cook over medium heat, stirring occasionally, until sugar dissolves and becomes syrupy, 3 to 5 minutes. Watch carefully to avoid scorching. Transfer to a plate. When cool enough to handle, separate nuts.

3. In a large bowl, combine lettuce, arugula, radicchio, and cheese. Drizzle on oil and vinegar. Toss until well mixed. Season with salt and pepper to taste. Divide among 8 plates. Sprinkle salads with fruit and nuts and serve.

351 CHESTNUTS AND CHEESE ON BABY LETTUCES

Prep: 15 minutes   Cook: none   Serves: 4

Honey helps heighten the subtle sweetness of fall chestnuts in this simple main course. Using canned chestnuts, as suggested here, saves lots of time roasting, shelling, and peeling. Of course, if you prefer, prepare 1 pound fresh chestnuts, which are usually available from September until February.

2 tablespoons raspberry vinegar
1 teaspoon mild honey
1 garlic clove, minced
3 tablespoons walnut oil
3 tablespoons extra-virgin olive oil
1 (10-ounce) can whole chestnuts, rinsed and drained (about 2 cups)

½ to ¾ cup crumbled blue cheese
Salt and freshly ground pepper
8 cups assorted baby lettuces

1. In a large bowl, whisk together vinegar, honey, and garlic until well blended. Slowly whisk in walnut and olive oils.

2. Add chestnuts and cheese to dressing. Toss until well mixed. Season with salt and pepper to taste.

3. To serve, arrange lettuce on a platter or on 4 individual plates. Mound chestnut mixture in center and serve.

352 ORANGE, BEET, AND ROQUEFORT SALAD

Prep: 15 minutes   Cook: 1 hour   Serves: 3 to 4

Beets and Roquefort go together beautifully, as this second recipe featuring the duo illustrates. This vividly colored salad makes the best of fresh produce available in winter, including beets, oranges, and Belgian endive. In smaller portions, it makes a delightful first course.

4 medium beets, trimmed
4 navel oranges
1½ tablespoons lemon juice
1½ teaspoons Dijon mustard
¼ teaspoon celery seed
¼ cup extra-virgin olive oil
Salt and freshly ground pepper

2 Belgian endive, thinly sliced
½ small red onion, thinly sliced and separated into rings
9 to 12 large spinach leaves
½ cup crumbled Roquefort cheese

1. Preheat oven to 350°F. Wrap beets in foil and bake until tender when pierced with a sharp knife, about 1 hour. When cool enough to handle, peel and slice thinly. Transfer to a medium bowl.

2. With a swivel-bladed vegetable peeler, remove zest from 2 oranges; mince finely. In a small bowl, combine orange zest, lemon juice, mustard, and celery seed. Gradually whisk in oil. Season with salt and pepper to taste. Pour half of dressing over beets and toss until evenly coated.

3. Remove peel, including white pith from all oranges; cut into segments. In a medium bowl, combine oranges, endive, and red onion. Drizzle on remaining dressing and toss until well mixed. Line 3 or 4 plates with spinach. Arrange a ring of beets around each plate and top with a smaller ring of oranges. Sprinkle cheese on top and serve.

---

353   ARUGULA-MONTRACHET SALAD WITH COUNTRY MUSTARD VINAIGRETTE

Prep: 15 minutes   Cook: none   Serves: 2

Mild, soft goat cheese tempers the sharp taste of arugula in this stunning salad. Its circular layers of ingredients resemble a sunburst pattern, giving it a special look for a party. If your arugula is very fresh, you can assemble the salad a day ahead. Keep it covered and refrigerated, and drizzle the vinaigrette over it just before serving.

2 tablespoons extra-virgin olive oil
2 teaspoons coarse-grained country mustard
2 teaspoons white wine vinegar
Salt and freshly ground pepper

4 cups torn arugula
1 spear of Belgian endive, shredded lengthwise
4 ounces mild goat cheese, such as Montrachet, crumbled or shaped into 2 equal ¾-inch-thick rounds

1. In a small bowl, whisk together oil, mustard, and vinegar until smooth and thickened. If needed, season with salt and pepper to taste. If not using within 2 hours, cover and refrigerate. Let return to room temperature before serving.

2. Divide arugula between 2 plates. Arrange endive in a spoke pattern on top of arugula. Drizzle dressing over endive and place goat cheese in center of each salad. Serve at once.

354   HARICOTS VERTS SALAD WITH GOAT CHEESE
Prep: 15 minutes   Cook: 2 minutes   Serves: 4

If the slender, tender French green beans known as *haricots verts* are not available, use the freshest, most tender green beans you can find and increase the cooking time accordingly. Because the beans hold up well when dressed and taste best at room temperature, this dish makes a convenient picnic, buffet, or party salad.

2 pounds haricots verts or slender green beans, trimmed
½ small red onion, thinly sliced and separated into rings
¼ cup extra-virgin olive oil
¼ cup balsamic vinegar

Salt and freshly ground pepper
¾ cup kalamata or other oil-cured black olives
6 to 8 ounces soft goat cheese, such as Montrachet, crumbled

1. In a large saucepan of lightly salted boiling water, cook green beans until crisp-tender, about 2 minutes. Drain, run under cold water, and drain again.

2. In a large bowl, combine green beans and red onion. Drizzle on oil and vinegar and toss until well blended. Season with salt and pepper to taste.

3. Divide salad among 4 plates and sprinkle olives and goat cheese on top. Serve at room temperature.

355   WINTER PEAR, GOAT CHEESE, AND HAZELNUTS ON WATERCRESS
Prep: 20 minutes   Cook: none   Serves: 4

6 cups shredded Boston lettuce
2 cups watercress, tough stems removed
4 small firm ripe pears, preferably Red Bartlett, cored and cut into ½-inch dice
½ cup chopped toasted hazelnuts

¼ cup hazelnut oil
2 tablespoons balsamic vinegar
Salt and freshly ground pepper
1½ cups crumbled mild goat cheese, such as Montrachet

In a large bowl, combine lettuce, watercress, pears, and hazelnuts. Drizzle on oil and vinegar. Toss until well blended. Season with salt and pepper to taste. Divide among 4 plates, sprinkle with cheese, and serve at once.

356 BELGIAN ENDIVE, SUN-DRIED TOMATOES, AND GOAT CHEESE ON ARUGULA

Prep: 15 minutes   Cook: none   Serves: 6

12 cups torn arugula
⅓ cup extra-virgin olive oil
3 tablespoons balsamic
   vinegar
   Salt and freshly ground
   pepper
3 medium Belgian endive
   spears

¾ cup sun-dried tomatoes
   packed in oil, drained
   and chopped
8 ounces mild goat cheese,
   such as Montrachet,
   crumbled

1. Place arugula in a large bowl. Drizzle with oil and vinegar. Toss until well blended and season with salt and pepper to taste. Divide among 6 plates.

2. Slice endive lengthwise into long thin strips and arrange in a spoke pattern over arugula. Sprinkle sun-dried tomatoes and cheese on top and serve.

357 MEDITERRANEAN SALAD WITH CHICKPEAS AND OLIVES

Prep: 20 minutes   Cook: none   Serves: 4

4 cups torn arugula
4 cups torn Boston lettuce
8 medium radishes, trimmed
   and thinly sliced
1 small cucumber, quartered
   lengthwise and thinly
   sliced crosswise
1 (8¾-ounce) can chickpeas,
   rinsed and drained

¾ cup crumbled feta cheese
½ cup pitted kalamata or other
   oil-cured black olives
¼ cup extra-virgin olive oil
2 tablespoons lemon juice
   Salt and freshly ground
   pepper

In a large bowl, combine arugula, lettuce, radishes, cucumber, chickpeas, feta cheese, and olives. Drizzle on oil and lemon juice. Toss until well blended. Season with salt and pepper to taste. Divide among 4 plates and serve at once.

358 MIXED GREEN SALAD WITH FETA CHEESE, PEPPERY PECANS, AND CARAMELIZED ONIONS

Prep: 10 minutes   Cook: 6 to 7 minutes   Serves: 4 to 5

2 tablespoons sugar	4½ cups watercress, tough
¾ teaspoon salt	stems removed
⅛ teaspoon cayenne	4½ cups torn butter lettuce
½ cup pecan halves	1½ cups crumbled feta cheese
½ cup extra-virgin olive oil	1½ cups Caramelized Onions
¼ cup rice vinegar	(recipe follows)
1 tablespoon honey	Freshly ground pepper

1. In a large nonstick skillet, combine sugar, ¼ teaspoon salt, cayenne, and 2 tablespoons water. Cook over medium heat, stirring, until sugar dissolves, 1 to 2 minutes. Add pecans. Cook, stirring constantly, until liquid evaporates and pecans are glazed, about 5 minutes. Watch carefully so that sugar does not burn. Transfer peppery pecans to a plate and let cool.

2. In a large bowl, whisk together olive oil, vinegar, honey, and remaining ½ teaspoon salt until smooth. Add watercress and lettuce and toss until evenly coated. Divide among 4 or 5 plates. Top with feta cheese, caramelized onions, and pecans. Season with pepper to taste. Serve at once.

359 CARAMELIZED ONIONS

Prep: 5 minutes   Marinate: 2 hours   Cook: 8 to 10 minutes
Makes: 1½ cups

The marinade used to flavor these onions is also used in cooking them. As the marinade evaporates, it coats and glazes the onions while intensifying in flavor.

¼ cup olive oil	1 large Vidalia or other sweet
¼ cup balsamic vinegar	onion, thinly sliced and
2 tablespoons sugar	separated into rings

1. In a shallow dish, stir olive oil, vinegar, and sugar until sugar dissolves. Add onion rings and toss well. Marinate at room temperature 2 hours or cover and refrigerate overnight, turning at least once.

2. Lift onions from marinade and place in a large nonstick skillet. Add ¼ cup marinade; discard remaining. Cook onions with marinade over medium heat, stirring frequently, until softened and glazed, 8 to 10 minutes. Transfer to a plate and let cool.

360 ROASTED VEGETABLE SALAD WITH OLIVES AND FETA CHEESE

Prep: 25 minutes   Cook: 20 minutes   Chill: 4 hours   Serves: 5 to 6

Here is a robust Mediterranean version of that old American standby—the layered overnight salad. If you have a glass bowl, create the layers of this salad carefully to show off its bright ingredients. Serve with crusty bread and extra-virgin olive oil.

4 small zucchini, cut into ¼-inch slices
2 medium red bell peppers, cut into thin strips about 1½ inches long
1 medium eggplant, quartered lengthwise and cut crosswise into ¼-inch-thick slices
1 pound mushrooms, cut into ¼-inch slices

2 tablespoons olive oil
½ cup firmly packed fresh basil leaves, torn if large
1 cup crumbled feta cheese
4 medium plum tomatoes, thinly sliced
1 cup Garlic-Basil Vinaigrette (recipe follows)
½ cup kalamata or other oil-cured black olives

1. Preheat oven to 450°F. In a large bowl, combine zucchini, bell peppers, eggplant, and mushrooms. Drizzle olive oil over vegetables, toss until evenly coated, and spread on a large baking sheet in a single layer. (If necessary, roast in batches or use 2 sheets.) Roast, turning at least once, until tender and lightly browned, about 20 minutes. Transfer to a 6-quart, preferably glass, bowl.

2. Top roasted vegetables with a layer of basil, cheese, and tomatoes. Drizzle dressing over salad, cover, and refrigerate 4 hours or overnight. When ready to serve, toss until well blended. Garnish with olives. Serve warm or at room temperature.

361 GARLIC-BASIL VINAIGRETTE

Prep: 5 minutes   Cook: none   Makes: about 1 cup

¼ cup minced fresh basil
¼ cup balsamic vinegar
2 garlic cloves, minced
1 teaspoon sugar

1 teaspoon salt
½ teaspoon black pepper
½ cup extra-virgin olive oil

In a small bowl, blend together basil, vinegar, garlic, sugar, salt, and pepper. Slowly whisk in oil. If not using within 2 hours, cover and refrigerate. Let return to room temperature before serving.

362 FETA-GLAZED SPINACH SALAD WITH DATES AND PROSCIUTTO

Prep: 15 minutes   Cook: none   Serves: 3 to 4

The subtle sweetness of dates is especially delicious when paired with salty prosciutto and a dressing made of feta cheese.

½ **cup crumbled feta cheese**
1 **tablespoon lemon juice**
2 **tablespoons extra-virgin olive oil**
8 **cups torn spinach**
4 **paper-thin slices of prosciutto, chopped**

½ **small red onion, thinly sliced and separated into rings**
½ **cup chopped pitted dates**
Salt and freshly ground pepper

1. In a blender or small food processor, blend together feta cheese, lemon juice, and 3 tablespoons water. With machine on, drizzle in oil and process until dressing is well blended.

2. In a large bowl, combine spinach, prosciutto, red onion, and dates. Toss lightly to mix.

3. Drizzle dressing over salad and toss until well mixed. Season with salt and pepper to taste and serve.

363 GOAT CHEESE–STUFFED SMOKED SALMON CORNETS ON DILLED CUCUMBERS

Prep: 20 minutes   Stand: 2 hours   Cook: none   Serves: 4

All of the parts of this sophisticated salad can be made hours ahead of time; all that's needed at the last minute is to toss the cucumbers with the dressing and assemble the plates. Be sure to rinse the cucumbers thoroughly to rid them of excess salt before dressing them, and, if you prefer, you can substitute milk for cream in the cornet filling.

2 **large cucumbers, peeled, halved lengthwise, seeded, and thinly sliced crosswise**
1 **tablespoon salt**
½ **cup nonfat plain yogurt**
1 **tablespoon minced fresh dill or 1 teaspoon dried**

1 **shallot, minced**
⅛ **teaspoon black pepper**
7 **ounces mild goat cheese, such as Montrachet**
¼ **cup heavy cream or milk**
12 **thin slices smoked salmon (about 6 ounces)**
Red leaf lettuce leaves

1. In a colander, sprinkle cucumbers with salt and toss until well blended. Let stand 2 hours. Rinse cucumbers well, drain, and pat dry with paper towels.

2. In a medium bowl, combine yogurt, dill, shallot, and pepper. Add cucumbers and toss until well blended. If not using within 30 minutes, cover and refrigerate.

3. In a medium bowl, blend goat cheese and cream until smooth. Roll smoked salmon into cornet or horn shapes and fill with goat cheese mixture. Divide cucumbers among 4 lettuce-lined plates and arrange 3 cornets around cucumbers. Serve at once.

364 MIXED BABY LETTUCES WITH WARM GOAT CHEESE IN PUFF PASTRY
Prep: 15 minutes   Cook: 20 minutes   Serves: 8

Sage-scented, soft goat cheese baked in rich puff pastry highlights this special salad. Accompany it with the best fruit of the season and a glass of wine. Puff pastry needs to remain cold until the moment it goes into the oven, so be sure to thaw the pastry in the refrigerator, not at room temperature, and chill it again before baking.

6 (4-ounce) logs mild goat cheese, such as Montrachet	½ cup extra-virgin olive oil
⅓ cup minced fresh sage (about 12 large leaves)	2 to 3 tablespoons balsamic vinegar
1 (17¼-ounce) package frozen puff pastry, thawed in refrigerator	½ teaspoon salt
	¼ teaspoon freshly ground pepper
1 egg, lightly beaten	16 cups assorted baby lettuces
	8 small plums, thinly sliced

1. Roll each log in sage. Unfold both pastry sheets. Cut off one-third of each sheet lengthwise. Align 2 smaller pieces together lengthwise and pinch them together to form a solid rectangle of pastry equal to 2 remaining sections. Place 2 logs of cheese end to end lengthwise on each piece of pastry and bring ends of pastry together, enclosing cheese. Pinch seams together carefully to seal. Place on a lightly oiled large baking sheet and brush with egg. Refrigerate 20 minutes.

2. Preheat oven to 425°F. Bake puff pastry logs until golden and puffed, about 20 minutes. Transfer to a rack and let cool at least 20 minutes. With a sharp serrated knife, slice each log crosswise into 8 pieces.

3. In a large bowl, whisk together oil, vinegar, salt, and pepper. Add lettuces and toss until well blended. Divide among 8 plates and arrange 3 slices of cheese in puff pastry on each salad. Arrange plums in slightly overlapping slices alongside. Serve at once.

365   RASPBERRY-SPECKLED WATERCRESS AND WARM GOAT CHEESE SALAD

Prep: 15 minutes   Cook: 5 to 6 minutes   Serves: 4

Sophisticated but easy to prepare, this salad is peppery, slightly sweet, and minty. Warm, smooth goat cheese melts in your mouth, providing stark contrast to crisp watercress and radicchio.

2 (4-ounce) logs mild goat cheese, such as Montrachet, at room temperature
⅓ cup fine dry bread crumbs
⅓ cup extra-virgin olive oil
2 tablespoons raspberry vinegar
½ cup chopped fresh mint
2 tablespoons honey
5 cups watercress, tough stems removed
3 cups shredded radicchio
Salt and freshly ground pepper
1 cup fresh raspberries

1. Preheat oven to 400°F. Cut goat cheese into 8 rounds about ½ inch thick. Roll rounds in bread crumbs and place on a lightly oiled baking sheet. Bake just until heated through, 5 to 6 minutes.

2. Meanwhile, in a large bowl, whisk together oil, vinegar, mint, and honey until well blended. Add watercress and radicchio and toss to mix. Season with salt and pepper to taste.

3. Divide salad among 4 plates. Arrange 2 warm goat cheese rounds in center of each salad. Sprinkle raspberries on top. Serve at once while cheese is still warm.

Index

Spinach fettuccine
calamari s. with, 100
in hay and straw s., 106
Squash, yellow (summer)
in roasted vegetable and toasted bread
s., 149
in vegetables à la grecque, 183
Squid. *See* Calamari
Steak and potato s. with fresh salsa, 143
Strawberry(-ies)
in fresh fruit mélange, 161
in pork tenderloin s. with pineapple
salsa, 209
spinach, and smoked chicken s., 214
vinaigrette, chicken s. with green
peppercorns and, 205
**Stuffed grape leaves with tomatoes and
feta cheese, 159**
**Succotash and barley s.,
South-of-the-border, 198**
Summer harvest bread s., 150
**Sunburst shrimp and fruit platter,
Indonesian style, 193**
Sun-dried tomato(es)
in artichoke and angel hair s., 158
Belgian endive, and goat cheese on
arugula, 251
and crab s., 169
dandelion, and potato s., 154
halibut s. with avocado and, 78
vinaigrette, 101
in grilled portobello mushroom and
rigatoni s. with goat cheese, 101
Sweet and hot curried chicken s., 38
Sweet potato
ham, and hazelnut s., 144
in swordfish and chips s. Caribe, 80
Swiss cheese
in chef's s. with Thousand Island
dressing, 13
in deli chef's s., 166
in Reuben s., 167
Swordfish
and chips s. Caribe, 80
soba noodle s. with poached, 215

Tabbouleh, 24
shrimp, 122
Taco s., 30
Tapenade, 103
rotelle and grilled fresh tuna s. with,
103
Tarragon-Dijon vinaigrette, 228
leek s. with, 228
Technicolor tortilla toss, 188
Thai-style salads and dressings
cool chicken-noodle s., 212
ginger-lime dressing, Thai, 91
Mongolian lamb s. with Thai curry
paste, 60
pork in lettuce cups with snow peas
and mandarin oranges, 70
shrimp and papaya s., 91

Thousand Island dressing, 13
chef's s. with, 13
Three-bean s. with ham, classic, 22
Three-flavor Asian vinaigrette, 90
in crispy Asian shrimp slaw, 90
Tofu
broiled, and spinach s. with creamy
sesame-ginger dressing, 234
in gado-gado, 22
ranch dressing, 179
in dilled and grilled chicken-potato
party s., 178
**Tomatillo and fresh corn s. with
shredded chicken, 43**
Tomato(es)
s. with arugula and poached garlic, 184
in asparagus under wraps, 174
aspic
with avocado and shrimp, 95
with crab, 165
in bow ties with blue cheese, mixed
greens, and caper vinaigrette, 185
bulgur and lentil s. with ham and, 120
in caponata with tuna fish, 16
in Caprese, 20
and charred chicken s., with herbed
Roquefort vinaigrette, 40
in chef's s. with Thousand Island
dressing, 13
cherry
in Cajun-spiked salmon on greens, 86
in corn and pepper summer s., 180
in falafel and cucumber s. on a pita
platter, 176
in Greek shrimp and rice s., 124
in instant aioli s., 165
in marinated steak s. in potato baskets,
64
in one-bowl, two-bean Italian s., 162
in potato s. Provençal, 146
in Cobb potato s., 145
in dilled and grilled chicken-potato
party s., 178
dressing
creamy, 152
creamy, in white bread and shellfish
s., 152
in fava and cannellini bean s. with
Mediterranean accents, 134
-fennel vinaigrette, 76
Italian sausage and cannellini s. with,
75
in gazpacho bread s., 153
in Greek s., 29
grilled garlic bread, and fontina s., 155
ham and bean s. with mint and, 71
in Italian chop-chop, 21
in macaroni and mozzarella s., 105
minty couscous with olives, feta cheese,
and, 108
in s. Niçoise with grilled fresh tuna, 31
in puttanesca s., 111
in Salmagundi, 26

Dedication
    To my husband, Warren Foster, whose
passion for champagne is surpassed only by his
insistence on iceberg lettuce.

Acknowledgments
    To Susan Wyler, for providing this in-
triguing, timely topic and for guidance during its
development.
    To my mother, Wynnis Perkerson, and
my sister, Anne Thomas, for unconditional listening
and support.
    To colleagues and friends who listened
and sampled, who provided ingredients and ideas:
Braiden Rex-Johnson, Nancy Sutter, Pat Gervais,
Keun Hii and Theo McCulloch, Dixie Mitchell, Jack
Bollerud, Mary and Don Robertson, Sid Thompson,
Gyvonne and Jim Britten, Lois Melville, Donna
Bailey, and Glenn Hoshal.